NUTSHELLS

Contract Law

NUTSHELLS

Contract Law

Fergus Ryan

ROUND HALL

THOMSON REUTERS

Published in 2006 by
Thomson Reuters (Professional) Ireland Limited
(Registered in Ireland, Company No. 80867. Registered Office and
address for service 43 Fitzwilliam Place, Dublin 2)
trading as Round Hall.

Printed in Great Britain by
CPI Group (UK) Ltd, Croydon, CR0 4YY

ISBN: 978-1-85800-171-5

A catalogue record for this book is available from the British Library.

PREFACE

As the name suggests, the *Contract Law Nutshell* encapsulates, in a format that is both succinct and accessible, the core principles, concepts and cases of Irish contract law. A particular focus is placed on the application of contract law, with practical examples interspersed throughout the text. The overall objective is to illuminate otherwise abstract points in a manner that, it is envisaged, will assist the student in understanding the key principles of contract law.

The book is aimed primarily at two types of student: first, those who seek an introduction to contract law, a primer identifying the key principles and cases that apply in this field; and second, students who, having studied contract law in depth, wish to revise for upcoming examinations.

While contract law is a subject of some considerable vintage, its application in modern commercial contexts is of crucial significance. As such, contract law tends to be an intensely intricate subject, with an overwhelming abundance of interesting caselaw, commentaries and comparative materials. For almost every rule there is a plethora of exceptions, and for each of those exceptions, another raft of caveats.

Given its nature and size, this text focuses on the most significant and helpful examples of contract law jurisprudence. As such, this text does not hold itself out as an all-encompassing review of the intricacies of contract law. It is hoped, nonetheless, that students will find this introduction useful in their study of contract law, in particular in providing a sound basis for the further study of cases, legislation and commentaries, and in revising the fundamental principles of the law in this arena.

Sincere thanks are due to a number of people: in particular, to Catherine Dolan, Susan Rossney, Fergal Cunningham and the staff of Thomson Round Hall, to Bruce Carolan and Stephen Carruthers at DIT, and to Chris Roufs for their support and above all their patience during the completion of this text. Sole responsibility for errors and opinions, of course, lies with the author, who has endeavoured to ensure the accuracy of this text as of September 1, 2006.

Fergus Ryan

TABLE OF CONTENTS

TABLE OF LEGISLATION

Post-1922 Statutes

Statutory Instruments

x   *Contract Law*

TABLE OF CASES

NORTHERN IRELAND

UNITED STATES AND CANADA

OTHER

1. Introduction

1.1 Introduction

Contract law concerns the various rights and duties that arise from agreements. In general (though in some cases such analysis may not be appropriate), it concerns obligations that are "freely assumed" by the parties to the contract. Thus, while the law of torts generally concerns rights and obligations imposed by operation of law, contract law is considered to deal primarily with freely assumed duties.

Contract law thus provides one of the two legal pillars of the free market, the other being the law of property (which governs the ownership of land, goods and intellectual property). Contract law sets out the conditions under which goods and services may be exchanged by private persons. It regulates and enforces bargains entered into between free agents. Although it generally does not concern itself with the content of these bargains, it nonetheless sets out certain rules determining how such bargains come into effect (the formation of a contract), how certain terms are incorporated into a contract, the interpretation of such terms, and the consequences of a breach of contract.

1.2 The basis for contract law

Various academic theories exist regarding the basis for contract law. In fact, there is some considerable debate (and very little clarity) on the precise doctrine underpinning the law in this area. Given space constraints, it is not possible to explore these theories in full, though it is worth noting the key features of each:

- **Promise theory.** Some theorists suggest that contract law fundamentally concerns the creation of promises and the circumstances under which such promises will be enforced. The question that then arises is which promises will be enforced and which will not be.
- **Bargain theory.** Others rely on a theory of bargain that assesses contracts in terms of the mutual obligations assumed by the parties. This theory centres on an exchange—each party gives up something in exchange for a benefit flowing from the other party. Where there is such a bargain, all else being equal, the courts should enforce the exchange.

1

- **Reliance theories.** Some commentators suggest that contract law aims to protect the expectations of parties who have acted in reliance on particular representations—in other words, if a party relies on a promise, by for instance, doing something that she would not otherwise have done, the promise should be enforced.
- **Marxism.** Others, by contrast, claim that contract law reflects the priorities of the ascendant class, and in particular, that it supports the economic goals of people in power. Marxist theorists, in particular, hold that classical contract law reflects the values of those who benefit most from the free market, often at the expense of vulnerable sub-groups in society.
- **Critical legal studies.** A final category, the critical legal studies movement, asserts that contract law is not in fact a coherent and cohesive doctrine, but reflects many competing and conflicting priorities and concerns. At root, this movement holds that contract law represents an uneasy compromise between several competing theories, and in particular between individualism (holding that people should be free to make their own decisions) and collectivism (asserting the importance of the common or collective good over that of the individual).

This last theory is worth dwelling on—students will find, in the study of contract law, many apparent contradictions. For every case establishing a rule, one will inevitably encounter another creating an exception to that rule. Contract law may, in fact, frequently prove quite uncertain. The results of specific cases as often as not turn on their specific facts, a point to bear in mind when studying the many contrasting cases encountered in this field.

1.3 The origins of contract

Although contract law is of some considerable vintage (students continue to study cases going back to the 1600s), it did not rise to prominence as a discipline until the mid-to-late 1700s. From mediaeval and feudal times up to the early eighteenth century, markets (particularly in essential goods) were strictly controlled. Prices for essential goods were often fixed, and significant penalties were meted out in respect of commercial practices which today might be considered best model practice for high-performance businesses. In such pre-modern societies, obligations generally arose not as a result of agreement between parties, but in consequence of the status of an individual, the place or position that they held in society. Thus, most obligations were imposed by law and custom. Duties generally arose, then, from the particular relationship of the parties, and not from their free will.

1.3.1 Freedom of contract

From the mid 1700s onwards, however, the concept of "freedom of contract" came to prominence. This reflected in large measure the philosophical, political and economic changes of the time (the most notable being the shift from a predominantly agricultural to an increasingly industrialised society). This trend coincided with growing support for liberal thought, which posited that provided no harm was done thereby, individuals should be entitled to make up their own minds as to what best suited their interests.

The doctrine of freedom of contract holds that the parties to a contract (in particular if they have equal bargaining power) should be free to assume whatever obligations they wish. Individuals, it was believed, should be free within minimal limits to bargain for what they desire and correspondingly free of all duties save those assumed through mutual agreement. This "contractualism" suggests that obligation, to the greatest extent possible, should be the product of individual free will rather than external imposition. People should, in sum, be free to shape their own destinies. Governments should intervene only where necessary to facilitate such free decisions and to enforce the resulting agreements in cases of breach. The courts (it is said) should only intervene where there was some flaw in the *process* by which the contract was made. The substantive result of the contract, by contrast, was a matter for the parties alone.

1.3.2 The rise of "welfarism"

The reality, many suggest, is that freedom of contract facilitates unfair exchanges particularly where there is an inequality of bargaining power between the parties. A stark example of the pitfalls of freedom of contract arose in *Lochner v New York* 198 US 45 (1905). In this case, the US Supreme Court struck down legislation setting maximum working hours for bakery staff, the majority of the court reasoning that these laws interfered with the freedom of employer and employee to contract. This was despite the compelling evidence of the serious damage caused to bakers' health owing to oppressive levels of heat and dust. The minority, including Justice Holmes, concluded that state intervention was, in fact, perfectly appropriate as it offered the bakers "… protection against the superior bargaining power of their employers".

In fact, by the mid twentieth century, the thinking that prevailed in *Lochner* had lost considerable currency. Conscious of the potential for exploitation, parliaments throughout the world increasingly restricted freedom of contract with a view to protecting vulnerable persons in contractual contexts, particularly in circumstances where the parties were not of equal bargaining power. This trend is evidenced most vividly by the exponential rise in consumer protection laws and laws governing the employment relationship. Judges too have proved more reticent to enforce unfair contracts, as evidenced by their sceptical approach to exclusion clauses (see Chapter 14).

In short, throughout the mid to late twentieth century, the State considerably pared down the concept of freedom of contract. It has shifted from a "contractualist" approach that allows the parties to determine their own bargains, to a "welfarist" perspective, that considers it appropriate and necessary to act so as to protect certain vulnerable persons. In contrast with its predecessor, the welfarist perspective often inquires into the substantive fairness of the bargain. In other words, this new perspective is concerned not merely that the process of contractual formation is fair but also that the results of the contract are in the best interests of all concerned.

1.4 Specialisation and contract law

In the process of growing regulation, niche areas have emerged, governed by specific rules. Indeed, out of the original realm of contract law have sprung a variety of quite distinct disciplines governing specific types of contract. A good example is employment law, where both common law and legislation have created a highly specialised domain of legal regulation. The rules of employment law are largely determined by the State—in other words, they are generally imposed, rather than assumed. Consumer law has experienced similar changes, with many of the terms of consumer contracts being determined by legislation rather than agreement. Correspondingly, the areas to which classical contract law apply have narrowed considerably. Although it might not be fair to say, as Dean Gilmore once suggested, that "contract is dead", its significance has been greatly diminished by increasing government regulation.

1.5 Common law and codification

Nonetheless, and despite these trends, much of what is now considered to be within the domain of contract law is still governed by the common law and equity (that is, by laws developed in the courts). With some notable exceptions (particularly in relation to employment and consumers) there is comparatively little legislation in this area. How long this will last is an open question. In most continental states, contract law is "codified", that is, it is contained in written codes, clearly delineating the applicable rules. Similarly, in many of the US states, "restatements" of contract law have served in all but name to codify contract law. Given the importance of contract law in inter-state commerce, it is not unlikely that the European Union will attempt, in the near future, to establish a common code of contract. The growing intervention of legislation into contracts concerning consumers is evidence of a broad trend towards codified regulation of contracts.

1.6 The "objective" approach in contract law

Before tackling some of the technicalities of contract law, it is worth noting that, when assessing the intention of the contracting parties, contract law generally takes an objective approach. Contract law typically looks to the "manifest intention" of the individual, as evidenced by their outward conduct. In other words, instead of seeking to peer into the minds of the individual (the subjective approach), judges look to their actions and words as evidence of their contractual intention. The law asks what the "ordinary reasonable person" observing these actions and words would assume was the intention of the parties. In *Smith v Hughes* (1871) L.R. 6 Q.B. 597, Blackburn J. observed that:

> "... [i]f, whatever a man's real intention may be, he so conducts himself that a reasonable man would believe he was assenting to the terms proposed by the other party, and that other party upon that belief enters into the contract with him, the man thus conducting himself would be equally bound as if he had intended to agree to the other party's terms ...".

Take the following example. Muiris offers to sell his Spanish villa to Sinéad for €1. In fact, and unknown to Sinéad, Muiris intends this as a joke. Nonetheless, if Sinéad accepts the offer in good faith, Muiris may well be bound to sell, unless in all the circumstances an ordinary reasonable person would have realised, looking at the behaviour of the parties, that the offer was a joke. The fact that in Muiris's mind, this was merely intended as a joke would be irrelevant, if outwardly this appeared to be a reasonable and serious offer.

2. Offer

2.1 Introduction

This chapter, and the chapters that follow, cover how a contract comes into being. Generally, for a contract to be formed there must be a "bargain" between at least two persons. As such, a contract cannot be made by one person acting alone (thus, a will is not a contract). Nor may a contract arise between two or more persons who are fundamentally at variance regarding the content of the proposed agreement.

The process of bargain is most often analysed using a framework in which one party makes an "offer" which another person (sometimes called the "offeree") unconditionally "accepts". This method of analysis can sometimes prove technical and artificial. In essence, the key question is whether the parties have unconditionally agreed to assume certain obligations towards each other. Nevertheless, at common law, a contract continues to be viewed as the product of two elements: an offer and a corresponding acceptance.

An offer may be defined as an unambiguous statement indicating an intention or willingness to contract on specified terms. As observed in *Storer v Manchester City Council* [1974] 3 All E.R. 824, an offer "... empowers the persons to whom it is addressed to create a contract by their acceptance". An offer may be converted into a contract by the unconditional acceptance of the offer by the person to whom it is made.

2.2 Some preliminary points

2.2.1 The form of the offer

An offer may be made orally or in writing, or may be inferred from the gestures or conduct of a party. Take for instance, the situation that occurs at many newsagent checkouts. A tired shopper silently places a chocolate bar on the shop counter, and hands the required cash to the cashier. The cashier, who is gossiping with a friend on her mobile, takes the money and gives the customer her change. Although no words have been exchanged, the shopper's gesture may fairly be taken to constitute an offer to purchase the confectionery, which offer has been accepted by the cashier's subsequent action.

2.2.2 An offer may be made to the world at large

A single offer may be made to one or more persons. Theoretically, there is no upper limit on the number of persons to whom a single offer may be made. Nor is it necessary that an offer be made to any specified or named persons. It is possible, for instance, to make an offer to the world at large. For instance, if Ahmed were to offer to pay €500 to anyone who will walk from Dublin to Waterford, it would be open to any number of people who accepted the challenge to collect the sum offered. The fact that Ahmed might not be able financially to satisfy all completed contracts is irrelevant.

2.3 The differences between a unilateral offer and a bilateral offer

Contract law distinguishes between a unilateral offer and a bilateral offer. This distinction is important in certain contexts. For instance, somewhat different rules apply as regards the revocation of an offer and the acceptance of an offer depending on whether the offer is unilateral or bilateral.

The key differences lie in (a) the manner in which an offer may be accepted and (b) whether one or both parties are bound by the resulting contract.

(a) A bilateral offer presupposes acceptance in the form of a promise. A unilateral offer, by contrast, requires for its acceptance the performance of a specified act (or, in some cases, refraining from a particular act). For instance, if Ernie offers Bert €4,000 in exchange for a promise to sell Bert's car, this is a bilateral offer. Bert may accept by promising to sell the car for that price. By contrast, if Joe offers Barbara €500 if she runs 10 km a day for one week, that is a unilateral offer; Barbara accepts the offer by performing the contemplated act, running 10 km each day. Once she has completed the task, (but not before) the contract is formed.

(b) An easy way to distinguish a unilateral from a bilateral offer is as follows: if, once the contract comes into being, only one of the parties is required to do something, the contract (and the offer on which it was based) is unilateral. If, however, both are obliged to act, the contract is bilateral. For instance, in the first example above, once Bert and Ernie agree on the sale, both are bound under the contract: Bert to sell the car and Ernie to buy it. However, in the second example, Barbara accepts the contract by performing the stipulated act, running 10 km each day. Although she is not obliged to complete this task, once she has done so, the contract is formed.

Once this happens, she is not obliged to do anything further under the contract. Only Joe is bound by the contract—he must pay Barbara for her efforts, as agreed.

The classic example of a unilateral offer arises where a reward is offered for the return of an item, such as a lost wallet. Another example arises where an offer is made to pay €1,000 to any person who performs a certain task, such as to climb Ben Bulben. In those circumstances, the offer is unilateral. It requires as a precondition to acceptance, the performance of an act, the act of returning the wallet to its owner or of climbing Ben Bulben. Although, no one is obliged to perform either task, once the contemplated act is performed, the contract is deemed to have been created.

Carlill v Carbolic Smokeball Company [1893] 1 Q.B. 256, provides an unusual example of a unilateral offer. In this case, the defendant company placed a newspaper advertisement for the sale of a "smokeball". Correct use of the smokeball, the advert claimed, would protect the user from a series of ailments, including influenza (the flu). Indeed, the manufacturers were so confident in their product, they promised that anyone who used it and contracted the flu would be paid £100 in compensation. Having used the smokeball, but nonetheless caught the flu, Mrs Carlill sued for the promised sum. Despite the defendant's claim that no offer had been made, the court ruled that the advert constituted a unilateral offer which had been accepted by satisfaction of the conditions of performance—contracting influenza while using the smokeball, as had occurred in this case. The court relied in particular on the advert's statement that as proof of the company's sincerity, £1,000 had been lodged in a bank to pay for any claims made. Thus, the company was bound to pay Mrs Carlill £100.

2.4 Distinguishing offers from other phenomena

An offer is sometimes confused with certain other phenomena. An offer must, in particular, be contrasted with an "invitation to treat". Whereas an offer generally comprises an indication of willingness to enter into a contract on certain terms, an invitation to treat comprises an indication that one is willing to *consider offers* from other persons. An invitation to treat is best defined as a statement that one is willing to take offers for the purchase or sale of an item. The person issuing the invitation to treat is thus not making an offer but inviting others to make her an offer that she may or may not accept.

2.4.1 A statement of opinion or a quotation or estimate of price
A statement setting out one's opinion, hope or expectation is not an offer. For instance, in *Harvey v Facey* [1893] A.C. 552, a statement that £900 was the lowest cash price that would be accepted for a particular property ("Bumper Hall Pen") was deemed to constitute an opinion as to the likely price the owners would accept if they were minded to sell. It was not however, an offer to sell at that price. (See also *Anderson v Backlund* 159 Minn. 423 (1924); *Clifton v Palumbo* [1944] 2 All E.R. 497.)

Nor, generally speaking, does a quotation or estimate of a likely price for goods amount to an offer. In *Boyers v Duke* [1905] 2 I.R. 617, for instance, a statement of the lowest price at which canvas would be sold was held to be an estimate only and not an offer to sell at that price. That said, in *Dooley v Egan* (1938) 72 I.L.T.R. 155, a quote for a medical cabinet was held to constitute an offer, a conclusion that may be explained on the basis that the quote was issued for "immediate acceptance only".

2.4.2 Letter of intent/statement of intention
An offer must also be distinguished from a statement of intention. The difference between the two is admittedly rather fine but significant in its implications. A statement setting out one's intention is not deemed to be an offer.

A good example of this is provided by *Gibson v Manchester City Council* [1979] 1 All E.R. 972. The plaintiff, who lived in a house owned by the defendant Council, wanted to buy his home. In reply to an enquiry, the Council wrote to Mr Gibson indicating that it "… may be prepared to sell the house …" for £2,180. The letter further stated that if he wished to make a formal application to buy the house, Mr Gibson should complete and return the enclosed application form. The House of Lords concluded, however, that the letter from the Council contained merely an invitation to treat, and not an offer. Although there was a specified price, the letter was otherwise relatively non-committal (a point underlined by use of the phrase "may be prepared" and the suggestion that Mr Gibson would have to make a formal application). (See also *Farina v Fickus,* [1900] 1 Ch. 331. See, however, *Storer v Manchester City Council* [1974] 3 All E.R. 824, where a more definitive letter regarding the sale of a council house was interpreted as containing an offer.)

2.4.3. The display of goods

The classic example of an invitation to treat arises in a situation very familiar to a regular consumer. For instance, a shopper, Marcy, goes into a music store in which CDs are placed on open display. She takes a copy of a CD by her favourite boyband and brings it to the counter. The cashier, a heavy metal fan who detests boybands, refuses on principle to sell it to her. Technically, Marcy would have no redress; the display of the CD constitutes an invitation to treat and would not typically be treated as an offer. It is in fact Marcy who is making the offer in this case, offering to purchase the CD, empowering the cashier to accept the offer (or to decline) on behalf of the shop.

Where stores display goods advertising their availability for sale, generally speaking such a display does not constitute an offer to sell, but rather an invitation to the public to make offers to purchase (an invitation to treat). Thus, in most consumer transactions it is usually the *buyer* who makes the offer and the seller who accepts.

This was established in the important UK case of *Pharmaceutical Society of G.B. v Boots Cash Chemists* [1953] 1 All E.R. 482. At the time of this case, it was illegal to contract for the sale of certain pharmaceutical products otherwise than in the presence of a qualified pharmacist. The defendant pharmacist (in a move that was quite novel at the time in question) had stocked its open shelving with such items. The key question in this case was whether the display of goods was an offer which the customer accepted by taking the goods off the shelf, in which case the contract would have been completed otherwise than in the presence of a qualified pharmacist. The English and Welsh Court of Appeal ruled that it was not. The offer in such a scenario was made not by the shop, but by the customer, who offered to buy the items by presenting them to the pharmacist, thus empowering the pharmacist to accept or reject the customer's offer. As such, no offence had been committed, the contract having been completed in the presence of the pharmacist. Likewise, in *Fisher v Bell* [1961] 1 Q.B. 394, a shop displaying flick knives for sale was deemed not to be offering such items for sale.

The Minister for Industry and Commerce v Pim [1966] I.R. 154 provides a sturdy Irish example of this rule, holding that the display of a coat in the defendant's shop window was not an offer to sell the coat but merely an invitation to treat. The defendant was thus not guilty of the offence of offering for sale an item "on credit terms" without simultaneously indicating what those terms were.

This is arguably a sensible result. A shop will invariably have limited stocks of an item. If a display were deemed to constitute an offer, the shop could potentially find itself liable to an unlimited number of potential buyers, despite the fact that its stocks of the product are depleted. There may be other good reasons for interpreting such transactions as involving an offer made by the buyer and not the seller. Take, for instance, an off-licence displaying cans of beer, wine and spirits on its shelves. Were such a display to be considered an offer to sell, contracts could potentially arise with persons who are not allowed to purchase alcohol.

2.4.4 Advertisements

As a general rule, the advertisement of an item is not an offer but rather an invitation to treat. It is worth noting, however, that where an advert turns out to be false, it may separately be in breach of the legislation banning misleading advertising: see, for instance, the Consumer Information Act 1978 (ss.6, 7 and 8) and European Directives 84/50/EEC and 97/55/EC.

An advert generally invites the customer to make an offer to purchase an item. For instance, in *Partridge v Crittendon* [1968] 2 All E.R. 421, a magazine advertised "Bramblefinch cocks and hens" for sale at 25 shillings each. This, the court ruled, did not constitute an offer to sell wildlife, an offence under British law. Similarly, in *Grainger & Sons v Gough* [1896] A.C. 325, the distribution by a wine merchant of a price list for various wines was deemed not to be an offer.

There are good policy reasons for such a result. The theory of "limited stocks" again applies in this context. Take, for instance, a cinema with a 1,000 seat capacity which advertises tickets for the premiere of a sequel to a wildly popular film. If the advertisement of the film were taken to constitute an offer, accepted by any member of the public who presents herself at the cinema, the cinema owner could potentially be liable in contract to many more persons than she can safely fit in the cinema. If she refused entry, she could be liable to thousands of disappointed fans. If she honours the contract, liability may arise under health and safety legislation.

There are however, some notable exceptions to this perspective. Generally speaking, the more explicit and unconditional the advertisement the more likely it is that it will constitute an offer. In particular, if the advertisement states that if a person performs a particular act, she will receive a particular specified benefit, it is likely that the advertisement will be interpreted as an offer. The decision in

Carlill v Carbolic Smokeball Co. (discussed above at para.2.3) is a classic (albeit somewhat bizarre) example of this exception.

In *Lefkowitz v Great Minneapolis Surplus Store* (1957) 86 NW 2d. 689, the defendant had placed an advertisement for fur stoles (worth $139.50) in a Minneapolis newspaper, indicating that on a specified day it would sell the remaining stoles for $1 each on a first come, first served basis. When Mr Lefkowitz attempted to buy the stole, he was refused on the basis that the offer was intended for women only, though this intention was not stated in the advertisement. On the facts before it, the court concluded that the advertisement being sufficiently "clear, definite, and explicit" and having "left nothing open for negotiation" constituted an offer (that was not, moreover, conditional on the gender of the purchaser).

2.4.5 Auctions

Special rules apply to the advertisement of an auction. *Harris v Nickerson* (1873) L.R. 8 Q.B. 286, is authority for the proposition that an advertisement to the effect that an auction will take place at a specified place and time is a declaration of intention only, and not an offer to hold the auction. In particular, potential bidders who, acting on the advertisement, arrive at the auction intending to bid, cannot claim that they have thus accepted the offer to hold an auction. In this context, it is generally said that the advert is an invitation to the public to attend and make a bid. The attending bidder makes an offer which the auctioneer may choose to accept (by dropping the hammer and "closing" bids the auctioneer is deemed to have accepted the highest bid on behalf of the vendor).

However, where an auction does go ahead, different rules apply. Where the auctioneer has not set a reserve price for the item being auctioned (a price below which the item will not be sold), and has indicated that she will sell to the highest bidder, this is deemed to be an offer to sell at the highest offered price. (See *Tully v Irish Land Commission* (1961) 97 I.L.T.R. 174; *Warlow v Harrison* (1859) 1 E & E 309.) In theory, anyone who attends and bids at such auction is deemed to have accepted the offer. In such a case, however, only the person who made the highest bid may sue for recovery of the items (or damages for a refusal to sell).

2.4.6 Tenders

A good example of an invitation to treat arises where an organisation invites tenders for the supply of goods or services (for instance, where a county council seeks tenders for the building of a road, or where a company requests tenders for the supply of stationery). Those who view the advert are invited to pitch (usually in open competition) for the work. A request for tenders, then, is not generally deemed to be an offer; instead, those who respond are usually deemed to be making an offer to perform the work, which offers may be accepted or rejected as the case may be.

In general, there is no obligation to accept the highest or lowest bid. In fact, the organisation requesting tenders is usually free to decline all bids. In *Spencer v Harding* (1870) L.R. 5 C.P. 561, for instance, the defendant had invited tenders for the purchase of stock. The highest bidder, whose bid was declined, sued claiming that his bid constituted an acceptance of an offer to sell. The Court of Common Pleas concluded that the invitation for tenders did not amount to an offer, and in particular that there was no obligation on the defendant to accept the highest bid. One way of ensuring that this will be the case is by inserting "a privilege clause" reserving the right to decline all offers, however favourable.

Where, however, an invitation to tender *expressly indicates* that the best bid (the highest offer in the case of a tender inviting people to buy items, the lowest in the case of a tender inviting people to supply goods or services) will be accepted, this will constitute an offer. In *Harvela Investments v Royal Trust of Canada* [1985] 2 All E.R. 966, the defendant invited two parties to tender for the purchase of shares, indicating that it bound itself to accept the highest offer. In such a case, the House of Lords ruled, the invitation was in fact a unilateral offer which was accepted by the party making the highest bid.

In the course of its ruling, the House of Lords indicated its disfavour for what are called "referential tenders", a tender that promises to top the best bid by a specified amount. A referential tender, the House concluded, was not a proper tender. The tender process is designed to attract the best possible genuine bid; if each party knew what the other was tendering for, this might not be possible. Furthermore, if each party were able to make a referential bid, it might not be possible to determine the identity of the best bid.

2.5 The termination of an offer

An offer, once made, may come to an end in any one of a number of ways. Once it has been terminated, it can no longer be accepted. By the same token, however, once an offer has been accepted, it is no longer possible to terminate the offer, as a contract has come into being.

2.5.1 Rejection

An offer will be terminated if the person to whom it is made rejects the offer. Such rejection may be express or implied. It is important, however, to distinguish between the rejection of an offer and an enquiry as to the openness of the offeror to alter the terms of the offer. In *Stevenson, Jacques and Co. v McLean* (1880) 5 Q.B.D. 340, an enquiry was made as to the possibility of changing the terms for the acceptance of an offer. The enquiry was deemed to be a request for further information only, and not an outright rejection of the offer.

An offer may almost always be rejected. As a byproduct of the broad principle of freedom of contract, every offeree has the right to reject an offer for whatever reason he or she sees fit. This freedom, however, is restricted in part by the Equal Status Acts 2000–2004, which prevent the rejection of an offer on certain grounds, *e.g.* the race, religion or sexual orientation of the offeror. In addition, Art.82 of the European Community Treaty and the Competition Acts 1991–2002 prohibit sellers who have a monopoly over an item from refusing to supply that item without good reason. Where a seller enjoys a dominant position in a particular market, it is precluded from abusing that position.

Once an offer has been rejected, it is not possible subsequently to accept the same offer, even if the offeree has changed her mind. It is not possible, in other words, to "revive" a rejected offer. A fresh offer will have to be made.

2.5.2 Making a counter-offer

A counter-offer is a response to an offer that does not meet the terms of the offer. The making of a counter-offer (like a rejection) serves to terminate the original offer. For instance, in *Hyde v Wrench* (1840) 3 Beav. 334, Wrench offered to sell property to Hyde for £1,000. Hyde responded indicating that he would only pay £950, a counter-offer which terminated the original offer. In such circumstances it was not possible for the offeree subsequently to accept the original offer.

A counter-offer is also made where a person purports to accept an offer but in fact adds new terms. For instance, in *Jones v Daniel* [1894] 2 Ch. 332, Daniel had offered to purchase land from Jones for £1,450. Jones agreed to the price, but presented Daniel with a contract containing terms that Daniel had not previously seen. This attempt to introduce new terms meant that Jones had not accepted the offer but had made, instead, a counter-offer.

2.5.3 Death or incapacity of offeror

The rules in this context are not certain. There is some debate on this point, but it appears that the death or incapacity of the offeror may serve to terminate the offer if certain conditions are met.

- If the offeror dies, and the offeree is aware of the death, it appears that the offer is terminated. *Coulthart v Clementson* (1879) 5 Q.B.D. 42.
- If the offeree was not aware of the death, the offer may still be accepted but not if it contemplates personal performance by the deceased. *Re Whelan* [1897] 1 I.R. 575, *Bradbury v Morgan* (1862) 1 H. & C. 249.

Correspondingly, on the death of an offeree, the offer to that person lapses automatically—see *Reynolds v Atherton* (1921) 125 L.T. 690—though surviving offerees may still accept.

2.5.4 Revocation

An offer, once made, may be withdrawn or "revoked" at any time prior to acceptance though not after the offer has been accepted. Revocation basically involves the withdrawal of the offer by the person by whom it was originally made. The offeror need not give any reason for the withdrawal of the offer (though a revocation based on grounds set out in the Equal Status Acts 2000–2004 (see above) would be illegal).

This is the case even where the offeror has indicated that the offer will remain open for a stipulated time or indeed indefinitely. Notwithstanding such a statement, it is still open to the offeror to revoke the offer before the deadline passes. Unless there is a separate enforceable contract to keep the offer open, the offeree cannot complain that the offer was withdrawn before the deadline for acceptance. In particular, an indication that an offer will be kept open for a certain period of time will only prove effective if it is supported by consideration. (See *Routledge v Grant* (1828) 4 Bing. 653.)

To take effect, a revocation must be communicated to the persons to whom the original offer was made. In other words, a revocation will only be effective from the time it is communicated to the offeree. Such communication may be explicit ("I withdraw the offer") or implicit. For instance, a revocation may be communicated where the offeree is informed of behaviour or events that are inconsistent with the continuance of the offer. *Dickinson v Dodds* (1876) 2 Ch. D. 463 establishes that it is not necessary that the offeror herself communicate the revocation. It is sufficient that the offeree has actual knowledge of the revocation or behaviour that is inconsistent with the continuance of the offer.

In *Dickinson v Dodds,* the defendant had originally offered to sell a property to the plaintiff. The offer was to be accepted by a specified deadline. The plaintiff subsequently discovered from a third party that the property had been sold to a different person, before the deadline had expired. Although the offeror had not personally informed the plaintiff of the revocation, the third party's information was deemed to amount to effective communication to the offeree of the fact of revocation.

Revocation must be communicated before acceptance occurs, as evidenced by *Byrne v Van Tienhoven* (1880) 49 L.J.Q.B. 316. On October 1, 1879, the defendants (based in Wales) posted a letter to the plaintiff (located in New York) offering to sell the latter 1,000 boxes of tinplates. The letter arrived on October 11, and on the same day the plaintiff telegrammed its acceptance, following this up with a letter posted October 15. However, on October 8, the defendant had posted a letter withdrawing the original offer, but this did not reach New York until October 20. Acceptance by post or telegram is deemed to occur at the point of dispatch (*i.e.* when and from where the letter/telegram is posted). (See para3.7 below.) Revocation, however, does not occur until it is communicated to the offeree. In this case, the offeree did not find out about the revocation until October 20. In summary, acceptance occurred on October 11, the day the telegram was sent, 9 days before the revocation became effective. The offer thus had been accepted before it was officially revoked.

With a unilateral offer somewhat different principles may apply. If such an offer is made to the world at large, reasonable steps must be taken to inform the public of the revocation. In principle, this means that the revocation must be communicated by a method equally as effective as that by which the original offer was advertised. For instance, if an offer is made in a prominent newspaper advertisment, its withdrawal more than likely would need to be similarly publicised.

2.5.5 *Lapse of time*

Where a deadline has been set for the termination of an offer, the offer clearly lapses once the deadline passes. As Carroll J. noted in *Parkgrange*

Investments v Shandon Park Mills (unreported, High Court, May 2, 1991), "... [a] purchaser who ignores a time limit for accepting an offer runs the risk that it will lapse". Indeed, as noted above, it is generally possible to validly withdraw an offer, even where a set deadline has not passed.

Nonetheless, even where there is no deadline set, an offer may nonetheless terminate if a reasonable time has passed since the offer was made. In *Commane v Walsh* (unreported, High Court, May 3, 1983), O'Hanlon J. indicated that an offer would lapse where it was not accepted within a reasonable timeframe. For instance, in *Ramsgate Victoria Hotel v Montefiore* (1866) L.R. Exch. 109, five months was deemed too late for the acceptance of an offer to buy shares. Montefiore, having applied to purchase shares, received a response five months later, a delay which, in the opinion of the court, served to terminate his original offer.

The timeline may itself be indicated in the offer—for instance, in *Dooley v Egan* (1938) 72 I.L.T.R. 155, the offer was advertised as being for "immediate acceptance only" requiring a very swift response. What is or is not a reasonable time will otherwise depend on the circumstances. For example, an offer by a restaurant to purchase a consignment of freshly harvested organic vegetables would presumably have to be accepted by the seller in a matter of days. Price volatility may also dictate what is or is not a reasonable timeframe. With rising costs of property, for instance, an offer to sell land might be interpreted as being valid only for a few months.

2.5.6 Failure of a precondition

If an offer is predicated on the satisfaction of a condition, which fails prior to acceptance, the offer cannot be accepted. For example, Zander offers Zelda €100 for a concert ticket. Before Zelda accepts, the concert is cancelled. The offer is thus terminated, as a precondition to its purchase—that the concert proceeds as planned—has failed. In *Financings Ltd v Stimson* [1962] 1 W.L.R. 1184, the defendant offered to buy a car on hire-purchase terms. Before the offer was accepted, the car was stolen and, when recovered, was found to be badly damaged. The court implied a condition that the car be sold in good condition, a condition that had failed before acceptance. As such, the offer was terminated before acceptance.

3. Acceptance

3.1 Introduction

A contract comes into being where an offer is accepted, without condition, by the person to whom it is made. Acceptance, once communicated, concludes the formation of contract. Of course, as will become evident in forthcoming chapters, a contract may not be enforceable or may not be valid for other reasons but once an offer is accepted, it is nonetheless concluded.

3.2 Some preliminary points on acceptance

3.2.1 An offer may only be accepted by a person to whom it is made

A person may only accept an offer where, under the terms of the offer, it has been made to that person. It is, however, possible to make an offer to more than one person, or to the public at large—anyone who meets the conditions of the offer may thus reap the benefits of a contract. For example, if Raoul offers €50 to anyone who hops down Grafton Street, any person who does so may collect the €50. If he offers the money only to any red-haired person who does so, a blond man would not be able to collect the €50, as he does not meet the conditions of the offer.

It is a question of fact whether an offer made collectively to several people can be accepted by only one of those persons alone. For instance, if a magazine offers to give €10,000 to a charity if *all* the members of a boyband run the marathon, it would not be liable if only one member did so. It would be if the offer stipulated that *any* member do so.

3.2.2 An offer cannot be accepted in ignorance of the offer

There can be no acceptance where the offeree acts in ignorance of the offer. *Fitch v Snedaker* (1868) 38 NY 248 provides authority for this proposition. Snedaker had offered a reward for the return of his lost dog. Fitch found the dog and returned it to Snedaker, but had done so unaware of the offer of a reward. Fitch was thus not entitled to claim the money as he had acted in ignorance of the offer.

Similarly, in the Australian case of *R. (The Crown) v Clarke* (1927) 40 C.L.R. 227, Clarke sought to claim a reward offered to persons giving information on the murder of two policemen. Although he had initially been aware of the ad, on the facts, Clarke was held to have panicked and forgotten about the reward, giving information simply "to save his own skin". At the time he acted, because of his panicked state, he had not been cognisant of the offer and thus could not claim. That is not to say that a person acting with a motive other than reward is thereby prejudiced. In *Williams v Carwardine* (1833) 4 B. & Ad. 621, the plaintiff had supplied information about a murder to the police. Although Ms Williams was aware at the time that an offer had been made for the giving of information, she had acted out of goodwill, anxious to ease her conscience before she died. However, being aware of the offer and having met its terms, she was nonetheless entitled to claim the $20 reward, despite her motive.

A somewhat similar principle arises from *Taylor v Laird* (1856) 25 L.J. Exch. 329. The captain of a ship, mid-voyage, had resigned his position but, unknown to the defendant, had continued to do work on the ship. Taylor was, however, unable to sue for services rendered as the work had been performed without the knowledge of the ship's owners. In other words, Laird had no opportunity to either accept or reject Taylor's offer of work, as it had not been communicated to the defendant.

3.2.3 An offer may be accepted at any time before the offer is terminated, but not thereafter
See above at para.2.5.

3.2.4 An offer may be terminated at any time before it is accepted, but not thereafter
See above at para.2.5.

3.3 Methods of acceptance

3.3.1 Acceptance must be unconditional
In order to give rise to a contract, the acceptance must be made unconditionally, that is, in precisely the same terms as the offer. If the terms of the offer and the terms of an apparent acceptance differ, then there is in fact no acceptance but rather a counter-offer. This is sometimes called the "mirror image" effect: the acceptance must match the terms of the offer.

As Murphy J. observed in *Tansey v College of Occupational Therapists* (unreported, High Court, August 27, 1986):

> "Ordinarily a communication in the course of negotiations leading to a contract which contains conditions not previously agreed by the party to whom the communication is addressed

will fall to be treated as a new or counter-offer rather than an acceptance".

For instance, John makes an offer to James, indicating that he will sell his car to James for €5,000. James replies by letter stating that he will accept the offer but only if John pays James' car insurance for one year. This latter term not having been in the original offer, there is no acceptance: James has instead made a counter offer. It is now for John to decide whether to accept James' new offer.

In *Swan v Miller* [1919] 1 I.R. 151, in response to an offer to sell land for £4,750 plus a ground rent, the plaintiffs responded stating that they would pay £4,450, with no mention of the ground rent. As the plaintiffs' response did not match the offer, the plaintiffs were deemed to have made a counter-offer. Likewise, in *Tinn v Hoffman* (1873) 29 L.T. 271, an offer to sell 1,200 tons of iron received a response ordering 800 tons. The response, being in terms different from the offer, was held to be a counter-offer and not an acceptance.

Such a process of negotiation often involves what is called the "Battle of the Forms". Effectively, in the course of negotiations, each party puts forward terms and conditions, asserting that its terms should govern the contract. As such, during the course of negotiations several offers and counter offers may be made before acceptance occurs. The basic rule is that until one party accepts the other party's terms without conditions, there is no contract. In essence, "the last shot wins the battle"—the offer that is last made immediately before agreement is reached, governs the terms of the contract.

For example, in *British Road Services v Crutchley Ltd* [1968] 1 All E.R. 811, a driver working for the plaintiff company had delivered whisky to the defendant, for the purpose of storage. On delivery, the driver presented a delivery note to the defendant's agent, which note set out the plaintiff's standard "conditions of carriage". This note was in turn stamped by the defendant's agent, the stamp indicating that the goods were "Received under [Crutchley's standard] conditions". The driver accepted this note. The court concluded that by placing the stamp on the note, Crutchley had issued a counter-offer, asserting that its terms (and not the plaintiff's) would apply to the contract. The driver having accepted the stamped note, the contract was held to have been made on the defendant's conditions.

Another example of the battle of the forms arises from *Butler Machine Co. v Ex-cell-O Corp. Ltd* [1979] 1 W.L.R. 401. In this case, the plaintiff company issued an offer to sell a machine for £75,000. The terms of the offer included a clause allowing the plaintiff to increase the sale price should costs rise before delivery. The defendant responded asserting that the sale would proceed on its (*i.e.* the defendant's) terms, which did not provide for price variation. The plaintiff having signed and returned an acknowledgement slip confirming that it accepted the defendant's terms, was held to be bound by those terms. In other words, the plaintiff was deemed to have accepted the defendant's counter-offer, and was thus not entitled to invoke its price variation clause.

However, a counter-offer must be distinguished from a request or inquiry as to the terms of the offer, if it is clear that there will or may be acceptance regardless of the response to such inquiries. In *Stevenson v McLean* (see para.2.5.1), an inquiry as to whether the offeror would allow a purchase on credit was not deemed to constitute a counter-offer.

3.3.2 Exceptions
In some cases a statement that apparently deviates from the offer may nonetheless be treated as an acceptance:

- If the offeree suggests a new term that will benefit the offeror (as in *Quadling v Robinson* (1976) 137 C.L.R. 192, where the acceptance promised to pay on a date earlier than stipulated in the offer; the offeror could hardly complain that it was to receive an early payment).
- If the new terms would be inserted by law, regardless of the wishes of the party.

3.3.3 When is a unilateral offer accepted?
Special rules apply to unilateral offers. Where a unilateral offer is made, acceptance occurs through performance of an act (or, if relevant, refraining from doing so). What would happen if the offer was withdrawn after performance was commenced but *before* it was completed? If Jill, for instance, offered Caspar €500 if he walked from the Cliffs of Moher to the G.P.O. in Dublin, could she withdraw the offer after he started walking, for instance, as he passed through Enfield?

The classical view is that acceptance occurs only when there is *complete* performance of a contemplated act. Strictly speaking, it is technically possible to withdraw the offer before every element of acceptance is complete, even if performance has already commenced.

In theory at least, if Jill phoned Caspar while *en route*, calling off the deal, Jill would be entitled to do this as there can be no acceptance unless and until the contemplated act has been performed in its entirety.

The traditional view is set out in *Luxor (Eastbourne) Ltd v Cooper* [1941] 1 All E.R. 33. An estate agent was offered £10,000 if it found a buyer for a house. After the estate agent began making serious efforts to sell the property, but before a purchaser was found, the landowner revoked the offer. The House of Lords ruled that the estate agent had no claim over the £10,000 as the owner was entitled to revoke the offer at any time before the completion of performance.

However, certain dicta of Buckley L.J. in *Daulia Ltd v Four Millbank Nominees Ltd* [1978] 2 All E.R. 557 suggest that once the offeree commences performance, the offer cannot be revoked. (See also *Abbott v Lance* (1860) Legges N.S.W.R. 1283.) In *Errington v Errington* [1952] 1 K.B. 290, a father had promised his son and daughter-in-law that once they paid off the mortgage on his house, the house would be theirs. Before the mortgage was fully cleared, the father's executors attempted to revoke the offer: as performance had already commenced, the court ruled that the offer could not be withdrawn, even though it had not yet been accepted. Although this may be theoretically unsound, it is undoubtedly fair.

3.4 Indicating acceptance

An unexpressed mental intention to accept an offer, without more, is not sufficient to make a valid contract. In other words, acceptance cannot occur simply in the mind of the offeree. There must be some outward indication of acceptance. This may occur either expressly (by words) or implicitly (by conduct).

3.4.1 Express acceptance

A person may indicate acceptance expressly, that is by making a definitive statement, either orally or in writing, to the effect that she accepts the offer without condition. Such acceptance must explicitly indicate an intention to accept the offer in the terms in which the offer is made.

3.4.2 Implied acceptance

Acceptance may also be implied, or inferred from certain conduct. A good example might be where a shopper offers to buy a chocolate bar in a newsagent. The cashier is talking on her mobile phone. The shopper puts the bar on the counter, and proffers a euro. The cashier, still preoccupied with her phonecall, takes the euro, rings up the purchase on the till, and gives the shopper her change. The cashier's conduct constitutes implied acceptance. The fact that the parties have not spoken to each other is irrelevant—the conduct of the cashier indicates that the offer has been accepted.

Acceptance by conduct is a regular response to unilateral offers. For instance, in *Billings v Arnott* (1945) 80 I.L.T.R. 50, an employer had offered his workers half pay if they joined the army. In this case acceptance was deemed to have occurred where the plaintiff employee enlisted in the army. Although he had not expressly informed his employer of his decision, his conduct was sufficient to denote acceptance.

In *Western Electric v Welsh Development Agency* [1983] Q.B. 796, the defendant, by letter, offered work to the plaintiff. Instead of responding to the letter, the plaintiff, to the defendant's knowledge, began to perform the contemplated work. This action was deemed to constitute acceptance—again, though words had not been exchanged, the conduct of the plaintiff could only have been consistent with his implicit acceptance of the offer. Likewise, in *Brogden v Metropolitan Ry. Co.* (1877) 2 A.C. 666, a contract was deemed to have been accepted by the defendant's conduct in ordering coal and accepting it on receipt.

3.4.3 Acceptance by silence?

While a person may denote acceptance through conduct, silent inactivity in the face of an offer does not typically denote consent. If the offeree neither speaks nor acts in apparent acceptance of the offer then there can be no contract. As a general rule, unless the context clearly indicates otherwise, silence cannot constitute acceptance.

This is the case even where the offeror states that silence will be taken to be acceptance. The classic example of this principle arises from *Felthouse v Bindley* (1862) 11 C.B. (N.S.) 869. In this case, an uncle wrote to his nephew offering £30 and 15 shillings for the nephew's horse. In the letter, the uncle indicated that "if I hear no more about him, I consider the horse mine at that price". The nephew did not respond. A court held that the uncle had not been entitled to the horse as the nephew had not accepted his offer. Mere silence on the part of the nephew was not sufficient to give rise to a contract.

An Irish example of this rule is provided by *Russell & Baird v Hoban* [1922] 2 I.R. 159. In this case, the plaintiff had mailed a sale note to the defendant offering to supply material. In the correspondence, the plaintiff had indicated that if there was no response within three days, acceptance would be assumed. The court ruled that there was no contract, as silence did not denote consent.

The policy reasons for this rule are arguably well founded. Silence is generally ambiguous as to intention. It may denote indifference or indecision. It is, moreover, perfectly consistent with the possibility that the silent party was unaware of the offer. This being the case, it would arguably be unfair to penalise a party for their silence.

There are, however, some exceptional cases in which silence may be considered as indicative of acceptance.

- **If the parties agree that silence may be interpreted as consent, a contract may form as the result of silence.** In particular, if it is the offeree who suggests that silence on her part will denote acceptance, she thus assumes the risk that acceptance will occur unless she expressly rejects the offer. For instance, A offers to sell B his car for €5,000. B responds saying he's not sure "but if you don't hear from me by Monday, you may assume that I accept your offer". In such a case, because the offeree has agreed that his silence can be interpreted as acceptance, acceptance may spring from B's silence. (See *Re Selectmove* [1995] 2 All. E.R. 531.)
- **Where past dealings give rise to a legitimate expectation that silence will suffice.** Past dealings between the parties may also give rise to an expectation that silence indicates acceptance. Industry practice may also dictate that silence denotes consent, a good example being the insurance industry practice whereby a contract will often be renewed automatically unless the offeree expressly contacts the insurer to cancel the cover.
- **Where there is an implied contract for services.** A contract may be implied in circumstances where a person "X" performs an act for the benefit of another person "Y", provided that Y is aware of and does not object to the performance of the act. Provided that Y has a reasonable opportunity to object, and refrains from doing so, a contract may be implied. For instance, in *Western Electric v Welsh Development Authority* (see para.3.4.2), the defendant asked the plaintiff to perform certain works. The plaintiff did not respond, but nonetheless, to the knowledge of the defendant, turned up to perform the work. Despite its silence, the plaintiff was deemed to have accepted the offer.

3.4.4 *If the mode of acceptance is expressly stipulated*

However, if the offeror requires as a term of the offer that acceptance occurs in a particular manner, that condition must be complied with. For instance, if the offeror stipulates that the offer must be accepted in writing, by post, a phone call indicating acceptance may not suffice. However, if an equally effective method or better method is used this will suffice as acceptance. (See *Tinn v Hoffman* (1873) 29 LT 271.) For instance, if acceptance is stipulated to occur by post, and the acceptance occurs by couriered delivery of the acceptance, the acceptance will be satisfactory. Likewise, it is possible that an e-mailed PDF will be equally as effective as a fax.

Furthermore if the method of acceptance is stipulated for the benefit of the offeree, (the person accepting the offer) rather than the offeror, the offeree is not obliged to use the stipulated method of acceptance (see *Yates Building Co. v Pulleyn & Sons* (1975) 119 S.J. 370). However, a stipulation for silence cannot bind the offeree.

3.5 Acceptance must be communicated

An acceptance will not give rise to a contract unless and until the offeror is made aware of the fact of acceptance. In other words, acceptance must be communicated to the person who made the offer; it will not be effective until this occurs. The policy reason for this appears to be that the law wishes to avoid a situation where a person becomes bound by a contract without knowing it. It is suggested, for instance, that even where two people simultaneously post each other offers in the same terms, ("cross-offers"), each made in ignorance of the other, there can be no acceptance as each party is ignorant of the other's acceptance.

In *Entores Ltd v Miles Far East Corporation* [1955] 2 Q.B. 327, Lord Denning put forward a hypothetical example of this rule. Suppose A and B are standing on opposite sides of a river. A shouts an offer across the river to B. B shouts his acceptance in response, but due to a plane flying overhead, A does not hear B's message of acceptance. In such a case, because A is unaware of the acceptance, there is no contract. There can be no contract until the offeror is aware that the offeree has accepted.

Parkgrange Investments v Shandon Park Mills (unreported, High Court, May 2, 1991) provides a good Irish example of such a scenario. In this case the defendant had signed a contract of sale indicating its apparent acceptance thereof. In fact, the defendant did so only to obtain tax clearance in case the sale should actually go ahead. In particular, the defendant had failed to return the contract to the plaintiff. As such, the plaintiff remained ignorant of the acceptance. Carroll J. ruled that there had been no contract, partly because the defendant lacked the intention to accept. She also ruled, however, that the contract had not come into being, owing to the defendant's failure to communicate the acceptance to the other side.

3.6 Exceptions to the communication rule

There are certain exceptions to the rule requiring the communication of an acceptance.

3.6.1 Unilateral contracts

Unilateral offers are accepted through the performance of an act. As such, communication of acceptance is generally unnecessary. The acceptance occurs when the act is completely performed.

3.6.2 Where the terms of the offer permit acceptance without communication

If the offer itself states that communication of acceptance is not required, an uncommunicated acceptance will bind the offeror. The offeror is deemed to have accepted the risk of becoming bound by a contract without her knowledge.

3.6.3 Offeror's own fault

It is generally accepted that where the offeror fails to hear of the acceptance because of her own conduct, the offer may nonetheless be accepted. An example might include a situation where a note of acceptance is received, but not read. (See *The "Brimnes"* [1975] Q.B. 629.)

3.7 The postal rule

The most significant—and controversial—exception to the communication rule arises as a result of the "postal rule". This rule posits that when a letter of acceptance is sent through the post, the acceptance is deemed in law to have been made (a) at the time it was posted and (b) in the place it was posted. Acceptance takes effect not on receipt (as would normally be required) but at the point of postage. Literally then, where an acceptance is posted, the contract comes into being at the time it is inserted into the postbox.

The postal rule was first established in the English case of *Adams v Lindsell* (1818) 1 B & Ald. 681. Some Irish examples usefully demonstrate the operation of this rule. In *Sanderson v Cunningham* [1919] 2 I.R. 234, a Dublin-based plaintiff had offered to purchase insurance from a London insurer. The insurer accepted the plaintiff's offer by issuing an insurance policy by letter from London. The Irish Court of Appeal ruled that because the acceptance had been posted from London, the contract had been concluded in London. In *Kelly v Cruise Catering* [1994] 2 I.L.R.M. 394, an Irish employee was injured while working on a boat *en route* from Mexico to Texas. The Irish courts would only have the power to hear the case if the contract of employment was concluded in Ireland. In this case, the contract of employment was drafted in Oslo, but was signed by the plaintiff in Dublin, and returned to Norway by post. This being the case, the courts ruled that the contract was concluded in Ireland, because the acceptance had occurred at the point of postage, not at the point of receipt.

Remarkably, the postal rule takes effect even if the letter in question is lost or delayed in the post, the offeror assuming the risk that the acceptance will be lost in the post (See *Household Fire Insurance v Grant* (1879) L.R. 4 Ex. 216). This may not be the case, however, where the loss or delay results from the fault of the offeree, as, for instance, where the offeree has misaddressed the letter, or paid insufficient postage.

As discussed above at para.2.5.4, where a letter of acceptance is put in the post before notification of a revocation is received, revocation will not be effective. In *Byrne v Van Tienhoven* (see para.2.5.4), a telegram of acceptance was dispatched October 11, 1879 with a letter following sent on October 15. The defendant, however, had sent a letter revoking the offer, posted October 8 but it was only received by the offeree on October 20, 1879. Acceptance took place when the telegram was sent, or failing that, when the letter of acceptance was posted, October 11 or 15. A revocation, however, only takes effect when it is received, in this case, October 20.

3.8 Cases where the postal rule does not apply

3.8.1 Express exclusion of rule
It is always possible to exclude the application of the postal rule, simply by agreeing that communication of acceptance is a pre-condition to

the formation of a valid contract. This may be done by stipulating, as a term of the offer, that there will be no acceptance until the letter of acceptance is *received*: *Holwell Securities v Hughes* [1974] 1 W.L.R. 155. For instance, in *Nunin Holdings v Tullamarine Estates Property* [1994] 1 V.R. 74, the plaintiff had made an offer stating that a contract would form only on receipt by the plaintiff of the acceptance. After the acceptance was posted, but before the acceptance was received, the defendant telephoned revoking the acceptance: the rejection of the offer was deemed effective, as acceptance had not yet taken place.

3.8.2 Stipulation that another mode of delivery be used
The postal rule will not apply where the offeror has stipulated for a method of delivery other than the post, *e.g.* by telephone or courier.

3.8.3 Instantaneous communication
Although the postal rule applies to telegrams (see *Cowan v O'Connor* (1888) 20 Q.B.D. 640), it does not apply where the method of communication is instantaneous. *Entores Ltd v Miles Far East Corporation* (see para.3.5) is authority for the proposition that the postal rule does not apply to a communication by telex (a form of electronic communication whereby a message is typed into a special typewriter and conveyed via telephone lines to the recipient.) In this case, a telex was sent from Amsterdam to London indicating acceptance of an offer. The court ruled that because telexes offered the possibility of virtually instantaneous communication, the postal rule did not apply. Acceptance, thus, was only concluded on receipt of the telex message in England.

A fax is very similar to a telex, and in fact, operates by means of an analogue telephone line. This being the case, it is likely that the postal rule does not apply to fax messages, as the message is virtually instantaneous. It is also generally possible for the sender to check whether the faxed message was received. It is likely that this exception also applies to more modern methods of instantaneous communication, such as offers made while instant messaging, via webcam or by using the "click-wrap method" (where an internet user clicks on a box to indicate acceptance of certain terms and conditions).

It is not clear whether this exception applies to e-mail. While e-mail communication certainly can be quicker than regular post, it is not as instantaneous as a phone call. Most importantly, with e-mail, there is "mediated" delivery. In other words, if Buffy sends Bree an e-mail, it does not go directly from Buffy's PC to Bree's. It passes via telephone line to Buffy's SMTP server (which handles outgoing mail) and then (sometimes via a variety of servers and several alternative routes) to Bree's POP3 server (this handles incoming mail). The incoming mail sits on the server until Bree accesses her e-mail. It might also be argued that although one may check a fax or telex machine to see if there has been delivery, this is not immediately possible with e-mail. As such, the postal rule may apply to e-mail, though this point is nonetheless debatable. Some authors suggest that the postal rule is already considered to be anomalous and that as such, it may be more likely that the courts will not ultimately apply the rule to e-mail. The better view may be that judges will be anxious to confine the postal rule and will be reluctant to extend it to e-mail.

4. The Intention to Create Legal Relations

For a contract to come into being, a person must accept without condition an offer made by another person. At this point, where there is an offer accepted without condition, it can be said that there is a contract or "agreement" between the parties. Nonetheless, not all such agreements are automatically enforceable in law. In other words, although there may be an agreement, other conditions must be met before the contract can be enforced in a court of law.

One of these conditions is that the parties entering into the contract must exhibit an intention to create legal relations. This means that the parties have manifested through their actions or words the intention or belief that their contract would be legally binding. In other words, did the parties intend that, if broken or otherwise in contention, the contract could be enforced in a court of law?

The question is an important one. There are a great many agreements and arrangements that, though possessing many of the characteristics of a contract, probably are not intended to attract legal consequences. One example might be an agreement between two people to go on a date or meet up to go to the cinema. Such agreement may well comprise an offer and acceptance. Nonetheless, in such a scenario, although there may be agreement (possibly even supported by consideration, *e.g.* if one of the parties buys cinema tickets in advance), generally the parties would not reasonably be taken to have intended their agreement to have legal consequences. In other words, the parties probably did not contemplate the formation of a legal relationship, attracting legal remedies.

4.1 Two presumptions apply in this regard

- Where the agreement springs from a family, social or domestic relationship, it is presumed (unless the contrary is established) that the agreement is *not* intended to attract legal relations.
- Where the agreement is of a commercial nature it is presumed (unless the contrary is established) that the agreement *is* intended to attract legal relations.

As Budd J. noted in *Rogers v Smith* (unreported, Supreme Court, July 16, 1970):

"… in social and family matters agreements may be come to which do not give rise to legal relations because such a

30

consequence is not the intention of the parties and in family matters, an intention to remain free of legal obligations will be readily implied whereas in business matters the opposite result would ordinarily follow".

4.2 Family, domestic and social arrangements

The law presumes, then, that arrangements or agreements of a social or domestic nature or involving matters internal to a family or household do not generally attract legal relations. Unless the opposite intention is clearly stated, a presumption arises that such domestic or social arrangements are not intended to be legally enforceable.

4.2.1 Agreements between spouses

The key decision in this area is *Balfour v Balfour,* [1919] 2 K.B. 571, where an agreement by a husband to the effect that he would maintain his wife was deemed not to be legally enforceable. The Court of Appeal concluded that a presumption arose that the agreement—being one between husband and wife—was not intended to attract legal relations.

It is important to note, however, that at the time of the agreement, the marriage was still intact and the couple were on good terms. Such a conclusion would *not* apply where the parties made the agreement in the context of a relationship breakup. In summary, the less amicable the relationship at the time of the agreement, the easier it will be to displace the presumption. For instance, an agreement entered into in contemplation of present separation will be enforced. In *Courtney v Courtney* (1923) 57 I.L.T.R. 42, a separation agreement between a husband and wife was upheld as enforceable. (See also *Merritt v Merritt* [1969] 2 All. E.R. 760.)

4.2.2 Agreements between other family members

Two Irish cases involving family property arrangements are instructive in this regard.

In *Rogers v Smith* (unreported, Supreme Court, July 16, 1970), the Irish Supreme Court concluded that an understanding between a mother and her son did not attract legal relations. In this case, the mother had transferred the family business to her son, the plaintiff, in exchange for which the plaintiff promised that he would pay his mother a weekly sum in respect of household expenses. In response, the mother had told her son that "any money that I owe you when I am dead and gone you will probably take it from my estate". Budd J. nonetheless concluded that this arrangement was of "a purely family nature not intended to have [legal] consequences".

Likewise, in *Mackey v Jones* (1959) 93 I.L.T.R. 177, having worked his uncle's farm for some years, without payment, Mackey claimed that his uncle had promised him the farm on the uncle's death. The farm having been left to another relative, Mackey sued for breach of contract. Deale J. ruled, however, that no contract had arisen. The uncle's representation amounted to a statement of intention only, with no promissory effects. There was, the judge concluded, no intention to create legal relations. There was "… nothing more than a statement of intention or wish by the deceased … no promise was made."

Similarly, in *Jones v Padvatton* [1969] 1 W.L.R. 328, a mother and daughter entered into an agreement under which the mother agreed to maintain and accommodate her daughter, if the latter undertook studies for the Bar. The presumption that family arrangements did not attract legal relations was not, on the facts, displaced. The agreement in this case was based on the familial relationship of the parties, and there was nothing to indicate that the normal presumption had been ousted in this case.

4.2.3 Rebutting the presumption

This presumption may, however, be rebutted (displaced) by evidence that legal relations were intended. In short: the less amicable the relationship between the parties, the more distant the relationship and the more business-like the agreement, the more likely it is that the intention to create legal relations will arise, even between family members.

Hynes v Hynes (unreported, High Court, December 21, 1984) establishes that where the agreement involves matters of a business nature, the agreement is more likely to attract legal relations. In the latter case, an agreement to transfer a business from one brother to another was upheld as legally enforceable notwithstanding the relationship of the parties.

According to *Leahy v Rawson* (unreported, High Court, January 14, 2003), moreover, for the presumption to apply, the relationship must be a close and probably a legally recognised relationship (such as that between parent and child or between spouses); in that case the relationship between the plaintiff and her non-marital partner's brother was deemed insufficiently close to attract the presumption. The brother had agreed to do work on the plaintiff's home: this agreement was upheld as one attracting legal relations

In several cases, agreements between friends regarding the sharing of competition winnings have been upheld, notwithstanding the relatively informal nature of the arrangements. For instance, in *Simpkin v Pays* [1955] 3 All E.R. 10, a lodger, living in the defendant's house, won £750 in a Sunday newspaper competition. The defendant and her granddaughter, who had helped the lodger complete and pay for the entry, were held to be entitled to a share in the prize money. It seems then that an understanding regarding the distribution of competition winnings will be enforced.

4.3 Commercial agreements

In strong contrast with the situation that applies to domestic arrangements, contract law generally assumes that unless there is a clear statement to the contrary, the parties to a commercial or business contract intended to create a legal relationship. In fact, it is quite unusual to find a commercial contract that is not intended to attract legal relations.

This is the case even where the negotiations leading to the contract were quite informal. It is possible, for instance, to make a binding agreement over a round of golf, or between cocktails at a business lunch. For instance, in *J. Evans & Son (Portsmouth) Ltd. v Andrea Merzario Ltd* [1976] 2 All E.R. 930, an impromptu visit by a sales representative, making a courtesy call to a client, led to the conclusion of a binding contract, notwithstanding the informality of the arrangement. Likewise, in *Esso Petroleum v Commissioner of Customs and Excise*, [1976] 1 All E.R. 117, a binding contract was deemed to arise from a transaction in which football tokens were offered to anyone who purchased four gallons of the plaintiff's petrol. According to Lord Simon "... the whole transaction took place in a setting of business relations...", the purpose of the offer being commercial: Esso wanted the public to buy its petrol.

There are however, some exceptions to the general rule that commercial agreement attract legal relations:

4.3.1 Exaggerated statements

Certain statements, made in the course of contractual dealings, may by their very nature not be intended to give rise to contractual liability. In particular, some statements made in the course of advertising cannot realistically be interpreted as having contractual force. For instance, a representation that a deodorant or cologne will have women or men (or both) chasing after you in romantic adulation or that a washing powder will clean your whites to the point that they are visible from space, would not reasonably be interpreted as a contractual promise. Such representations amount to a "trader's puff", obvious exaggerations designed to draw in the punters but not meant to be taken seriously. (See *Smith v Lynn* (1954) 85 I.L.T.R. 57.)

Whether such statements give rise to legal relations, is however, a matter of fact. The question to be asked is not whether the person making the representation intended it to be binding. The question is instead, based on objective criteria: would the ordinary reasonable person take this statement as a serious promise? In *Carlill v Carbolic Smokeball Co.* (see para.2.3), for instance, the court concluded that a promise that the use of a smokeball would prevent the user from contracting the flu was a genuine offer. The fact that the defendant had laid aside £1,000 to pay to users who did contract the flu was deemed to confirm the defendant's seriousness in making this offer.

4.3.2 Joke offer

A similar principle applies to contracts made in jest, that is, as a result of what the parties intended to be a joke. The contract will not be enforceable if (but only if) it would have been clear to a reasonable bystander that agreement was meant to be a joke. The fact that one or other party to the contract did not seriously contemplate a sale will not be conclusive in this regard. The question is whether or not, from an objective standpoint, the parties can reasonably be deemed to have made a serious contract. In this regard context is crucial.

4.3.3 Honour clauses/gentlemen's agreements

Even in a commercial context, the presumption in favour of the intention to create legal relations can be displaced by a very clear expression of lack of legal intention. In other words, the parties may exclude the possibility of legal consequences by expressly stating that a breach of contract will not result in legal liability. A clause ousting legal jurisdiction in this way is sometimes called an "honour clause". The resulting agreement is often known (rather quaintly) as a "gentleman's agreement": an agreement that is binding only as a matter of honour, and not as a matter of law.

A classic example of such a clause arose in *Rose and Frank Co. v Crompton Bros.* [1923] 2 K.B. 261. In this case, the parties had agreed that the plaintiff would be permitted to distribute the defendants' goods in the United States. The agreement however contained an "honourable pledge clause" stating that:

"This arrangement is not entered into, nor is this memorandum written, as a formal or legal agreement, and shall not be subject to legal jurisdiction in the law courts of the United States or of England, but it is only a definite expression and record of the purpose and intention of the three parties concerned to which each honourably pledge themselves with the fullest confidence, based on past business with each other, that it will be carried through by each of the three parties with mutual loyalty and friendly co-operation."

Such confidence had clearly been misplaced, the defendants having withdrawn from the agreement. The English Court of Appeal concluded, however, that because of the honour clause set out above, the agreement could not be enforced. By this clause the parties had, the court ruled, unequivocally ruled out an intention to create a legally binding contract, and thus had agreed that a breach would not result in legal liability.

A similar clause served to exclude legal consequences in *Jones v Vernon's Pools Ltd* [1938] 2 All E.R. 626, a case involving a football pools coupon. The coupon contained a statement to the effect that any agreement or transaction in that case "… shall not be attended by or give rise to any legal relationship, rights, duties or consequences whatsoever or be legally enforceable or the subject of litigation". Any agreement arising would be "binding in honour only", a condition that excluded the creation of a legal relationship.

It is evident, however, from *Edwards v Skyways* [1964] 1 W.L.R. 349 that those wishing to avoid the creation of a legal relationship in a business context must express that intention clearly and unambiguously. In other words, in a commercial context, a very explicit statement is required to prevent a contract from giving rise to legal relations.

4.3.4 "Letters of comfort"

A "letter of comfort" is similar in many respects to an honour clause. In short, a letter of comfort is a document designed to reassure its recipient regarding certain matters, without subjecting the writer to a contractual liability. Such a letter, in summary, simply sets out the current state of mind of the writer; it does not amount to an enforceable promise. While it may be useful in reassuring the recipient, the terms of the letter are not intended to give rise to a legal relationship.

Whether or not a statement amounts to a letter of comfort depends on the wording of the letter. A good example of the effects of a letter of comfort arose in *Kleinwort Benson v Malaysia Mining Corp. (MMC)*

Bhd. [1989] 1 All E.R. 785. In this case, the plaintiff bank had agreed to lend money to a subsidiary of the Malaysia Mining Corporation (MMC). In the course of negotiations for the loan, the bank received a letter of comfort from MMC stating that:

> "… it is [MMC's] policy to ensure that the business of our subsidiary is at all times in a position to meet its liabilities to you under the above arrangements."

Despite this reassurance, the Court of Appeal concluded that this statement did not bind the defendant. The letter was not, in fact, purporting to make a binding promise. It was simply stating the company's policy, a policy that might be changed or adjusted in response to novel circumstances.

It is important to note, however, that there is no concrete rule precluding a letter of comfort from giving rise to legal relations. Whether or not such a letter creates a legally binding promise is a matter to be discerned primarily from the language used. The simple fact that the words "letter of comfort" have been used, while evidentially relevant, may not conclusively prevent the agreement from having legal implications.

4.3.5 "Subject to contract"

Where, particularly in contracts for the sale of land, an agreement is expressed to be "subject to contract", the agreement generally will not attract legal relations. The phrase is best viewed as a statement to the effect that the relevant arrangement is not a binding contract and that the arrangements are conditional on a final contract being concluded and signed by both parties.

There has, however, been some amount of vacillation on this point, the courts equivocating with regularity on the precise effect of these words. The *locus classicus* is *Thompson v The King* [1920] 2 I.R. 365, where an offer containing the words "subject to contract" was made by telegram, in response to which the plaintiff had communicated his acceptance. The Court of King's Bench concluded that the use of the phrase "subject to contract" precluded the formation of a binding contract. The parties had not, it ruled, agreed to a final settlement and had postponed the final agreement to a later date. In *Mulhall v Haren* [1981] I.R. 364, Costello J. likewise suggested that the phrase "subject to contract" precluded the enforcement of a contract, the parties having indicated that the matter was still subject to negotiation.

For a while, the courts drifted from this view. In *O'Flaherty v Arvan Property* (unreported, High Court, November 3, 1976), for example, the parties had agreed on the terms orally, with no mention of the agreement being subject to contract. An oral contract for the sale of land will not be enforceable unless there is a written note evidencing its content. (See below at para.10.5.) In this case, subsequent to the oral agreement, a note of the contract was drawn up containing the phrase "subject to contract". The High Court nonetheless ruled that because the parties themselves had not used this phrase during their negotiations, it had no effect. Unless the parties to the contract agreed that a subsequent binding contract was contemplated, the action of a solicitor or other agent in adding the term "subject to contract" to a note evidencing the agreement did not prevent the agreement from having legal effects. In other words, the use of the phrase was not conclusive if on the facts the parties intended their agreement to be full and final, a point further underlined by *Casey v Irish Intercontinental Bank* [1979] I.R. 364 and *Kelly v Park Hall Schools* [1979] I.R. 340.

Nonetheless, in the wake of the Supreme Court decision in *Boyle v Lee and Goyns* [1992] I.L.R.M. 65, the better view would appear to be that the use of the phrase in a note of the contract is conclusive, and that a contract cannot be enforced where a note of the contract contains these words. This decision appears to overrule or at least severely restrict the operation of the rulings in *O'Flaherty, Casey* and *Kelly,* by suggesting that a note of an agreement, containing the words in question, cannot be contradicted by oral evidence that the parties in fact intended their contract to be conclusive. There is a ring of sense to this conclusion: a note denying the existence of a final contract could hardly be fairly used to enforce the very contract it denies.

There is, however, no particular magic in the use of this specific phrase. Its absence is not conclusive as to the enforceability of a contract: other phrases may also suffice to prevent a provisional agreement from being enforced. Provided that the note clearly indicates that further negotiations are contemplated, the parties will not be bound. For instance, in *Silver Wraith v Siúicre Éireann* (unreported, High Court, June 8, 1989) an agreement was expressed to be "subject to full lease terms being agreed." On the facts, the court concluded that there was no final contract, that the parties intended further detailed negotiations before their bargain was concluded.

4.3.6 An agreement that contemplates the making of a further agreement

Where an agreement necessitates or contemplates the making of a further contract, it is more than likely that the first contract will not (on its own) give rise to legal relations. A good example arises from *Cadbury Ireland v Kerry Co-op and Dairy Disposal Co. Ltd.* [1982] I.L.R.M. 77. Dairy Disposal Co. (DDC) was the owner of several creameries that supplied milk for Cadbury's chocolate factories. In anticipation of a likely expansion in Cadbury's Irish operations, DDC and Cadbury had agreed that the former would ensure an adequate supply of milk should Cadbury go ahead with its plan to increase production. DDC subsequently sold some of its creameries to Kerry Co-op. As a condition of the sale, Kerry Co-op had agreed with DDC that the former would supply Cadbury's needs, subject to price and quantity of supplies being agreed between the two companies. Though Cadbury was not involved in this agreement, it sought to enforce Kerry Co-op's apparent promise to supply. The High Court, nonetheless, declined to hold Kerry Co-op liable. Barrington J. concluded that the contracting parties had assumed that the relevant clause would be supplemented by an agreement between Cadbury and Kerry Co-op. In other words:

> "… the agreement contemplated a further agreement between [Cadbury] and [Kerry Co-op] to give it business efficacy".

At the very most, the judge observed, there was a commitment to enter into honest negotiations for a legal trading agreement with Cadbury, an agreement that never transpired.

The English case of *May and Butcher Ltd v R.* [1934] 2 K.B. 17 provides another useful example. In this case, the parties had agreed to transfer certain goods, leaving the price and timing of the sale "to be agreed from time to time." The House of Lords concluded that the agreement was not enforceable, as it was incomplete, several crucial matters being left for further negotiation.

4.4 *De minimis non curat lex*

Before leaving this topic, it is worth considering, briefly, the principle *de minimis non curat lex*. This means that a court will generally be reluctant to enforce a contract where the subject matter is trifling, or where the case is of little real consequence. For instance, if A contracts to buy a chocolate bar worth 50c belonging to B, and B reneged on this agreement, A would more than likely not be entertained should he choose to take a case. The loss is minimal, and judges (quite appropriately) have more serious matters to consider.

5. The Requirement of Certainty

5.1 Introduction

A contract will not be enforced unless its terms are sufficiently clear and certain. Thus, the terms of a contract should generally not be vague, ambiguous or uncertain or insusceptible to clarification.

For instance, in *Scammell v Ouston* [1941] A.C. 251, a contract agreeing that the balance for the purchase of a van would be paid "on hire-purchase terms" was deemed too vague to be enforced. Given the diversity of hire purchase arrangements that might be entered into, it was ultimately unclear to the court what was meant in this context by the phrase "hire-purchase terms". Similarly, in *Loftus v Roberts* (1902) 18 T.L.R. 532, a contract promising to pay an actor a "West End salary to be mutually agreed between us" was held to be uncertain as to the salary, (as it was again unclear that there was any such thing as a standard "West End salary"—a leading actress and a chorus girl would receive significantly different rates) and thus unenforceable. (For a more recent example see *Malcolm v University of Oxford* [2001] 2 Lloyd's Rep. 76.)

Some Irish examples might also prove illuminating. In *Mackie v Wilde* [1998] 2 I.R. 578, the plaintiff had agreed to issue the defendant 25 annual fishing permits and "a few day tickets" for fishing. The Supreme Court ruled that as the quantity of day tickets available was uncertain, the contract could not be enforced. The promise to supply annual fishing permits, moreover, could not be severed from the agreement regarding the day tickets: thus the whole contract was rendered unenforceable. Likewise, in *Central Meat Products v Carney,* (1944) 10 Ir. Jur. Rep. 34, the failure to agree certain crucial matters in a contract for the sale of cattle prevented the contract from being enforced. (See also the *Cadbury* case discussed above at para.4.3.6.)

At a minimum, there should be clarity as to the three Ps: the "parties" (who is contracting), the "price", and the "property" or subject matter of the agreement. That is not to say, however, that unless every contingency is provided for, the contract will be doomed. It may not always be feasible, especially in a contract that is intended to endure for an indefinite time, to provide for every possible eventuality. Some flexibility is required. Indeed, the courts will generally lean in favour of certainty.

5.2 Methods of clarification

Notwithstanding these precedents, the courts in general have proved quite reluctant to rule that a contract is unenforceable. Indeed, in practice the courts tend to lean towards clarification of contractual terms, making every effort to ascribe a clear mening to particular terms, where possible. Over the years, a variety of techniques have been developed by which judges may avoid a finding of uncertainty:

5.2.1 Where there is a provision for clarification

Very often, the terms of the contract itself provide a mechanism for clarification of the terms. For instance, in *Foley v Classique Coaches* [1934] 2 K.B. 1, a contract provided that the price to be paid under the contract would be agreed from time to time. Despite this uncertainty, the contract was upheld on the grounds that the agreement itself provided that any dispute over the price was to be resolved by an arbitrator.

5.2.2 Parol (oral) evidence

In some cases, clarity may be provided by the introduction of evidence as to orally expressed understandings between the parties. In *ESB v Newman* (1933) 67 I.L.T.R. 124, the defendant had agreed to indemnify a customer of the ESB in respect of her liability to pay for electricity. The customer in fact had a number of accounts with the ESB, in respect of a variety of premises, and it was unclear initially whether the defendant had agreed to indemnify the customer in respect of all accounts or just one. Using oral evidence, however, the court concluded that the agreement related to only one premises.

5.2.3 Terms may be implied by Statute

The provisions of legislation (such as the Sale of Goods and Supply of Services Act 1980) may rectify an apparent ambiguity by implying certain terms into a contract. This is discussed further below at para.15.2ff.

5.2.4 Terms may be implied by reference to principle of reasonableness

In some cases, the courts may imply terms into a contract by reference to the principle of reasonableness. In such cases, the courts look to what one might reasonably infer from the context in which the agreement was made and the conduct of the parties. The question to be asked here is whether it is reasonable to assume that the parties intended this term to arise. Is the term implicit? A useful test applied in many cases is the "officious bystander" test—would an officious (albeit neutral) bystander, observing the behaviour and statements of the parties, have reasonably assumed such a term to have been included? Another way of stating this is as follows: if the officious bystander were to have asked the parties if they intended to include such a term, how would the parties have reacted (beyond telling the former to mind his own business)? If they would have said "yes of course" the term will most likely be included. (See para.13.2.2.)

5.2.5 Terms that give business efficacy to a contract

In some cases, the courts will imply into a contract terms that are reasonably necessary to give the contract "business efficacy", in other words, to give effect to the commercial expectations of the parties. This is discussed further at para.13.2.2—in particular, see the discussion of *The Moorcock* (1889) 14 P.D. 64, which is very pertinent in this regard.

5.2.6 Terms may be implied by a previous course of dealing or by the custom of a trade

A term may be implied into a contract by reference to prior dealings, provided the prior dealings are sufficiently frequent and consistent as to the inclusion of the term. For instance, in *Spurling v Bradshaw* [1956] 1 W.L.R. 461, an exclusion clause was deemed to be incorporated into a contract in circumstances where it had been expressly included in prior contracts between the parties. Although the clause was not expressly notified to the defendant until after the particular contract was concluded, the clause was deemed to be incorporated, as it had consistently been included in previous dealings between the parties.

Such implications may serve to clarify an otherwise uncertain contract. The custom of a trade may also supply such clarity, if both parties are familiar with such customs, and provided the customs are sufficiently well established. In *Hillas v Arcos* (1932) 147 L.T. 503, for instance, the contracting parties were deemed to be bound by terms common to the timber business, of which both parties had considerable experience. A similar conclusion arose from *Lynch Roofing Systems (Ballaghaderreen) Ltd v Bennett and Son* [1999] 2 I.R. 450, where an arbitration clause was implied into a contract, such clauses being common in the building trade.

6. Consideration

6.1 Introduction

Consideration is a particular peculiarity of the common law. The requirement of consideration is indeed somewhat controversial, leading some commentators to suggest that it should be abolished. Nonetheless, unless a contract is incorporated into a deed made under seal, consideration is required in order to render the contract legally enforceable.

To elaborate, even where there is a valid offer and an unconditional acceptance, as well as an intention to create legal relations, a contract will not be enforceable in a court of law unless at least one of the following conditions is met:

- The contract has been made in a deed under seal which has been signed by both parties. A deed is a formal legal document containing a seal (usually denoted by a circle enclosing the letters "L.S."). Where a contract is contained in deed which has been "signed, sealed and delivered" no consideration is required.

OR

- The contract is supported by consideration. The principle broadly arising is that while a person may be *morally* obliged to fulfil her promises, the law will only enforce a promise where the person to whom the promise has been made (the "promisee") has given something in exchange.

6.2 What is "consideration"?

In this context, the term "consideration" has a special meaning unique to contract law. Consideration is quite simply something of tangible value that is given or foregone in exchange for a promise. This may include, for instance, money, a good or item of property, a service or a promise to deliver any of the above. Generally, the law requires that the person to whom the promise is made must, in exchange, suffer some sort of loss or detriment, however slight. Unless a contract is made under seal, a promise will only be enforceable if it is supported by consideration.

The concept of consideration is somewhat vague and nebulous. It effectively draws on the notion that a contract must involve some sort of exchange, something of value given in return or foreborne in exchange for a promise. In *Currie v Misa* (1875) L.R. 10 Ex. 153, Lush J. defined consideration as "... some right, interest, profit or benefit accruing to one party, or some forbearance, detriment, loss or responsibility, given, suffered or undertaken by the other". *O'Keefe v Ryanair Holdings* [2003] 1 I.L.R.M. 14 provides a relatively expansive recent example. The plaintiff was the one millionth customer of a well-known airline, and had been promised free flights for life in recognition of this event. In exchange, Ms O'Keefe had participated in publicity, appearing in the media, conduct that constituted, in the High Court's view, consideration. The plaintiff had surrendered, the court noted, her anonymity and privacy for the benefit of the airline, conduct which was sufficient to support a contract.

6.3 Consideration must move from the promisee

In order for the contract to be enforceable, the consideration must "move from the promisee". This means that a person to whom a promise is made may not enforce a contractual promise unless that person herself has personally provided consideration. It is not possible, thus, for a promisee to rely on consideration provided by a third party. For instance, Arthur promises Bertha €20 if Bertha cleans Constance's car. Constance would not be able to enforce such a promise as she has not provided any consideration for the promise (cf. para.8.2).

Tweddle v Atkinson (1861) 1 B. & S. 393 provides a classic example of this rule. In that case, Mr Tweddle was happily engaged to a young lady. In anticipation of the couple's marriage, the plaintiff's father and future father-in-law had promised each other that they would both give money to the plaintiff, once the couple had wed. However, before the money was paid, the plaintiff's father-in-law had died. The plaintiff sued for the promised money, but as the plaintiff himself had not provided any consideration for the promise he was not entitled to stake his claim.

The Irish case of *McCoubray v Thompson* (1868) 2 I.R.C.L. 226 reinforces the application of this rule. In this case, the owner of land had agreed to donate the land to the defendant. The owner did so on the express condition that the defendant pay to the plaintiff, McCoubray, a sum of money. The donor having died, McCoubray sued for the sum promised but, as consideration had not been provided by the plaintiff, he was deemed unable to rely on the contract.

6.4 Consideration need not move to the promisor

It is not necessary, however, that the person who made the promise receive any benefit from the consideration. In fact, it is perfectly feasible for a third party to receive the benefit arising, if any. While the promisee may only rely on a contract for which she has herself provided consideration, it is not necessary that the promisor receive any profit or benefit from the provision of consideration. In other words, consideration need not move to promisor. It is enough that the promisee has suffered some detriment or inconvenience as a result of the provision of consideration.

The US case of *Hamer v Sidway* 124 NY 538 (1891) provides a pertinent example. In this case, an uncle offered to pay his nephew $5,000 if he rejected alcohol, smoking and gambling and thus lived a life of virtue while he was studying at university. The promise was deemed to be enforceable on the basis that the nephew had foregone these "vices", even though his uncle was not likely to get any tangible benefit from his forebearance. (It is worth considering whether there would have been good consideration if the nephew had no interest in these matters.) Similarly, in *Jones v Padvatton* [1969] 1 W.L.R. 328, at the request of her mother, a woman gave up her job in the US to study in England. Although the mother did not stand to benefit from this arrangement, the consideration was valid (though the court held that there had been no intention to create legal relations).

6.5 Consideration must have some tangible value

Consideration must, however, consist of something that the law regards as having some objective or tangible value (though the value may be next to nothing). The law does not, for instance, regard prayers, or a promise to say prayers, as good consideration. In the case of *O'Neill v Murphy* [1936] N.I. 16, for instance, the Northern Ireland Court of Appeal refused to enforce a contract under which a religious order of nuns were to pray for the intentions of a builder who was to carry out repairs to their convent. Prayers were too intangible, the court reasoned, to amount to good consideration. (Is this a fair conclusion? If the builder perceived that he was getting a benefit from such prayers, however intangible, was it not fair to hold him to his bargain?)

Equally, in *White v Bluett,* (1853) 23 L.J. Ex. 36, a son's promise to stop complaining to his father was deemed unenforceable, such a promise having no objectively quantifiable legal value. Similarly, in *Bret v J.S.* (1600) Croz. Eliz. 756, the natural love and affection that a mother has for her son was deemed to provide inadequate consideration for the mother's promise to pay for her son's lodgings. The court nonetheless resolved that the son's agreement to remain in lodgings with the plaintiff amounted to sufficient consideration for the mother's promise. (See also *Eastwood v Kenyon* (1840) 11 A. & E. 458.)

6.6 The consideration must have some value, but that value may be minimal

Provided that the consideration has some tangible value, it is irrelevant that the value of the consideration is minimal. In other words, the law does not generally concern itself with the fairness or adequacy of the bargain made. Take the following example: Arthur agrees to sell Bertha his 2006 Mercedes (in prime condition) for just €1. Assuming that the contract is not the product of any sharp dealing, the courts would enforce it, notwithstanding the clear imbalance in Bertha's favour.

The philosophy underpinning this perspective is decidedly free market in its origins. The parties alone make the bargain and it is up to them alone to defend their best interests, to get the best bargain possible. As Blackburn J. observed in *Bolton v Madden* (1873) L.R. 9 Q.B. 55, "… [t]he adequacy of the consideration is for the parties to consider at the time of making the agreement, not for the court when it is sought to be enforced". Thus, even if a bargain heavily favours one of the contractors at the expense of the others, the courts will generally not intervene unless the imbalance is the result of some procedural flaw.

There may be good policy reasons for such an approach. First, the courts consider that what is or is not a fair price for a product is a subjective matter, dependent on several variables to which the court may not be privy. Second, the courts are reluctant to set themselves as the arbiters of a fair market value: arguably the courts are not equipped to determine what is or is not a fair price. On the other hand, this stance may leave many vulnerable contractors open to abuse, with little chance of protection from the courts. (Though as will become evident later, several defences and legislative measures exist and may serve to mitigate such unfairness.)

Returning to consideration, the value need not equate to that received in return—it may be merely nominal. Indeed the term "peppercorn rent" is sometimes used to describe an item of nominal value given in return for a promise. It is sometimes said then, that the consideration may be *sufficient* without being *adequate*. For instance, in *Thomas v Thomas* (1842) 2 Q.B. 851, a widow paid £1 a year in exchange for the occupation of a house, the market rental value of which was considerably more than this nominal sum. Nonetheless, the court concluded that even this very paltry sum constituted consideration, notwithstanding the fact that considerably more could have been obtained on the open market.

A useful example arises from *Chappell and Co. Ltd. v Nestlé Ltd* [1960] A.C. 87. In this case, the purchasers of a chocolate bar made by Nestlé could buy a record of "Rockin' Shoes" by sending Nestlé one shilling and six pence together with three empty chocolate wrappers. Chappell and Co., who owned the copyright in this song, sued Nestlé for royalties arising from the promotion. In doing so, Chappell claimed that the monies made by Nestlé should include not only the price collected for each record but also the cumulative value of the wrappers, which, they argued, formed part of the consideration for the agreement to post the record. The House of Lords concluded that, although Nestlé considered them to be of no value, the wrappers formed part of consideration. In other words, however trifling it may have been, the wrappers had some tangible value, and this was enough to render them good consideration.

Sometimes judges stretch to find valuable consideration where it is arguable that the benefit derived from a contract is wholly one-sided. In *North Ocean Shipping v Hyundai* [1979] Q.B. 705, for instance, currency fluctuations had resulted in a significant reduction in the value to the defendant of the price agreed in respect of a ship that the defendant was building for the plaintiff. As a result, the shipbuilder asked for, and obtained, a reluctant agreement from the plaintiff to pay an extra 10 per cent. The plaintiff owed the shipbuilder for the ship, but the shipbuilder had agreed to give the plaintiff a credit facility in respect of this debt. When the price was increased by 10 per cent, the shipbuilder correspondingly increased by 10 per cent the amount covered by the credit note. The shipbuilder's action was deemed to amount to good consideration. The plaintiff was being allowed to owe the defendant 10 per cent more than before, which, with respect, can hardly be considered a benefit. Similarly, in *Haigh v Brooks* (1839) 10 Ad. & El. 309, the court ruled that a note of guarantee constituted valid consideration even when that guarantee was not enforceable at law. Although the piece of paper received was in fact of minimal value, the court reasoned that it amounted to consideration regardless.

On the other hand, in *Lipkin Gorman v Karpale* [1991] 3 W.L.R. 10, gaming chips issued by a casino were deemed not to constitute consideration. The House of Lords reasoned that the chips were simply used as a tool for gambling and did not in themselves constitute something of value given in exchange for a promise—in fact the chips remained the property of the casino throughout.

It is worth noting, additionally, that although the inadequacy of consideration may not be relevant in the formation of a contract, it may provide cogent evidence of fraud or unconscionability. For instance, in *Noonan (A Ward of Court) v O'Connell* (unreported, High Court, April 10, 1987), the sale of land at a grossly inadequate price, 50p, was struck down as unconscionable on the basis that the vendor, a man suffering from senile dementia, had been the victim of unconscionable bargain. (See para.18.5.)

6.7 Insufficient consideration

6.7.1 Past consideration is no consideration

Consideration cannot be used to support a contract where the consideration was given or acquired in the past, before the promise was made. In other words, one cannot rely on a benefit already given as consideration for a subsequent promise. Take the following example: unbeknownst to Bertha, Arthur washes his neighbour Bertha's car, as an act of neighbourly goodwill. If Bertha were subsequently to agree to pay Arthur €10 for having done so, Arthur's original unsolicited act of goodwill would not constitute good consideration, as the consideration was given before the contract was made.

The classic example of this rule is provided by *Roscorla v Thomas* (1842) 3 Q.B. 234. In this case, the defendant sold a horse to the plaintiff. *After the sale,* the defendant stated that the horse was "sound and free from vice". The horse in fact turned out to be quite vicious and the plaintiff sued upon this apparent warranty. However, having been stipulated subsequent to the sale, the warranty was not supported by consideration and could thus not be relied upon. (Today, such a term would be implied into every consumer contract unless the defect was brought to the attention of the buyer. See para.15.2.2 below.)

Two further Irish examples bear out this ruling. In *Morgan v Rainsford* (1845) 8 Ir. E.R. 299, improvements to property which had already been made before a contract was entered into were deemed insufficient consideration for the contract. In *Provincial Bank of Ireland v O'Donnell* (1932) 67 I.L.T.R. 142, moreover, the court ruled that monies loaned by a bank in the past did not amount to consideration supporting a subsequent contract.

An important exception. *Lampleigh v Braithwait* (1615) Hob. 105 provides an important exception to this rule. In short, the past consideration may be considered good consideration where:

- the past consideration was given at request of the promisor; and
- compensation had been anticipated for the service given.

In this case, Braithwait had asked Lampleigh to travel to London to obtain for him a royal pardon. Lampleigh duly obliged, and on his return with the pardon, Braithwait had promised to pay Lampleigh £100. While the consideration for this promise (obtaining the pardon) was technically past, the court found that the promise was nonetheless enforceable. As Braithwait had asked Lampleigh to obtain the pardon, and it was implicit that it would be paid for, Braithwait was now bound to fulfill his promise. (See also *Re Casey's Patents: Stewart v Casey* [1892] 1 Ch. 104.)

The conditions for the satisfaction of this exception were endorsed by Lord Scarman in *Pao On v Lau Yiu Long* [1980] A.C. 614:

1. The act was carried out at promisor's request.
2. There was an understanding that the promisee would be remunerated.
3. The promise to pay, had it been promised in advance, would have been enforceable.

6.7.2 A promise to do what one is already obliged by law to do is not good consideration

One cannot validly offer as consideration something that one is already obliged to do. In other words, if (independently of the contract) a person is already obliged to perform an act, or desist from certain conduct, such performance or desistance cannot constitute good consideration.

In *Collins v Godefroy* (1831) 1 B. & Ad. 950, for instance, the plaintiff had been promised six guineas to testify in a case, in respect of which he had already been subpoenaed to give evidence. The plaintiff, in short, would have been obliged to give evidence regardless. Thus, the giving of evidence did not constitute good consideration for the promise. Similarly, in *Stilk v Myrick* (1809) 2 Camp. 317, after some of their shipmates had deserted, the remaining sailors on a ship demanded and were promised extra pay to perform extra duties. However, under their contract the sailors had already contracted to do whatever was required of them to sail the ship. As the sailors were already obliged to perform these extra duties, if called on to do so, the promise was not supported by consideration. (By contrast, in *Hartley v Ponsonby* (1857) 7 E. & B. 872, a similar promise made to a crew of sailors remaining following substantial desertions was deemed enforceable. The remaining crew was so small as to increase significantly the danger of sailing the ship.)

The basic question to be asked is whether or not the promisee would have had to perform the contemplated tasks regardless of the contract. If she would have been obliged, there is no consideration. If, however, the promisee performs tasks that would not otherwise have had to be carried out, there is good consideration.

For instance, in *Glasbrook Brothers v Glamorgan County Council* [1925] A.C. 270, the Welsh police had been asked to guard a mine during a mineworkers' strike. Although the police had offered to pay occasional visits to check up on the mine, the mine owners had insisted on a permanent police presence and had agreed to pay £2,200 for this extra service. The mineowners subsequently reneged on this promise, arguing that the police were already obliged to provide such protection. Nonetheless, the House of Lords ruled that because the mineowners had been afforded a service over and above that which the police reasonably believed to be appropriate, consideration did exist.

A similar principle applies in relation to police supervision of sporting events. An Garda Síochána generally would be obliged, as part of its public duty, to monitor situations where large crowds congregate. However, where a particularly heavy presence is required because of an event voluntarily organised by a private body, as in *Harris v Sheffield United F.C.* [1988] Q.B. 77, the English courts have taken the view that the heavy police presence goes above and beyond the call of regular duty. Thus it is possible for the Gardaí as a body of persons to extract extra compensation in exchange for providing police protection above and beyond that usually called for. (Is this a policy decision? Sporting clubs make a substantial profit from such events and it is arguable that they should be obliged to pay to police these games.)

In short, the courts require that there be some extra service above and beyond that which is required by law. For instance, in *Ward v Byham* [1956] 2 All E.R. 318, a mother of a child was deemed to provide good consideration for a promise by the father to pay her £1 per week in exchange for her caring for their child. Although a person is already obliged, by law, to care for any child in her custody, the mother had agreed to do more than this: she had promised to make sure the daughter was happy and to allow the daughter to choose her preferred place of residence.

6.7.3 Part payment of a debt

Where a person owes money, a contract to pay less than the amount of a debt due must be supported by fresh or additional consideration. Otherwise, even where a creditor agrees to take less than is owed, there will be no consideration. Payment of part of a debt is thus not good consideration for an agreement to forego the remainder of the debt unless something new is given in consideration for the agreement. In *Foakes v Beer* (1884) 9 A.C. 605, as a result of a judgment against him, a Dr Foakes owed Mrs Beer £2,090 plus interest. A subsequent agreement to pay £500 and the remainder in instalments (making no mention of the interest) was deemed not to be enforceable as payment of part of the debt was not good consideration for an agreement to forego the whole debt.

Both the principle and an important exception are established by *Pinnel's Case* (1602) 5 Co. Rep. 117a. In this case, a Mr Cole owed Pinnel £8 10s, due on 11 November. On October 1, Pinnel had accepted £5 2s 6d in full settlement. Although the court concluded that "... payment of a lesser sum on the day in satisfaction of a greater cannot be any satisfaction for the whole ...", the fact that the payment had been made before the deadline supplied fresh consideration:

> "... a change in time or mode of payment, or the addition by the debtor of a tomtit or canary or the like will suffice to constitute [fresh] consideration ..."

There are certain exceptions to the rule that part payment does not constitute good consideration:

- Where the claim is disputed: in such a case, the parties may decide that it is preferable to settle the matter rather than proceed to court. In such a case, the settlement will be supported by consideration.

- Where the amount of the claim is genuinely disputed or is uncertain, an agreement to part pay the debt may be valid.
- Where the amount paid is the result of a composition with creditors on liquidation or bankruptcy.
- Where the payment is made by a third party: For instance, in *Hirachand Punamchand v Temple* [1911] 2 K.B. 330 an army officer owed a moneylender a sum of money. The moneylender accepted from the officer's father an offer of an amount less than the debt "in full settlement" of the whole debt. Because someone other than the officer had paid the debt, the settlement was binding on the moneylender. Any other conclusion, the court reasoned, would permit a fraud to be committed on the father. (See also the very similar case of *Welby v Drake* (1825) 1 C. & P. 557.)

6.7.4 Pre-existing contractual duty

In some cases, a person who is party to a contract may make a claim for extra funds, over and above those agreed in the contract. This may occur, for instance, where extra costs arise, or where the work takes longer or costs more than anticipated. In strict theory, where a person is already bound to do something by contract, an agreement to pay more money to do that same thing (without some alteration in favour of the person being asked to fork out more money) will not be supported by consideration. In other words, agreeing to do what one is already obliged to do does not constitute good consideration.

There is some evidence, however, that the courts are willing to be flexible in this regard. Particularly in long term contractual relationships, it may be difficult to predict costs, and as such, some "give and take" may be required after a contract is entered into. In *Williams v Roffey* [1990] 1 All E.R. 512, for instance, the plaintiffs having agreed to perform building work, subsequently found that the agreed sum would not cover their costs. Finding themselves in financial difficulty, the plaintiffs requested a further £10,000 to finish the construction. Notwithstanding the fact that they had already agreed to complete the work under the initial contract, the Court of Appeal concluded that fresh consideration had been given in exchange for the agreement to pay the additional money. The court took a practical approach, reasoning that, although the plaintiffs were already obliged to finish the work, there was a real risk in this case that (without the extra finance) the work would not in fact be finished. The court further reasoned that, given the possibility that Roffey would incur penalty costs for late completion of the project, it was, in practice, receiving an additional benefit for payment of the money.

While this decision is difficult to square with the strict theory of consideration, *Williams v Roffey* represents a more practical and flexible approach to what constitutes consideration. The court recognised that in the circumstances, a real benefit had accrued to Roffey that the work, which might not otherwise be finished, was more likely to be completed.

There is an older exception to the principle that good consideration cannot flow from a promise to do what one is already contracted to do. This arises where one of the contracting parties promises a third party (*i.e.* someone who is not a party to the first contract) that the first contract will be honoured. For instance, Chris owes Mary €4,000 for her car. Chris then promises Joel that he will pay Mary €4,000, if Joel pays the insurance on the car. Although Chris is already obliged to pay Mary the €4,000, he has nonetheless provided good consideration for Joel's agreement to pay the insurance. This is because Joel now has a right to sue Chris should Chris fail to pay Mary, a right he did not have previously (remember that although consideration must flow from the promisee, it need not necessarily flow to the promisor, in this case Joel). Chris has, in other words, increased his potential liability; he is now obliged to two persons rather than just one

In *Shadwell v Shadwell* (1860) 9 C.B. (N.S.) 159, the plaintiff, a budding barrister, had been engaged to marry a young woman. In recognition, his uncle offered him £150 a year until he was earning 600 guineas a year, provided that he married his betrothed. At that time, a promise to marry was enforceable at law, and thus the plaintiff was already obliged to marry his wife-to-be. Nonetheless, as he had taken on an obligation to a person other than his bride, the uncle's promise was deemed to be enforceable (see also *Scotson v Pegg* (1861) 6 H. & N. 295).

7. Promissory Estoppel

7.1 Introduction

To be enforceable, a promise not made under seal generally requires consideration. It is possible, however, to prevent a person from reneging on certain types of promise, even in the absence of consideration. Where a person, A, makes a representation to B that she will not rely on her strict contractual rights, and B acts on this representation, B may (by means of promissory estoppel) legally prevent A from acting in contravention of the representation. This is called promissory estoppel: it is an equitable remedy preventing a person from going back on her word where she has indicated that she will not rely on her strict rights under the contract. Although it is closely related to estoppel by representation at common law, equitable estoppel is in fact a much broader and more flexible concept.

It is important to note that the estoppel does not arise simply on foot of a person's representation; the estoppel is said to arise because the person to whom the representation is made has relied on the representation. It is the reliance that gives rise to the estoppel, not the representation.

7.2 The *High Trees* principle

The classic example of this principle (and one which every student should study closely) is provided by the celebrated *High Trees* decision: *Central London Property Limited v High Trees* [1947] K.B. 130. In September 1939, the defendant had leased from the plaintiff a property in London, which the defendant subsequently sublet to tenants. With the onset of World War II and the Battle of Britain, many tenants left the city to escape the risk of bombing, with the result that much of the property remained vacant. Given the reduction in rental income, the defendant asked the plaintiff if he would agree to halve the rent payable. The plaintiff agreed. The defendant, however, had not provided any consideration for this reduction; the plaintiff had agreed simply out of goodwill and solidarity, and not as a result of any new bargain. Therefore, under standard contract law principles, the tenant would have been obliged to pay the deficit of rent not paid during the war.

The war having ended, the property returned to full occupancy, and the plaintiff sought to restore the original rent with effect from the last two quarters of 1945. The Court of Appeal ruled that the plaintiff was entitled to collect the rent for the last two quarters of 1945. As the conditions that led to the suspension of the full rent had ended, the plaintiff was entitled prospectively (*i.e.* from July 1945 onwards) to collect the full rent again.

The plaintiff had not claimed the deficit of rent which had not been paid between 1940 and 1945. Lord Denning nonetheless asserted that, had it wished to pursue this avenue, the plaintiff would *not* have been entitled to claim the full rent in respect of the duration of the war. The plaintiff had represented that it would accept half the rent, and the defendant acted upon that statement. Thus the plaintiff would not have been permitted to go back on its word—it was estopped from collecting the extra rent. However, this estoppel lasted only for so long as the conditions that led to the representation being made—the ongoing war— subsisted. Once the war had ended, the plaintiff was entitled to rent at the full rate.

The test to be applied here is as follows:

(1) A person X, makes a representation to another person Y to the effect that X will not rely on the strict terms of a contract previously made between the parties and

(2) Y relies on that statement

(3) In such circumstances, notwithstanding the absence of consideration, X will not be permitted to enforce the strict terms of the contract in contravention of the representation she has made.

In his decision, Lord Denning relied on the older case of *Hughes v Metropolitan Railway Company* (1877) 2 A.C. 439 in which a landlord was precluded from relying on an agreement requiring his tenants to restore a property to good repair within six months. After the agreement was made, the landlord and tenant commenced negotiations for the sale of the lease back to the landlord. In the light of these talks, the tenant indicated that it would not begin the repairs until the negotiations were complete. The negotiations having failed, and the six months having passed, the landlord sought the forfeiture of the lease for breach of the covenant to repair. The House of Lords ruled, however, that by entering into negotiations, the landlord had tacitly agreed to suspend the enforcement of the covenant. The tenants had relied on this understanding and thus it would inequitable to hold them to the original bargain. Lord Cairns stated that if a party to an agreement subsequently acts so as to lead the other party to believe that the strict rights arising from the contract will not be relied upon, or will be suspended,

> "... the person who might otherwise have enforced those rights will not be allowed to enforce them where it would be inequitable having regard to the dealings which have thus taken place between the parties".

7.3 Some Irish examples of estoppel

In *Kenny v Kelly* [1988] I.R. 457, a student who had obtained a place at University College Dublin, asked if she could defer entry to the University for one year. The University had represented to her that such a deferral was possible. The prospective student acted on this by paying part of her fees upfront and by taking the deferral. Barron J. thus ruled that the University could not subsequently go back on its word: it was estopped from denying her entry.

In the *Revenue Commissioners v Moroney* [1972] I.R. 372, the defendant's father had assigned the interest in land to his two sons. Although the deed of transfer indicated that the sons would pay for the transfer, in fact the father had indicated orally that no payment was due. On the father's death, the Revenue Commissioners claimed that the sons owed their father for the transfer. Kenny J. concluded that because the father had stated that his sons would not be liable to pay, and the sons had acted on this reassurance by signing the transfer deed, the father's estate could not pursue the debt.

7.4 There are certain conditions attached to the creation of an estoppel

Certain conditions must be satisfied in order to give rise to an estoppel. However, there is some debate regarding the applicability of these conditions. It is fair to say, indeed, that there are two distinct schools of thought in relation to estoppel: the orthodox perspective which claims that equity should offer relief only where strict conditions are met, and the liberal approach that takes a more flexible line. This can be a source of confusion for students: suffice it to say that there is a lot of debate about each of these conditions, though of late, the Irish courts appear to be leaning towards the more orthodox perspective.

The table below sets out the different perspectives arising in this context:

Promissory Estoppel	Orthodox Approach	Liberal Approach
Can it create a new cause of action?	No	Yes
Is a pre-existing legal relationship required?	Yes	No
Is detrimental reliance required?	Yes	No
Can it extinguish as opposed to merely suspend rights?	No	Yes

7.4.1 The estoppel must arise from a pre-existing legal relationship

Promissory estoppel, in its orthodox form, operates to suspend *existing* rights in the context of a contractual relationship, not to create new ones. In particular, it is said that for promissory estoppel to arise there must be a pre-existing legal relationship: estoppel cannot arise in a contractual vacuum. In this sense, promissory estoppel is sometimes said to be "a shield, not a sword". In other words, it provides a defence against the enforcement of contractual rights; it does not give rise to new actions where none existed before.

For instance, in *Combe v Combe* [1951] 2 K.B. 215, a man promised his ex-wife £100 a year in financial support, but reneged on this agreement. The wife had not provided consideration for this promise, but claimed that she was entitled to be paid on foot of the *High Trees* principle. The English Court of Appeal, however, denied her claim, holding that promissory estoppel only operated as a defence to a cause of action. In this case, the wife was attempting to use the representation to create a cause of action where none existed before. As Denning L.J. observed:

> "The principle does not create new causes of action where none existed before. It only prevents a party from insisting on his strict legal rights, when it would be unjust to allow him to enforce them ...".

Likewise, in *Chartered Trust (Ireland) v Healy* (unreported, High Court, December 10, 1985), Barron J. declined to accept that a cause of action could arise independently of a contract. Here the plaintiff was prevented from relying upon a void contract for the sale of a car. It attempted, instead, to argue that a similar obligation arose as a result of promissory estoppel. Barron J. ruled that a promissory estoppel could not give rise to a cause of action independently of the void contract. (A view confirmed in *Association of General Practitioners v Minister for Health* [1995] 2 I.L.R.M. 481.)

While this appears to be the generally accepted view in Ireland, the Australian case of *Walton Stores v Maher* (1988) 76 A.L.R. 513 suggests that a pre-existing relationship is not required. In this case, the parties had commenced negotiations for the lease of a property. On foot of these negotiations, the party hoping to lease the property started to perform construction work on the site, in anticipation of the sale. The prospective lessees were aware that this work was being performed, but when the work was 40 per cent complete, the lessees withdrew from negotiations. Even though there was no contract, the Australian High Court ruled that the lessees were estopped from withdrawing from the negotiations. In the circumstances, the court felt that it would be inequitable to allow such withdrawal.

7.4.2 The representation must be clear and unambiguous
This is not particularly controversial. The representation should be clear and unambiguous and not vague or susceptible to multiple interpretations. For instance, in *Keegan and Roberts v Comhairle Chontae Átha Cliath* (unreported, High Court, March 12, 1981), certain assurances were deemed too ambiguous to give rise to an actionable estoppel. (See also *Woodhouse A.C. Israel Cocoa v Nigerian Produce Marketing* [1972] A.C. 741.)

It is not enough to make a statement of intent, nor is inaction in pursuing one's contractual rights sufficient to imply an estoppel.

7.4.3 There must be an act of reliance
The third condition in relation to estoppel is that the party to whom the representation is made must have relied upon the statement. In *Daly v Minister for the Marine* [2001] 3 I.R. 513, for instance, the plaintiff had received a letter from the defendant, stating in error that the plaintiff was eligible to claim under a departmental fisheries scheme. The Supreme Court ruled that although this representation was made, there was no evidence of reliance in this case, and thus, no estoppel could arise.

Similarly, in *Ajayi v Briscoe* [1964] 1 W.L.R. 1326, the Privy Council refused to infer an estoppel from circumstances where there had been no reliance as the promisee had not "altered his position" on foot of the representation. This is a fundamental point—it is not the fact of the representation but the *reliance thereon* that gives rise to the estoppel.

The orthodox view moreover (though this is a point of debate) is that such reliance must be detrimental, in other words, that the reliance should put the promisee at a disadvantage. There is some debate on this point. For instance, in *W.J. Alan v El Nasr Export and Import Co.* [1972] 2 Q.B. 189, Lord Denning suggested that there is no support for the proposition that reliance should be detrimental. See also Lord Denning in *Brikom Investments v Carr* [1979] Q.B. 467 and the Australian High Court in *Walton Stores v Maher* (see para.7.4.1), both of which cases reject the need for detriment.

On the other hand, there is a large number of cases suggesting that reliance must involve some disadvantage to the promisee. (See, for instance, Lord Tucker in *Tool Metal Manufacturing v Tungsten Electric* [1955] 1 W.L.R. 761). Indeed, a preponderance of Irish cases, including *Morrow v Carty* [1957] N.I. 174; *McCambridge v Winters* (unreported, High Court, August 28, 1984); *Industrial Yarns v Greene* [1984] I.L.R.M. 15; and most recently *North Down Hotels v Province Wide Filling Stations* [1993] N.I. 261, all suggest that detriment is required. Most notably, the Supreme Court decision in *Daly v Minister for the Marine* (above) suggests strongly a requirement for detrimental reliance.

7.4.4 Inequity must exist

It is probably fair to say that without detriment, this next condition would be difficult to satisfy. As promissory estoppel is an equitable remedy, it is clear that an estoppel will only arise where injustice would otherwise ensue. In other words, equity acts to remedy an inequity: if no unfairness would result from the enforcement of strict legal rights, equity will not intervene. Equitable relief is, after all, discretionary and if no hardship would arise from the enforcement of the contract, an estoppel will not issue.

For instance, in *Williams v Stern* (1879) 5 Q.B.D. 409, the defendant had sold furniture to the plaintiff, who still owed him for the furniture. Although he had promised not to pursue the debt until a specific date, the defendant later reneged on this promise, and seized the furniture.

The court ruled that no estoppel arose, as the defendant was justified in acting as he did; if he hadn't acted, another of the plaintiff's debtors would have seized the furniture in question. As such, there was no inequity in acting to recover the furniture.

Similarly, in *D & C Builders v Rees* [1966] 2 Q.B. 617 Lord Denning suggested that promissory estoppel would not arise in favour of the defendants who had lied about their financial situation in order to extract a promise from the plaintiffs. In such circumstances it would be inequitable to allow an estoppel to arise.

7.4.5 Estoppel suspends but does not extinguish rights
Estoppel, in general, acts only to suspend a right and not to extinguish it. This is ably illustrated by the decision in *High Trees* where the right to pursue full rent was merely suspended for the duration of the war, and revived thereafter. Similarly, in *Tool Metal Manufacturing v Tungsten Electric* [1955] 1 W.L.R. 761, the owners of a patent agreed not to collect royalties on the patent during World War II. The right to compensation was suspended for the duration of the war, but was not extinguished for all time. Once the conditions leading to the estoppel expired, the estoppel also expired.

Ajayi v Briscoe Ltd. [1964] 1 W.L.R. 1326, furthermore, is authority for the proposition that an estoppel may be ended by the withdrawal of the representation on which it was based. In other words, the person who made the representation may prevent the estoppel by giving sufficient notice.

However, again some confusion arises in respect of this requirement: the decision in the *Revenue Commissioners v Moroney* (see para.7.3) suggests that in certain circumstances it may be possible for estoppel entirely to extinguish a right.

7.5 Distinguishing promissory estoppel from other similar concepts

7.5.1 Estoppel by representation
At common law a similar principle applies—estoppel by representation. For instance, in *McNeill v Miller* [1907] 2 I.R. 328, Mr McNeill, a car owner, left his car in with the defendant's garage to be repaired. Although the defendant had reassured McNeill that the car would be insured while in its care, this turned out to be untrue. On the basis of this reassurance, McNeill omitted to obtain insurance for the car. The car having been destroyed in a fire, the garage owner was "estopped"

from denying liability for damage to the car.

Traditionally, at common law, an estoppel would only operate where there was a statement relating to an existing fact and not where there was a statement of intention in relation to a future event. In *Jorden v Money* (1845) 5 H.L.C. 185, for instance, a statement was made to the effect that a person would not pursue a debt owing to the promisor. As this statement related to future conduct and not existing fact, at common law no estoppel would arise. See also *Munster and Leinster Bank v Croker* [1940] I.R. 185. It is clear from *High Trees*, however, that this restriction does not apply in equity: the representation may be as to future conduct as well as existing fact.

7.5.2 Waiver

Estoppel is also similar in certain respects to the equitable doctrine of waiver under which a person may be held to their bargain if they agree not to rely on strict contractual rights. In both *Hickman v Haynes* (1875) LR 10 C.P. 598 and *Charles Rickard v Oppenheimer* [1950] 1 K.B. 616, statements to the effect that goods would be accepted by customers later than originally promised served to "waive" the original deadlines. In other words, by agreeing to accept late delivery, the customers could no longer rely on the original deadines.

7.5.3 Proprietary estoppel

Promissory estoppel bears some relationship to proprietary estoppel, which concerns promises made *specifically* in respect of property. Where a person acts to their detriment on foot of a representation that they will thereby acquire an interest in property, the person may be able to claim an interest in the property on the basis of a proprietary estoppel. For instance, in *Smith v Halpin* [1997] 3 I.L.R.M. 38, a father had told his son that the family home "is yours after your mother's day". In reliance on this statement the son built an extension onto the house. Because of the son's reliance on his father's statement, the son was entitled to claim the house after his mother's death. (See also *Cullen v Cullen* [1962] I.R. 268.)

It appears that (unlike promissory estoppel) a proprietary estoppel may arise even where there is no pre-existing legal relationship between the parties (see *Re J.R.* [1993] I.L.R.M. 657 where the parties were unmarried). Furthermore, proprietary estoppel may give rise to an action in its own right—*Crabb v Arun District Council* [1975] All E.R. 865. In other words, it may be used as a "sword" rather than just a "shield".

7.5.4 *Legitimate expectation*

The doctrine of promissory estoppel shares some features in common with the public law remedy of legitimate expectations. (In fact, it has been suggested that legitimate expectation doctrine is derived from equitable concepts of estoppel—see *Webb v Ireland* [1988] I.R. 353). A legitimate expectation arises where a person relies on the statement of a public body, or on the past practices of that body. Although there is some overlap between these two concepts (as in *Kenny v Kelly* (see para.7.3) where both legitimate expectation and promissory estoppel were successfully alleged), it is important to note that legitimate expectations may arise only in a public law context (*i.e.* where the person who is alleged to have created the expectation is the State or an arm of the State).

8. Privity of Contract

8.1 Introduction

In Chapter 1, a distinction was made between torts law—where obligations arise by operation of law—and contract law, where, generally, obligations are freely assumed. It follows that a party may not be made liable without the consent of that party. For instance, if Jim agrees to pay Jane €40 for her DVD player, only Jim and Jane may enforce the contract. A third party, someone other than Jim or Jane, cannot sue or be sued on foot of such a contract. This is called the rule of "privity of contract" (only the "privy" parties are bound).

In short, unless a person is a party to a contract:

(a) she cannot be sued under that contract and
(b) she cannot rely upon or sue under that contract.

8.2 Examples of the privity rule

In *Tweddle v Atkinson* (1861) 1 B. & S.393, the plaintiff was engaged to marry G.'s daughter. In recognition of the impending marriage, G. entered into an agreement with the plaintiff's father, each promising the other that he would pay the plaintiff (who was not a party to the contract) a sum of money on marriage. G. subsequently died, and the executors of his estate refused to pay Tweddle. Nonetheless, as Tweddle was not a party to the contract, his claim failed. (G.'s father, of course, could have sued.)

Likewise, in *McCoubray v Thompson* (1868) 2 I.R.C.L. 226, a landowner who had contemplated transferring property to the defendant and plaintiff in equal shares, was persuaded to give all of the property to the defendant. The landowner and defendant agreed that, in turn, the defendant would pay the plaintiff, McCoubray, the value of half the property. Although he was the intended beneficiary, McCoubray could not sue for the money, as he was not privy to the contract. Similarly, in *Clitheroe v Simpson* (1879) 4 L.R. (Ir.) 59, a father and son agreed, as part of a property transfer to the son, that the latter would pay his sister a sum of money. The sister's estate was precluded from suing for this sum. Similarly, in *Beswick v Beswick* [1968] A.C. 59, a nephew had promised to support his uncle's wife after the uncle's death. As the widow was not a party to the agreement, she could not sue the nephew in respect of the promised allowance. (See also *Crow v Rogers* (1724) 1 Str. 592, *Mackey v Jones* (1959) 93 I.L.T.R. 177.)

The privity rule often poses problems where a contractor sub-contracts certain aspects of work to another party. Thus A may have a contract with B, who in turn sub-contracts with C. A may sue B and B may sue C, but in contract, A may not sue C, as these two parties are not party to a common contract. In *Murphy v Bower* (1868) I.R. 2 C.L. 506, Murphy had agreed to carry out construction work for a railway company. The railway company had in turn employed Bower to check and certify that Murphy's work was up to standard. Without certification, Murphy would not be paid. When Bower failed to certify the work, Murphy sued, but was unsuccessful. Murphy, not having been a party to the contract with Bower, could not sue the latter. (See also *Dunlop v Selfridge* [1915] A.C. 847.)

8.3 Comparison with consideration

At first glance, the privity rule appears very similar to the requirement that consideration move from the promisee. (See above at para.6.3.) Indeed many of the cases cited above may be invoked as examples of both the privity rule and the consideration requirement. Nonetheless, these are technically distinct requirements—a person may well provide consideration without being privy to the contract and *vice versa*. In *Kepong Prospecting v Schmidt* [1968] A.C. 610, a case appealed to the Privy Council from Malaysia, the Privy Council ruled that the privity rule applied notwithstanding the relaxation of consideration requirements in that jurisdiction. (See also *Dunlop v Selfridge* [1915] A.C. 847).

8.4 Exceptions to the privity requirements

Instinctively the results of the privity rule may seem harsh. Take *McCoubray v Thompson*—was it fair that Thompson should walk away with the money, despite his promise? Needless to say, several exceptions have developed in response to the apparent harshness of the rule.

8.4.1 Legislative exceptions

In some specific cases, the Oireachtas has softened the effects of the privity rule:

• Under s.11 of the Married Women's Property Act 1882 and s.7 of the Married Women's Status Act 1957, the privity requirement is relaxed in respect of life insurance and endowment policies. If the policy is (a) expressed to be for benefit of a spouse or child of the policy holder or (b) expressly states an intention to confer a benefit on the spouse or child, it may be relied upon by the spouse or child even if they are not a party to the contract.

- Married Women's Status Act 1957, s.8—where a contract names a husband, wife or child as the beneficiary of the contract, the spouse or child, though not parties to the agreement, may enforce the contract if it is expressed to be for their benefit.
- Under s.7 of the Road Traffic Act 1961, a third party who is injured in a car accident may claim from the insurance of the wrongdoer, even though the former is not a party to the insurance contract.
- See also s.13 of the Sale of Goods and Supply of Services Act 1980, under which a third party may sue in respect of the unroadworthiness of a vehicle. For instance, a passenger injured due to a fault in a car, may sue the manufacturer of the car in respect of such an injury.

In England and Wales, very considerable changes have been made to the privity rule as a result of the Contracts (Rights of Third Parties) Act 1999. If a contract either (a) expressly states that a named third party can sue on foot of the contract or (b) purports to confer a benefit on a third party, the third party may sue on foot of the contract.

8.4.2 *Trusts*

In certain cases, Equity permits the mitigation of the privity rule. It does so by implying a trust in favour of the named beneficiary. In other words, if A and B made a contract for the benefit of C, Equity would say that A and B held the benefit on trust for C. As the named beneficiary, C could then sue "the trustees" for the benefit.

Drimmie v Davies [1899] 1 I.R. 176 provides a good Irish example of this exception. A father agreed to transfer his dental practice to his son. In exchange, the son promised to support his mother and other family members, and in particular to pay certain annuities to them. The contract was deemed to have created a trust in favour of the mother and other family members, and as such, the latter were able to sue as beneficiaries under the trust. Likewise, in *Tomlinson v Gill* (1756) Amb.330, Gill had agreed to pay off the creditors of a woman's late husband. Although Gill had made the agreement only with the widow, the creditors not being privy to the contract, the creditors were nonetheless entitled to sue as beneficiaries under a "trust" created by the contract. (See also *Kenney v Employer's Liability Insurance Corporation* [1901] 1 I.R. 301.)

That is not to say that a trust will arise in every case where a third party is named as beneficiary. Judges have indeed proved less and less willing to allow the use of the trust device as an artificial means of avoiding the privity rule. There must be evidence of an intention to benefit the third party. (*Vandepitte v Preferred Accident Insurance Corp of New York* [1933] A.C. 70*)*. It may not, however, be enough that they wish to confer a benefit on that party. (*Green v Russell* [1959] 2 Q.B. 226). As *Cadbury v Kerry Co-op.* [1982] ILRM 77 demonstrates, it will generally be necessary also to establish that the parties intended to create a trust in favour of the third party.

8.4.3 Agency

Another way of avoiding the privity rule arises by means of the concept of agency. An agent is a person who acts not on his own behalf but on behalf of another person, called the "principal". In a contractual context, the agent's actions bind the principal. The principal moreover, is entitled to benefit from the contract as if she had made it herself. A good example arises in the case of a trade union, which, in industrial negotiations, is deemed to act as agent for its members.

An agent may be disclosed (where the other party knows that the agent is acting for a principal) or undisclosed (where the relationship of agent and principal is not revealed).

An agent moreover may act with:

* **express authority**: where the relationship of agency is expressly created by the parties, *i.e.* there is a clear agreement to this effect;
* **implied authority:** where the relationship of agency is implicit, where the conduct of the parties indicates that one party is necessarily acting as an agent of another party;
* **apparent authority:** where there is no actual relationship of agency, but where there is nonetheless good reason to believe that a party has authority to act as agent for another person.

In order for the acts of an agent to bind the principal there must be an intention to create the relationship of agency. (See *Sheppard v Murphy* (1867) 1 I.R.Eq. 490.) Here again there is a concern with the artificial application of this doctrine in order to prevent injustice flowing from the privity doctrine, and with this in mind, the courts have laid down a test for the creation of an agency relationship in such circumstances.

In *Scruttons Ltd v Midland Silicones* [1962] A.C. 446, the question arose as to whether a firm of stevedores (people who contract to unload a ship's cargo) could rely on a limitation clause in a contract between the carrier and a client. The House of Lords ruled that the third party was not entitled to claim the benefit of the limitation clause unless:

- the contract was clearly intended to protect the stevedores
- the carrier was clearly acting as agent for the purposes of securing a benefit for the principal (the stevedores)
- the agent had authority to act for the principal and
- consideration flowed from the principal.

The test was not satisfied in *Scruttons* as there was no evidence of an intention to benefit the stevedores. However, in very similar circumstances in *New Zealand Shipping v A.M. Satterthwaite and Co. Ltd. (The "Eurymedon")* [1975] A.C. 154, these conditions were satisfied such that a firm of stevedores was able to rely on a clause in a contract to which it was not a party. The plaintiff (based in New Zealand) had purchased a drilling machine from the seller (based in the UK). A firm was employed to transfer the machine to New Zealand. The firm in turn employed a company of stevedores to unload the machine. Owing to the stevedores' negligence, the drill was damaged. The stevedores tried to rely on a limitation clause in a contract between the carrier and consignors that meant that they could not be sued more than one year from the date on which the damage was caused. The Privy Council, having applied the four conditions laid out in *Scruttons,* concluded that a relationship of agency existed and thus the stevedores could rely on the clause. (See also *Borvigilant v Romina G* [2003] 2 All E.R. 736.)

An Irish example of this exception arose in *Hearn and Matchroom Boxing v Collins* (unreported, High Court, February 3, 1998). In this case, the first plaintiff—manager of boxer Stephen Collins—successfully relied on an agreement between the boxer and the second plaintiff, a management company. The court concluded that the latter had contracted as agent for Hearn and that Hearn could thus rely on the contract. The contract was intended to benefit Hearn, the company had clearly acted on his behalf and with his authority, and Hearn had furnished consideration by agreeing to work as Collins' manager.

8.4.4 Restrictive covenants in leases

A covenant is a promise contained in a lease or deed restricting the use of land for specified purposes. The rule in *Tulk v Moxhay* (1848) 2

Ph. 774 states that such a covenant "runs with the land". In other words, the covenant may bind people who were not party to the deed in which it was contained. See also *Whelan v Cork Corporation* [1991] I.L.R.M. 19.

8.4.5 Confidentiality clauses
Where a person enters into a confidentiality clause, it is possible to invoke the clause against a person who receives information in breach of the clause. (See *Oblique Financial Services Ltd v Promise Productions* [1994] I.L.R.M. 74.)

8.4.6 Implication of collateral contracts
In some cases, where A and B enter into a contract for the benefit of C, it may be feasible to imply a fresh contract (called a "collateral contract") between the third party and one of the contractors.

In *Shanklin Pier v Detel Products* [1951] 2 K.B. 854, the plaintiffs hired a contractor to repaint its pier. In turn the contractor bought paints from the defendants. The contractor however, bought the paint on the instructions of Shanklin Pier, who had received assurances from Detel that its paints, once applied, would last for seven to ten years. In fact the paint was of poor quality and faded within three months. The court ruled that although the contractor had bought the paint from Detel, there was a collateral contract between Shanklin Pier and Detel to the effect that the paint would last for ten years.

9. Capacity to Contract

A contract, as discussed above, requires the agreement of two or more persons. However, in order for a contract to be fully enforceable, all of the parties thereto must have the capacity to contract. In particular, a contract maybe avoided where one of the parties lacked the capacity to contract, for example, because of mental incapacity, intoxication or other similar impediments.

It is not necessary expressly to prove capacity in every case where a contract is made. The law generally assumes, unless the contrary is established, that adults entering into a contract have the full capacity to do so. In other words, the onus of proving absence of capacity is on the person who alleges such absence. In specific cases, however, it may be possible to establish lack of capacity—these are explored further below. Contract law regards certain vulnerable categories of person as deserving of protection and thus in certain cases, even where there appears to be full consent on the part of both contracting parties, the law may regard a party as being incapable of forming a valid contract or may otherwise limit such capacity.

9.1. Infancy: general

The most commonly experienced example of incapacity is infancy, that is, lack of age. Both common law and statute significantly restrict the capacity of infants to contract. An infant (also called a "minor") is an unmarried person who is under the age of 18. (See Age of Majority Act 1985. Prior to 1985 the age of majority was 21, and indeed some older cases in this context involve persons above 18 but under 21). The definition of infant excludes persons under 18 who are married, though given that 18 is also the minimum legal age for marriage, such cases rarely, if ever, arise.

Contracts made with infants may be divided into three categories (the "three Vs"): those that are "void", those that are "voidable" and those that are "valid".

- **Void *ab initio***—if a contract is void *ab initio* (from the start) it has no legal effect from its very inception. Such lack of effect is "retrospective", that is, it dates from the creation of the void contract such that the contract is deemed never to have had legal effect.
- **Voidable**—a contract that is voidable is a contract that is deemed valid until it is avoided. Once it is avoided, however, such a contract

is deemed to be invalid with retrospective effect. In other words, once avoided, a voidable contract is deemed to be and *always to have been* void *ab initio, i.e.* from the date of its very creation. It is possible, however, for a party to lose the right to avoid by ratification on reaching the age of majority (where the binding nature of the contract is acknowledged by the former infant) or by delay in avoidance.

• **Valid**

9.2 Infants: void contracts

At common law, contracts with a minor, with some notable exceptions, tended to be voidable. This meant that the contract could be avoided, but only at the behest of the minor. However, with the enactment of the Infants Relief Act 1874, certain contracts with minors were deemed to be absolutely void. This meant that such contracts were of absolutely no legal effect from their creation and could not be enforced even at the instance of the infant.

The 1874 Act deems two types of contract to be void *ab initio*:

(a) Contracts for the repayment of money lent or to be lent *to an infant*

(b) Contracts for goods supplied or to be supplied *to an infant*

According to s.2 of the Act, such contracts are absolutely void. It is not possible, for instance, for the infant to ratify the contract after she reaches the age of 18 (as would be possible with a voidable contract). Nor is it possible for the infant to enforce such contract (although there are certain exceptions to this rule). It is worth noting however, that the Act does not apply where *services* are being supplied to an infant. Nor does the Act extend to situations where it is the infant who is supplying the goods, or is the creditor of the loan. The Act only applies where the loan or goods in question are supplied *to* an infant and not *by an infant to an adult*. Hence there is nothing stopping an infant from entering into a contract to supply goods *to* an adult or to loan money *to* an adult.

9.3 Exception: contracts for necessaries

In respect of contracts deemed to be void or voidable, an important exception applies where the goods or services in question are deemed by law to be "necessaries". Notwithstanding the Act of 1874, where necessary items are sold and delivered to an infant, the infant must pay a reasonable price for them.

A "necessary" is a common law concept which has been codified into statute by the Sale of Goods Act 1893. Necessaries are defined by s.2 of the Act of 1893 as "goods suitable to the condition of life of such infant or minor or other person, *and* to his actual requirements at the time of the sale and delivery". These are, in other words, basic items that one requires in order to maintain a decent standard of living: key examples would include food, clothing, accommodation and education (*e.g.* books for a student: *Soon v Wilson* (1962) 33 D.L.R. (2d.) 428). The supplier of the goods bears the onus of proving that the item in question is a necessary.

Clearly, an item that is merely for ornamentation or is purely an item of luxury would not be a necessary. In *Skrine v Gordon* (1875) I.R. 9 C.L. 479, a hunting horse was deemed not to be a "necessary" even for a gentleman of means, the judge noting that "...we all know that hunting is a good sport and a manly exercise, but still that only shows that it is a sport, and luxuries or amusements are quite distinct from necessaries". Similarly, in *Ryder v Wombwell* (1868) L.R. 4 Ex. 32, cufflinks encrusted with jewels were deemed not to be a "necessary" even for a wealthy infant. A video games console would be a good modern example of an item that is not a necessary.

Nevertheless, the fact that something is luxurious in and of itself does not automatically mean that it is not also a "necessary". Some good examples might include an expensive branded pair of trainers or a costly suit: both might be necessaries, despite the exorbitant price charged for such items. See *Chapple v Cooper* (1844) 13 M & W. 252: "Articles of mere luxury are always excluded though luxurious items of utility are in some cases included". Nonetheless, it is apparent that where one already possesses enough goods of a particular type, additional goods of the same type may not be deemed "necessary". In *Nash v Inman* [1908] 2 K.B. 1, an underage Oxford student (the age of majority at the time being 21) purchased 11 "fancy waistcoats" from a Savile Row tailor. Although clothes are generally deemed to be necessaries, it was established that the minor already had sufficient waistcoats and that the purchases in question were surplus to requirements. They were, in other words, not actually "needed" as the student already had enough waistcoats and were therefore not part of the "actual requirements" of the minor. Thus the contract was not enforceable.

Two points are very important to note in this regard:

- Even if an item is deemed to be a necessary, the infant is only required to pay what a court would regard as "a reasonable price" for the item. She may not, thus, be required to pay the full contract price. Indeed, even a contract for necessaries may not be enforced if its terms are generally to the detriment of the minor. (See *Fawcett v Smethurst* (1914) 84 L.J.K.B. 473.)

- The exception relating to necessaries applies only if the contract is executed (performed in full) and not executory (pending performance). In other words, the infant is only required to pay for necessaries where the goods in question *have been delivered to her*. If the goods have not yet been delivered, the infant is perfectly free to reject delivery, even of necessaries.

9.4 Infants: voidable contracts

Under the common law, certain contracts with minors are deemed (independently of the Act of 1874) to be voidable, that is, they may be avoided at the behest of the minor. This does not mean that the contract is automatically invalid: simply that the minor may choose to avoid the contract, if she sees fit. The contract cannot be enforced against the minor, even after she has come of age, unless the minor has ratified the contract on turning 18 or shortly thereafter. A contract may be ratified by conduct of the minor indicating that the contract is regarded as binding.

The most commonly encountered example of a voidable contract arises where a minor has entered into a contract of employment or apprenticeship. Nowadays, legislation (such as the Protection of Young People in Employment Acts 1977–1996) provides important safeguards for young people in the workplace. Yet, even before these Acts came into force, certain protections were available at common law. Where an infant entered into a contract of employment or of service, such a contract will be voidable unless it is, on balance, more to the benefit of the infant than to her detriment. It is not enough, however, that the contract contains some onerous terms. A contract will only be voidable if, viewed globally, it is to the overall detriment of the minor.

Examples of voidable contracts:

- In *Keays v Great Southern Railway* [1941] I.R. 534, a railway ticket sold to an infant contained a clause excusing the railway company from all liability should the infant be injured. The clause was deemed to be unenforceable against the infant as it deprived her "… of practically every right that she has against the railway company …" in respect of its negligence.

- In *De Francesco v Barnum* (1890) 45 Ch. D 430, a 14-year-old girl was apprenticed as a stage dancer under very harsh terms. The girl was obliged to do her instructor's bidding, could not perform without his consent, could be sent abroad at his whim and was prevented from marrying against his will. By contrast, the dance instructor had next to no obligations towards his apprentice. He did not have to employ her, and when he did, could pay her a pittance. He could, moreover, terminate the contract at any stage. This clearly one-sided contract was deemed to be voidable as it was on the whole very onerous to the girl.
- In *Shears v Mendeloff* (1914) 30 T.LR. 342, a contract between a young boxer and a manager was deemed voidable: the contract was wholly sided in favour of the manager, who was entitled to a quarter of the infant's purse (the infant having to foot any expenses arising), even though the manager was not obliged to secure him any fights.

Examples of valid contracts:

- *Roberts v Gray* [1913] 1 K.B. 520 establishes that where an infant receives instruction under a contract, the contract is more likely to be to her benefit. Here an infant was contracted to tour with the plaintiff, a professional billiards player, in return for which he would receive tuition in this sport. The contract was overall to the benefit of the infant, and thus enforceable.
- In *Doyle v White City Stadium* [1935] 1 K.B. 110, a licence given to a minor (the great Irish boxer Jack Doyle) by the British Boxing Board of Control was deemed enforceable. A clause in the licence permitted the forfeiture of a fight purse in a case where the Board's rules were breached. In this case, Doyle challenged a decision to deprive him of the purse in a fight where he was disqualified for an illegal blow. The court, however, concluded that the contract was overall to his benefit, the clause being included ultimately with a view to protecting the welfare of boxers, by incentivising the observance of certain rules.
- In *Chaplin v Frewin* [1966] Ch. 71, the son of the famous actor, Charlie Chaplin, entered into an agreement to sell his memoirs. He attempted subsequently to repudiate the contract. The contract was

nonetheless deemed overall to be to his benefit, the court reasoning that it allowed him to make a living so that he could support his wife and family.

9.5 Contracts involving recurring obligations

A contract requiring a minor to pay recurring periodic payments may be deemed voidable at the behest of the minor. A good example would include a rental agreement; an infant who rented an apartment, for instance, would be entitled to avoid such an agreement. (See *Davies v Benyon-Harris* (1931) 47 T.L.R. 424.) Similarly, a contract to pay insurance by instalments is voidable at the instance of a minor (*Stapleton v Prudential Insurance* (1928) 62 I.L.T.R. 56).

However, monies already paid by a minor under a voidable contract cannot subsequently be recovered unless the minor has received no benefit whatsoever under the contract. In other words, an infant who has already paid instalments or rent will not be able to reclaim such monies unless there has been a *total* failure of consideration. Thus, unless there is a full failure in consideration, monies already paid cannot be recovered by the minor, as she has received some benefit in return. For instance, a minor rents an apartment for one year, lives there for four months and then repudiates the contract. Although she will be entitled to to repudiate, she cannot recover for rent paid in respect of the time she has lived there. She has received a benefit (consideration) for her payments, and it would be unfair to allow her to recover payments already made. (*Blake v Concannon* (1870) I.R. 4 C.L. 323.)

9.6 Mental illness

In certain circumstances, the mental illness of a contracting party may render a contract voidable. It is not enough, however, simply to establish the presence of a mental or psychiatric illness. The condition must be such that the person did not know what she was doing. The other party, moreover, must be aware of the mental illness. The onus of establishing that the mental illness prevented a contract from forming is on the person alleging it. Even where incapacity is established, a contractor may still enforce a contract for necessaries, though the contractor may only seek to extract a "reasonable price" for the goods.

9.7 Intoxication

An intoxicated person is liable under a contract made while intoxicated unless:

- the intoxication was such that the party did not know what he was doing **and**
- the other contracting party was aware of the intoxication *per se* (although it is not essential to establish that the other party was aware of the level of drunkenness, or the fact that the intoxicated party did not know what she was doing.)

Intoxication may arise from drunkenness, or drug use, though it is irrelevant whether the state of intoxication arose as a result of a voluntary or involuntary act. As with insanity, the onus of proof is on the person alleging intoxication. See *White v McCooey* (unreported, High Court, June 24, 1976).

Even where incapacity is established, however, a contract for necessaries may still be enforced against the incapacitated party. Section 2 of the Sale of Goods Act 1893 allows a contract for necessaries to be enforced against a person who was mentally ill or intoxicated at the time of the contract.

A contract with a person of diminished capacity, even if it is not invalid under these rules, may, in the alternative, be struck down for unconscionability where (a) one of the parties is in a position of relative disadvantage due to age, poverty, insanity or intoxication, (b) the other party is aware of this disadvantage and (c) the contract is of significant disadvantage to the first party. (See.para.18.5 below.)

9.8 Non-Irish nationals

Generally speaking, persons have full capacity in Irish law to enter into contracts whether or not they are nationals of or resident in Ireland. Formerly, non-EU nationals faced certain restrictions under the Land Act 1965 (s.45) when purchasing rural land in Ireland. These restrictions have, however, been abolished by the Land Act 2005.

A further minor exception applies when the State is at war. In such circumstances a citizen of the opposing state (regardless of her own sympathies—she may oppose her own government) is precluded, under Irish law, from making a contract or suing under a contract. These principles do not apply, however, to a non-Irish national who takes it upon herself personally to attack the state. For instance, in *Pedlar v Johnstone* [1920] 2 I.R. 450, a US citizen took part in the 1916 Rising. Although he was considered to have acted against the interests of the United Kingdom (though arguably for the greater good of Ireland), the court did not consider him an enemy alien: the US was not at war with the United Kingdom. The rule, moreover, does not apply to a person lawfully resident in Ireland nor does the rule preclude "an enemy alien" from defending an action taken against her by another person.

9.9 Incorporated bodies

A distinction is made in law between a "natural person" and a "legal person". A natural person is a human being who has full legal personality. The term "legal person", by contrast, generally refers to a body incorporated by law, such as a company. The body thus incorporated is deemed to be a legal person, with a legal personality separate from that of its shareholders, employees or founders.

A body may have been incorporated in one of three ways:

* By Royal Charter: Trinity College Dublin, for instance, gains it incorporated status from a charter issued by Elizabeth I
* By a specific Act of Parliament (such as the Dublin Institute of Technology, set up under the DIT Acts 1992–1994)
* Under the Companies Acts 1963–2003

An incorporated body generally may buy and sell, contract and sue, like any natural person. It is however, restricted by its memorandum and articles of association (the documents establishing the company): a company may only act in a particular way if its memorandum and articles permit it to act in that manner. It is not permitted to act *ultra vires*, that is, outside the powers conferred by its memo and articles (*Ashbury Railway Carriage and Iron Co. v Riche* (1875 L.R. 7 H.L. 653)). The company does not, in short, have capacity to act outside its powers: any contract made in defiance of the *ultra vires* rule will be void.

Nonetheless, s.8 of the Companies Act 1963 and art.6 of the European Communities (Companies) Regulations 1973 (S.I. No. 163) provide relief for a person dealing in good faith with a company acting outside its powers. Unless the person dealing with the company was aware of the fact that the company was acting *ultra vires*, the company will be held to its bargain.

9.10 Convicts

The Forfeiture Act 1870, s.8, renders a "convict" incapable of contracting, either expressly or by implication. A convict for these purposes is a person found guilty of treason or a "felony" (a category which has been abolished) who has been sentenced to penal servitude.

9.11 Immunity for foreign diplomats

As a general rule, foreign diplomats and envoys are immune from suit. Foreign States cannot generally be sued in the domestic courts of another jurisdiction. Certain exceptions and conditions nonetheless exist. See the Diplomatic Relations and Immunities Act 1967.

9.12 Where capacity is specifically provided for

In certain cases the law specifically provides that certain types of person, natural and legal, are capable of making contracts:

- **Married Women.** Under the Married Women's Status Act 1957 married women are expressly entitled to make contracts, and to sue or be sued under such contracts. (Married women were formerly prevented from making contracts on their own behalf.)
- **The State (Ireland):** The State is a legal person, and, as such, may sue and be sued on foot of a contract. The State basically has the same capacity and potential liability as an ordinary ("natural") person. The State cannot claim immunity from suit. Likewise, a contract made with a Government Department may be enforced against that Department—see s.2 of the Ministers and Secretaries Act 1924.
- **European Community:** the European Community has (under the European Community Treaty, Arts 281 and 282) a separate legal personality and legal capacity equivalent to that of a natural person. It can, in particular, enter into contracts, and sue and be sued under a contract.
- **Persons who are illiterate:** Inability to read a contract or lack of proficiency in the language of the contract is not a defence to a claim under a contract. In *Barclays Bank v Schwartz* (*The Times,* August 2, 1995) a Romanian man claimed that he was not bound by a contract which he had signed, because the contract was in English, a language which he was unable to speak well. The Romanian was nonetheless deemed to be bound by the contract.

10. The Formalities of Contract

10.1 Introduction

A "formality" is a condition relating to the manner in which a contract is brought into being. In order for certain types of contract to be valid or enforceable in a court of law, certain formal procedures have to be followed. In older times, formality was very important in contract. With the passing of time, however, formality has largely given way to less ceremonious, more practical ways of doing business. In fact in modern contract law, (despite the perception some might have of contracting) the formalities precedent to the creation of a valid contract are minimal, with very little ceremony involved. Exceptions to this principle do exist, but are limited.

It is possible, for instance, for a contract to come into being as a result of an informal discussion, while chatting in a pub for instance or during a social dinner. Additionally, the law does not require for the formation of a contract that any special form of words be used. In other words, provided that the parties make their shared intentions clear, there is no prescribed "formula" needed for the creation of a contract.

In particular, in most cases an oral contract—that is an agreement arising from spoken discussion with no writing involved—is generally sufficient in law to create a valid contract. This point is ably exemplified by the decision in *Pernod Ricard v FII Fyffes PLC* (unreported, High Court, October 21, 1988), in which an oral agreement for the multi-million pound sale of shares was held to be enforceable, notwithstanding the lack of a written contract. The parties orally agreed all essential elements of the sale; as such, the Supreme Court concluded, the agreement was enforceable.

10.2 Benefits of formality

Although it is generally not necessary to do so, there are certainly some practical benefits in writing down the terms of a contract:

- It makes people think about what they are doing—it brings home to them the significance of the act of contracting. People are generally more reticent and cautious when writing down their agreements.
- It avoids the evidential problems often associated with oral contracts—when a contract is in writing, it is easier to establish its contents and indeed its existence.

- It avoids the need to rely on memory alone, particularly over long periods of time.

10.3 Contracts that must be evidenced in writing

While an oral contract will generally suffice, there exist several categories of contract that unless encapsulated in or evidenced in writing will not be enforceable in a court of law. These are set out below.

10.4 Sale of Goods Act 1893, Section 4

This provision stipulates that any contract for the sale of goods worth more than €12 (formerly IR£10) should be in writing or evidenced in writing (in other words there should be written evidence of the contract).

Section 3 of the Sale of Goods Act 1893 states that a contract may be made in writing or orally or by a mixture of both or may be implied from the conduct of the parties. Section 4, however, states that a contract for the sale of goods worth more than €12 will not be enforceable unless there is some note or memo of the contract made and signed by the party to be charged or his agent in that behalf.

At first glance, this requirement seems quite remarkable. Potentially, were it not for some very broad exceptions, s.4 would render many normal commercial dealings, some very trifling, virtually unworkable. Notably, s.4 has been abolished in England and Wales, and at the very least, it is arguable that the minimum threshold should be increased to reflect inflation. However, the exceptions to s.4 are quite broad and in practice considerably reduce the impact of this (otherwise cumbersome) requirement.

Exceptions

10.4.1. If the buyer actually receives and accepts all or part of the goods sold
Section 4(3) of the Act drops the writing requirement where the buyer has accepted delivery of some or all of the goods that are the subject of the contract. For these purposes, acceptance occurs where the buyer performs any act in relation to goods that recognises the pre-existing contract. The rationale appears to be that by accepting the goods, the buyer has implicitly recognised the existence of the contract. A common example arises where a person purchases goods in a supermarket. The buyer offers to purchase the goods (by placing them on the conveyor at the cashdesk), and the cashier accepts the offer by

scanning the goods. Yet even though the transaction normally would involve at least €12 worth of goods, because the buyer receives the goods virtually instantaneously, no written contract is required.

Receipt of part of the goods is sufficient to satisfy s.4(3). For instance, in *Tradax Ireland v Irish Grain Board* [1984] I.R. 1, the buyer had received 8,000 tonnes of an order totalling 25,000 tonnes of grain. The Supreme Court concluded that in accepting delivery of part of the grain, the contract was rendered enforceable without the need for written evidence.

For this exception to apply, however, the buyer must in fact accept the goods. A seller could not, for instance, avoid the rule by delivering the item unbeknownst to the buyer. In *Hopton v McCarthy* (1882) 10 L.R.(Ir.) 266 a coach builder in Tipperary ordered timber goods from London. These were delivered by rail but never collected from the railway station, the buyer having refused receipt and returned the invoice to London. It was held that the exception did not apply in these circumstances.

10.4.2 If something tangible is given in earnest
An example of this exception might arise where a deposit has been placed in relation to the purchase of goods. This may explain why many businesses will require the placement of a deposit for goods that are not being immediately collected.

10.4.3 If the buyer has tendered payment in full or in part and it has been accepted by the seller
The requirement for written evidence may be waived where the buyer had tendered some or all of the payment for the goods. It is essential, however, that the seller accepts such payment. For instance, in *Kirwan v Price* (1958) Ir. Jur. Rep. 56, the plaintiff alleged that he had made an agreement with the defendant to purchase a chestnut horse for £300. The defendant, however, argued that the sum agreed was £350 and she, thus, refused to sell. Although the plaintiff sent a cheque for £300, the defendant declined receipt of the cheque and immediately returned it to the plaintiff. As no acceptance had occurred, the absence of written evidence was fatal to the enforcement of this (admittedly vague) contract.

It is worth noting that acceptance may be implicit as well as explicit, as occurs where there is passive receipt in circumstances where it is clear that the act denotes acceptance.

10.5 Statute of Frauds (Ir.) 1695, section 2

The Statute of Frauds 1695, while of considerable vintage, introduced important formal requirements in relation to certain contracts, in particular contracts for the sale of land. The Statute (another word for an Act of Parliament) represented a response to concerns that people were lying in court to prove contracts that didn't exist. In the 16th and 17th centuries, contract cases frequently turned on fraudulent statements and perjury, with the result that the legislature acted so as to require written evidence of certain types of contract.

The Statute essentially requires that a contract to which it applies will not be enforced unless there is written evidence of the contract's existence. It is important to note that the contract itself need not be written, but it is essential that there is at least a note establishing its existence and setting out its key terms. Absent such evidence, the contract may be valid, but it cannot be enforced in a court of law.

10.5.1 Types of contract to which the Act applies

a. A surety or guarantee agreement

A surety or guarantee agreement arises where a person promises to pay the existing debt of a person, should that second person default on the debt. Such an agreement, to be enforceable, must be written or evidenced in writing.

A surety or guarantee agreement must be distinguished from an indemnity. When a person issues a guarantee or surety, she agrees to pay the debt of a third party only if that person *defaults* on the debt. In such a case, liability is merely secondary—it arises only if the primary debtor fails to pay. By contrast, a person giving an indemnity agrees to take primary responsibility for the payment of the debt or contingent debt, thus relieving the original debtor of the obligation to pay. In particular, if a person offers an indemnity against a particular contingency and it occurs, that person must pay up front. While a surety agreement must be in writing, an indemnity need not be.

b. Contracts the consideration for which is marriage

Where a party enters into a contract where the consideration is provided by an agreement to marry, the contract must be in writing. Given that it is no longer possible to enforce an agreement to marry (see Family Law Act 1981), it is likely that this requirement will have very little relevance in modern contract law.

c. Contracts not to be performed within a year

Where obligations under a contract are likely to continue for more than one year, the contract must be evidenced in writing. In other words, unless the parties intend to perform their contractual duties within a year, the Statute of Frauds will apply (*Farrington v Donoghue* (1866) I.R. 1 C.L. 675). Given that, over time, memories may fade, there is some justification in this rule, providing as it does for contractual relationships that may continue over significant periods of time.

For instance, in *Naughton v Limestone Land Co.* [1952] Ir. Jur. Rep. 19, an agreement that bound the plaintiff to work for the defendant for four years following his studies was held to be unenforceable for lack of written evidence. The plaintiff had agreed to study modern land drainage for three months, after which he would work for the defendant for four years. As the agreement was merely oral, and contemplated performance over four years and three months, the contract could not be enforced as it was not evidenced in writing. While it may be possible to sever separate elements of a long-term contract, enforcing those duties that do not outlast one year, the court declined to do so in this case.

In determining whether this rule applies, however, it is important to consider the intention of the parties. Even if a contract outlasts one year, if the parties originally intended that it be performed within a year, written evidence will not be required.

d. Contract for the sale of land or any interest therein

A contract for the sale of land or any interest in land (*e.g.* a lease) requires, if it is to be enforceable in a court of law, a written contract or in the alternative, written evidence of its terms. This is perhaps the most commonly encountered example in modern times of the application of the Statute of Frauds. Usually, until formal written contracts are signed and exchanged, an agreement to sell land is not enforceable (unless there is a note or memo of the contract, in writing, signed by the parties). Thus, even where potential homebuyers have put down a deposit on a house, and orally arranged its purchase, there is a risk that (absent a written note of their agreement) they will be "gazumped" by a buyer offering more money for the same property.

10.5.2 Sale of land – part performance

Specifically in relation to contracts for the sale of an interest in land, an important exception arises. Where an oral agreement for the sale of land has been performed in full or in part, the requirement of writing may be overlooked. In such a case, equity considers that the part-performance provides evidence of the existence of the contract, and thus allows the contract to be enforced. Another possible rationale lies in equity's concern to prevent the Statute of Frauds itself being used as an instrument of fraud, as a means of justifying unconscionable conduct.

The classic example of part-performance is where a person, on foot of an oral contract, is permitted to move onto the property which is the subject of the contract. For instance, in *Kingswood Estate v Anderson* [1963] 2 Q.B. 169, the plaintiff persuaded the defendant to move out of her existing accommodation and into new accommodation. The plaintiff promised that the defendant and her son could stay in the new accommodation for as long as they both lived. Although the contract was not evidenced in writing, it was deemed enforceable on the basis of part-performance, in this case the act of moving from the old house to the new house at the request of the plaintiff. (See also *Kennedy v Kennedy* (unreported, High Court, January 12, 1984).)

Likewise, in *Rawlinson v Ames* [1925] Ch. 96, the parties orally agreed that the defendant would lease an apartment from Rawlinson. At Ames' request, Rawlinson made some modifications to the flat, which Ames inspected. The parties' acts were deemed to constitute part-performance of the contract, relieving them of the obligation to provide written evidence of the contract.

The acts of part-performance must have been carried out by, or at the request of, the party seeking to deny the enforceability of the contract. At the very least, the latter must have been aware of and must have acquiesced in the acts of part-performance. The party seeking to enforce the contract must, moreover, provide unequivocal evidence of the contract's existence. The acts in question must be consistent with the existence of the contract. (See *Silver Wraith v Siúicre Éireann* (unreported, High Court, June 8, 1989); *Mackie v Wilde* [1998] 2 I.R. 578.) Paying for the land (*e.g.* a deposit) will usually not be sufficient in itself to satisfy the part-performance requirement, though there are some exceptions to this view. (See *Steadman v Steadman* [1976] A.C. 536.)

10.5.3 What constitutes a note or memo for these purposes?
It is not necessary that the parties intend, by their actions, to create a memorandum of the agreement. In *Tradax v Irish Grain Board* [1984]

I.R. 1, for instance, the note of a contract for the sale of grain was contained in part in a letter from the defendant purporting to repudiate (reject) the relevant agreement. In these circumstances, even though the defendant hardly intended to make itself bound by the agreement, the letter nevertheless had this effect, providing in part the required note of the contract. That said, the use of the phrase "subject to contract" in such a note may have the effect of precluding the enforcement of the contract (see para.4.3.5 above).

The note or memorandum of agreement need not be particularly formal, though it must always be signed by the person against whom enforcement of the contract is sought. For instance, in *Doherty v Gallagher* (unreported, High Court, June 9, 1975) the details of the sale of a property were appended to the bottom of a cheque. This was held to be sufficient as a note of the contract.

The note or memo must, however, at the very least identify the "parties, the property and the price" (*per Godley v Power* (1961) 95 I.L.T.R. 135).

- **The parties to the contract:** It is sufficient, even if the parties are not precisely named, that they are sufficiently identifiable. (*Bacon v Kavanagh* (1908) 42 I.L.T.R. 120). In *Law v Roberts* [1964] I.R. 292 a court concluded that although a party's correct name had not been used in a note of a contract for the lease of a property, the identity of both parties was sufficiently clear from the correspondence and surrounding evidence.

- **The price:** In *McQuaid v Lynam* [1965] I.R. 564, the failure to set out the amount of rent involved meant that the note of a contract was not valid. It is sufficient, however, if the note affords some method of identifying the price

- **The subject matter of the contract—***i.e.* **what is being sold or bought:** In *Law v Roberts* [1964] I.R. 292, the vendor complained that the note of a contract did not sufficiently identify the precise property interest that was being sold. The court nonetheless concluded that the subject matter of the contract was sufficiently clear, as the purchaser, in this case, had indicated a willingness to accept whatever interest the vendor possessed.

- **The essential details of the agreement accurately stated:** If the parties have separately indicated the presence of other essential features of the contract, the memo must also make reference to these features.

A note or memorandum may comprise more than one document which, though not sufficient as separate documents, may be read together as evidence of the contract. This is called the "joinder of documents". For instance, in *McQuaid v Lynam* [1965] I.R. 564, a receipt for a payment and an application for a loan were read together as constituting a memorandum of an agreement to rent premises. In *Tradax v Irish Grain Board* [1984] I.R. 1, the plaintiff had orally agreed to purchase barley from the defendant. The court relied on a letter purporting to reject this oral agreement together with a telex containing the details of the contract as jointly constituting a memo for this purpose. The letter had referred to the terms of the contract and to the earlier telex.

This latter fact is of crucial importance: for two or more documents to be read together, there must be a sufficient acknowledgement in one document of the existence of the other document(s). In other words, there must be something connecting the documents together, such as a reference in one document to the other. In *Kelly v Ross* (unreported, High Court, April 29, 1980), for instance, a court refused to read nine documents together as constituting a memo of a contract as none of the documents contained sufficient reference to any of the others.

In order for a party to be bound by a contract, the note or memorandum must be signed by that party (or an agent acting on her behalf), as evidence of the authenticity of the agreement. It is not enough that the note contain a person's name—the person must have signed and have intended to sign the note. The signature may, however, be given in electronic form, if the person to whom it is offered consents to the use of an electronic signature (Electronic Commerce Act 2000, s.14). A rubber stamp may also constitute a signature for this purpose, as may a mark attached by an illiterate person, if either is intended to act in place of a person's signature.

10.6 Deasy's Act 1860, section 4 (Landlord and Tenant Law Amendment (Ireland) Act 1860)

Deasy's Act applies to any lease or any contract with respect to land where it is intended to create the relationship of landlord and tenant for any period of time not being from year to year or any lesser period. Such an agreement must either be executed by deed or be evidenced by a note in writing signed by the landlord or her authorised agent.

10.7 Bills of Exchange Act 1882

A "bill of exchange" is defined by the 1882 Act as "… an unconditional order in writing, addressed by one person to another, signed by the person giving it, requiring the person to whom it is addressed to pay on demand or at a fixed or determinable future time a sum certain in money to or to the order of a specified person, or to bearer". A good example of a bill of exchange is a cheque.

Certain formal requirements apply to bills of exchange:

* The bill must be in writing (s.3);
* It must be signed by the person giving it (s.3);
* The sum of money involved must be clearly stated (s.3);
* The drawee (in the case of a cheque, the bank at which the account is held) must be identified with reasonable certainty (s.6); and
* Unless the bill is made payable to the bearer of the bill (the person who possesses the bill, for the time being) the payee must be identified or identifiable with reasonable certainty (s.7).

10.8 Family Home Protection Act 1976

Where a family home, as defined, is involved, the Family Home Protection Act 1976 stipulates certain formal requirements designed to protect economically weaker spouses. The Act applies only to a "family home", defined as a dwelling in which a married couple reside or have resided, or where the spouse whose protection is in issue resides or resided. Additionally, the Act applies only to married couples, and not to non-marital partners. The Act precludes the sale of the home, or any part thereof or interest therein, without the prior consent in writing of non-disposing spouse. Absent this consent, any dealings with the house, any conveyance, including a mortgage or charge, a lease, or a contract for its sale or lease, will be void, *i.e.* of no legal effect.

The effects of the Act are tempered in certain important respects:

* The Act only applies to the family home of married persons or of a married spouse;
* The Act cannot be invoked more than six years after the property has been sold, provided that the non-owning spouse is no longer resident in the house;
* The requirement of consent can be dispensed with by a court, if consent is being unreasonably withheld;
* The Act does not apply to a purchaser who had no notice, actual, constructive or imputed of the failure to obtain consent;

- The Act does not apply where a husband and wife jointly contract to sell a house;
- The Act does not apply where the land is conveyed by operation of law or by a party other than one of the spouses. (*e.g.* through the creation of a judgment mortgage by a court, or following on foreclosure by a bank).

11. Electronic Commerce

11.1 Introduction

Nowadays, more and more transactions are made using electronic methods. In recent years, in particular, the internet has become increasingly popular as a tool in the purchase and sale of goods and the supply of services. Although some specific issues arise regarding the application of contract law in this context, generally no distinction is made between a contract entered into online and a printed contract signed by the parties. The principles of contract law are, indeed, equally applicable to contracts made online as they are to written or oral contracts. It is possible, in particular, to denote consent by means of an electronic signature. Similarly, a person who clicks a website icon denoting their acceptance of stated terms and conditions, (the "click-wrap" method) will, in principle, be bound by those conditions. All consumer laws that apply to regular contracts also apply with equal force to electronic contracts (the Electronic Commerce Act 2000, s.15).

11.2 The formation of a contract

Building on several EU Directives, the Electronic Commerce Act 2000 clarifies a number of points in relation to contracts entered into online. The main purpose of the Act is to confirm the effectiveness of electronic methods in the creation of contracts.

Broadly speaking, the rules regarding the formation of a contract by electronic means do not differ from those applying generally. The Act of 2000 nonetheless serves to clarify a number of points relating to electronic contracts:

- Unless the parties specify a particular non-electronic method of communication, an offer or acceptance may be made by electronic means.
- Unless the parties otherwise agree, an electronic communication is deemed to have been "dispatched" or sent for the purposes of contract law at the point in time where it enters an information system or the first information system (generally a "server") outside the control of the sender.
- Unless the parties otherwise agree, and subject to the terms of S.I. No. 68 of 2003, where a person has designated an information system for the purpose of receiving electronic communications (*e.g.* by supplying an e-mail address) an electronic communication

is deemed to have been received at the point when it enters that information system (*i.e.* when it becomes possible for the recipient to access the communication, whether the person has in fact accessed the information or not). Under the European Communities (Directive 2000/31/EC) Regulations (S.I. No. 68 of 2003), however, where a person wishes to contract online for the provision of a service provided at a distance, an order in respect of the service must be acknowledged electronically. (An order need not be acknowledged, however, where made by e-mail.) Both the order and the acknowledgement are deemed to have been received once the intended recipients are able to access the order and acknowledgement, respectively. Unless made by e-mail, the person placing the order must be given an opportunity to rectify any input errors in the order.

- If the party in receipt has not designated an information system, a message is deemed to have been received when it comes to the attention of the recipient.
- Regardless of its actual place of origin, an electronic communication is deemed to have been received at or sent from the place where the sender or recipient has her usual place of business, or (in the case of a consumer) where she normally resides. For instance, if an e-mail is sent from a laptop or mobile phone while a businessperson is out of the office, it is nonetheless deemed to have been sent from the location of the sender's office.
- It is unclear whether the postal rule applies to the use of e-mail (see para.3.8.3). Although in theory, e-mail not being totally instantaneous, the postal rule may apply, judges will most likely not extend this anomalous rule beyond its original confines.

11.3 The legal effects of electronic forms of communication

The Electronic Commerce Act 2000 serves to clarify some points in relation to the use of electronic means in the context of contract law:

- **The legal effect of electronic methods:** Section 9 of the Act stipulates that information supplied (wholly or partly) in electronic form will not be denied legal effect solely on the basis that it is conveyed electronically. Similarly, s.19 states that a contract cannot be denied effect simply because it is, in whole or in part, contained in electronic form. The parties may, however, agree otherwise, for instance by stipulating for a non-electronic means of communication.

- **Formalities:** Where a contract is required to be in writing, or evidenced in writing, writing contained in electronic form (*e.g.* an e-mail) will suffice for this purpose (s.12). However, two general caveats apply: first, it must be established that it is reasonable to expect that the information would be accessible in electronic form by the person to whom it is directed (*i.e.* that the person has access to e-mail); secondly, the person receiving the information must have consented to receiving the information in that form (s.12(2)). Additional conditions (for instance, as to the specific software that should be used, or the procedures that should be followed) may be added where the writing is required by a public body.
- **Electronic signatures:** Where a contract requires a signature, an electronic signature will be equally as effective as a handwritten signature. An electronic signature is defined as "data which serves as a method of authenticating the purported originator and which is attached to, incorporated in or logically associated with other electronic data". (This may comprise, for instance, a username and password.) However, the person requesting the signature must have consented to receiving the signature in electronic form. Again, additional conditions may apply where the signature is required by a public body.
- **Witnessing signatures:** Where, by law, a signature must be witnessed, the advanced electronic signatures of both the signer and witness will suffice for this purpose. An advanced electronic signature is a signature that is uniquely linked to the signatory and capable of identifying her, created using means that are solely under the control of the signatory and linked to the data in such a way that any subsequent change in the data may be detected. The signature must, moreover, be certified as valid by a certification service provider (*i.e.* a body that can affirm the validity of the signature). The document must also contain a statement that the signature is to be witnessed. Again, the recipient of the signature must consent to the receipt of the signatures in that form.
- **Seal:** A document that is required to be made under seal will be deemed to be under seal if signed using an advanced electronic signature. The document should state that it is required to be under seal.

11.4 Documents to which the Act does not apply

The Electronic Commerce Act 2000 does not apply to certain types of document, most notably wills, deeds creating a trust, enduring powers of attorney, deeds transferring property and affidavits.

12. The Terms of a Contract: Express Terms

12.1 Introduction

This particular part of the text concerns the "substantive" content of a contract, namely the "terms" thereof. In general, it is for the parties to a contract to determine its contents. The subject matter, price and other conditions depend almost entirely on the agreement of the particular parties. In line with the overriding philosophy of freedom of contract, judges generally prove most reluctant to interfere in the creation of contractual terms: it is for the parties alone to make their own bargain.

Nonetheless, certain rules and principles apply in relation to the terms of contracts. In particular, judges may be called upon to determine whether statements, made in the course of contractual negotiations, form part of a contract, or whether they are external thereto. In other cases, judges may be asked to consider whether certain terms should be implied into a contract, an issue considered in Chapter 13. As will be discussed in Chapter 14, particularly stringent rules apply to exclusion and limitation clauses, whereby parties purport to exempt themselves from liability under a contract or set quantifiable limits to their liability.

12.2 Can oral statements form part of a contract?

In general (though with some notable exceptions—see Chapter 10 above) a contract may be made orally or, alternatively, in writing, or by a combination of both written and oral statements. In particular, there is generally no legal difference between a contract made orally and a written contract: both are equally valid (though it will, of course, be easier to prove the content of a written contract).

12.3 Term or representation?

The next question to be addressed concerns the status of certain statements made during the course of contractual negotiations. Where a written contract is entered into, and deemed to represent "the whole of the contract" between the parties, such problems rarely arise. In such a case, the contents of the written document exclusively set out the terms of the contract.

However, where a contract is made orally, or by a combination of written and oral statements, determining the content of the contract may prove more elusive. In this regard, a distinction is made between two types of statement made in the course of contractual negotiations:

- **"Term"**: A statement may be deemed to be a "term" of the contract (sometimes also called a "warranty"). If so, it is considered to form an integral part of the contractual document, a binding promise. If a term is breached, the appropriate remedy is provided by suing for breach of contract.
- **Representation:** While a representation may prove instrumental in inducing a person to enter into a contract, it does not form part of the contract. In other words, the content of the representation has no contractual effect. Where a representation turns out to be untrue, or is not fulfilled, the appropriate remedy lies in suing in tort for misrepresentation.

Whether a statement becomes a term of a contract, or qualifies as a mere representation, is a question of fact to be decided based on the circumstances of each case. However, a number of tests may be applied to determine whether such a statement forms part of a contractual agreement.

12.3.1 Is the statement one of belief or one of fact?

If, objectively speaking, the statement merely indicates the belief or opinion of the person making the statement, it is unlikely to form part of the contract. For instance, in *Anderson v Backlund* 159 Minn 423 (1924), the vendor of land expressed his opinion that there would be plenty of water to sustain the land he was selling, as he had "yet to see the rains fail in Minnesota". This was held to be a statement of opinion rather a statement of fact (the situation might have been different if the vendor had been a meteorologist). In each case, however, the issue is to be determined by reference to the facts of the case. In *McGuinness v Hunter* (1853) 6 Ir. Jur. 103, a statement to the effect that a horse was "all right and I know nothing wrong about him" was held to be a term of the contract to sell the said horse.

In circumstances where a false statement is made knowingly, the courts may be somewhat more likely to regard the statement as giving rise to a term, particularly if it was used to induce the creation of a contract. However, even where the error was innocent, the statement may still form part of the contract. For instance, in *Bank of Ireland v Smith* [1966] I.R. 646, a statement (innocently made in error) that land was sown with barley (and otherwise prepared for agricultural use) was deemed to be a term of a contract for the sale of land, this being an error of fact, albeit innocent.

12.3.2 Have the parties stipulated that the statement forms part of the contract?

A statement will be a term of the contract if the parties have expressly stipulated that it should be incorporated. If, on the other hand, the matter is not mentioned at the time that the contract is concluded, it is less likely that incorporation has occurred. In this regard timing is crucial. In *Routledge v McKay* [1954] 1 W.L.R. 615, a written contract for the sale of a bike made no mention of its age, though the matter had been discussed some four weeks earlier. The court concluded that the earlier statement (which had misrepresented the age of the bike) did not form part of the contract.

12.3.3 How crucial was the statement in the conclusion of the contract?

In *Bannerman v White* (1861) 10 C.B. (N.S.) 844, the purchaser of hops had asked if they had been treated with sulphur, adding that if they had been he would not have been interested in their purchase. The plaintiff incorrectly stated that they had not been so treated. Given the importance attached to this matter by the defendant, the statement that the hops were untreated was deemed to be a term of the contract. Similarly, in *Couchman v Hill* [1947] 1 All E.R. 103, the buyer of a heifer stressed the importance he attached to the fact that the heifer had not been "served" by a bull. When the heifer turned out to be pregnant, the court concluded that a statement to the effect that the heifer had not been served was a term of the contract.

12.3.4 Does the person making the statement have a special skill or knowledge?

Where a person purports to exercise a particular skill or knowledge, greater weight may be attached to a statement made by that person within their area of expertise. For instance, if Joe, an experienced dealer in antique radios, sells a radio stating that it is a "1935 model", it is likely that this statement as to age will be deemed a term of the contract. This would be less likely where a person who admits to having no knowledge of antique radios expressed an opinion as to the age of the radio in question.

For instance, in *Dick Bentley Productions v Harold Smith Motors* [1965] 2 All E.R. 65, an experienced car dealer stated that a car had been driven 20,000 miles since its engine had been changed (the true figure was 100,000 miles). The dealer's statement was held to be a term of the contract. Likewise, in *Schawel v Reade* (1912) 46 I.L.T. 281, the purchaser of a horse was assured that the horse was sound, though the horse in fact had an eye defect. Given the experience of the horse dealer in such matters, and his reassurance that "the horse is perfectly sound", the court concluded that the statement as to the horse's health was a term of the contract.

By contrast, where a person does not purport to have any particular expertise, her statements are likely to carry less weight. For instance, in *Oscar Chess v Williams* [1957] 1 All E.R. 325, a private individual (relying on the car's registration book) innocently misstated the age of a car he was selling. Given his lack of expertise in such matters, the statement was not deemed to amount to a term of the contract. (See also *Hummingbird Motors v Hobbs* [1986] R.T.R. 276.)

12.3.5 How much time elapsed between the making of the statement and the conclusion of the contract?

Timing is also crucial. If the statement was made directly before the contract was made, it is more than likely that the statement is a term. If it was made some weeks earlier (as in *Routledge v McKay*, para.12.3.2 above, where the statement as to the age of the bike was made four weeks before the contract was concluded), it is less likely to be a term. The time lag is relevant in determining whether the statement is a term of the contract though it will not always be conclusive: in *Schawel v Reade* (1912) 46 I.L.T. 281, for instance, a four week gap between the making of a statement as to the health of a horse and the conclusion of a contract did not preclude the earlier statement from forming part of the contract.

In all cases, however, a statement will not form part of the contract (and indeed will not be actionable as a misrepresentation) unless it is made *before* the contract is concluded. In both *Roscorla v Thomas* (1842) 3 Q.B. 234 and *Olley v Marlborough Court* [1949] 1 K.B. 532, statements made after a contract was concluded were deemed not to form part of the respective contracts. (See also paras 6.7.1 and 14.4.1.)

12.3.6 Emphasis in statement

The more emphatic and certain a statement is, the more likely it is that it will form part of the contract. Correspondingly, the vaguer a statement is the less likely it is that the statement will be incorporated. For instance, in *Schawel v Reade* (1912) 46 I.L.T. 281, the seller of a horse assured its buyer in very strong terms that the horse was in good health. When the buyer went to inspect the horse, the vendor intervened stating that "You need not look for anything: the horse is perfectly sound. If there was anything the matter with the horse I should tell you". The emphasis in the statement convinced the buyer to stop his own inspection of the horse. The statement was thus deemed to be a term of the contract.

By contrast, if the buyer is asked to check for herself the veracity of a statement, it is less likely that the statement will form part of the contract. In *Ecay v Godfrey* [1947] 80 Lloyd's Rep. 286, the seller of a boat stated that he believed the boat to be sound, but nonetheless recommended that the buyer should, prior to purchase, engage a professional to verify this. In such circumstances, the seller's statement was deemed not to form part of the contract.

12.3.7 If the contract was put into writing, did the parties intend the written contract to be conclusive?

It may well be that, on the facts, the parties intended that the written contract would be conclusive, and that any oral statements would not form part of the contract. Determining whether this is the case is a question of fact, but obviously if the parties have expressly stated that a written document is intended conclusively to represent the entirety of a contract, then it is unlikely that statements external to that document will form part of the contract.

12.4 Where written and oral terms conflict: The "parol evidence" rule

12.4.1 The "parol evidence" rule explained

A contract may often consist of one or more written documents supplemented by oral statements. Where, however, a conflict arises between the written and oral terms of a contract, the "parol evidence" rule accords precedence to written statements over oral statements. As noted in *Bank of Australasia v Palmer* [1897] A.C. 540:

> "Parol evidence cannot be received to contradict, vary, add to or subtract from the terms of a written contract or the terms in which the parties have deliberately agreed to record any part of their contract".

The parol evidence rule dictates that where a contract is "reduced into writing", evidence of extrinsic matters (including but not limited to oral statements) cannot replace, add to, alter or contradict the terms of the written document. "Parol evidence' includes anything external to the document in which the contract is written, including discussions between the parties, earlier drafts of the contract, letters exchanged between the parties—in short anything external to the document in which the final contract is said to be contained.

For instance, if a written contract states that the contract price for the purchase of a car is €5,000, it would not be possible to contradict this by adducing evidence that the parties had orally agreed that the price would be €6,000. The written terms of the contract prevail.

The classic example of the application of this rule arose in *Henderson v Arthur* [1907] 1 K.B. 10. A written lease stated that the rent on a property would be payable in advance. Oral evidence established, however, that the parties had, prior to the conclusion of the contract, orally agreed that the rent would be payable in arrears. The Court of Appeal nonetheless concluded that the rent was payable in advance: the oral evidence could not be used to contradict the written terms of the contract. The parol evidence rule was applied in Ireland in the case of *Macklin and McDonald v Greacen & Co.* [1983] I.R. 61, where the Supreme Court declined to admit parol evidence to contradict a written contract for the sale of a pub licence.

In practice, however, the parol evidence rule is subject to a plethora of exceptions that heavily undermine the effectiveness of the rule. There are in fact a number of ways, notwithstanding the rule, to introduce parol evidence.

12.4.2 Rectification
Where a written document:

- purports to be a written record of a prior oral agreement and
- fails to record that agreement accurately

a principle of equity permits oral evidence to be introduced to rectify the terms of the written document. Effectively, equity permits the written document to be altered so as to reflect the true nature of the oral contract. This applies, however, only where it can be established that the written document was intended to constitute a record of the prior oral agreement, and that the written document differs from the oral contract.

12.4.3 Interpretation of ambiguous terms
If the express written terms of a contract are unclear or ambiguous,

extrinsic evidence may be admitted to clarify its true meaning. Parol evidence may also be adduced to cast light on the broader context in which a contract was agreed. For instance, in *Revenue Commissioners v Moroney* [1972] I.R. 372, extrinsic evidence was admitted to show that a written contract that appeared to be for the sale of property was in fact a transfer by gift. Similarly, in *Chambers v Kelly* (1873) 7 I.R.C.L. 231, extrinsic evidence was introduced to clarify that a contract ostensibly according felling rights in respect of trees on the plaintiff's lands in fact only applied to *some* of those trees and not all of them. In *Ulster Bank v Synnott* (1871) 5 I.R. Eq. 595, a security was lodged against "acceptances made" on the defendant's account. Parol evidence was used to establish that this included future acceptances as well as those made in the past.

Correspondingly, parol evidence will most likely not be permitted where the contents of a written contract are clear and unambiguous. (See *Kinlen v Ennis UDC* [1916] 2 I.R, 299; *Marathon Petroleum v Bord Gáis Éireann* (unreported, Supreme Court, July 31, 1976)). In particular, the courts probably will not allow such evidence flatly to contradict a clear written statement of unambiguous meaning.

12.4.4 Custom or trade usage

In specific localities and in particular trades, a word or phrase may take on a special meaning, and oral evidence may be introduced to clarify that meaning. For instance, in *Smith v Wilson* (1832) 3 B. & Ad. 728, as a result of a rather quirky local tradition, the phrase "1,000 rabbits" was interpreted as denoting "1,200" rabbits (much like a baker's dozen comprising 13 rather than 12). Parol evidence is thus admissible as evidence of the idiosyncratic meaning that is ascribed to words by reference to local customs. Understandings common to a particular trade may also serve to clarify the terms of a written document, as in *Wilson Strain v Pinkerton* (1897) 3 I.L.T.R. 86. In that case, oral evidence established that on the retirement of a Belfast roundsman who sold bread door to door on credit terms, it was common practice in the trade for his employer to take over any outstanding debts.

12.4.5 Where the written document "does not record the totality of the contract"

The parol evidence rule, it appears, only applies where the parties have intended that the written document would record "the totality of the contract", *i.e.* that it is considered to represent the whole of the transaction (the "entire agreement". If it can be shown, however, that the parties in fact intended that the contract would consist of the written document read in the light of other documents or oral statements, the parol evidence rule does not apply. In *Couchman v Hill* [1947] 1 All E.R. 103, for instance, the plaintiff had received oral assurances that a heifer he was purchasing had not been serviced by a bull. In fact, the heifer was pregnant and subsequently died in childbirth. While the sale catalogue had also confirmed the heifer as being "unserved" the conditions printed in the catalogue stipulated that all "lots were sold with all faults, imperfections and errors of description". The court nonetheless concluded that the catalogue had to be read in the light of the oral assurances made to the plaintiff. Together, the catalogue and these assurances made up a "whole" contract. The plaintiff was thus entitled to sue for a breach of contract.

In short, if the written contract is not intended to be comprehensive or conclusive, oral evidence will be admitted. In *Clayton Love v B. & I.* (1970) 104 I.L.T.R. 157, the Supreme Court ruled that a contract was not intended to be reduced wholly and exclusively to one written document. By written agreement, the defendant had agreed to transport frozen food across the Irish Sea. By phone, the plaintiff clarified that the food had to be transported at sub-zero temperatures. This being the case, the court permitted oral evidence of the phone call to supplement the instructions contained in the written agreement. (See also *Howden v Ulster Bank* [1924] I.R. 117.)

12.4.6 Oral statement limiting or qualifying operation of contract
Oral evidence may be introduced to show that a contract was intended to be conditional upon the occurrence of a particular event. For instance, in *Pym v Campbell* (1856) 6 E. & B. 370, parol evidence was successfully adduced to establish that the sale of an invention was conditional on approval of the invention by an independent engineer.

12.4.7 Collateral contract
Where it can be shown that the parties intended to enter into two separate contracts, one written contract and another "collateral" contract consisting of written words or oral statements, both will be enforced separately. In *Godley v Power* (1961) 95 I.L.T.R. 135, for instance, during negotiations for the sale of a pub, the parties had agreed that any bottles stored on the premises at the time of sale ("the stock in trade") would be included in the sale. Though the stock in trade was not properly referenced in the written memo of the agreement to sell the pub, the Supreme Court nonetheless ruled that the parol evidence

rule did not apply. The court reasoned that there were in fact two contracts here: one for the sale of the pub, and a collateral contract for the sale of the stock in trade. Likewise, in *City and Westminster Properties v Mudd* [1959] Ch. 129, while a written agreement stipulated that leased premises were to be used for business purposes only, the parties had orally agreed that the tenant could also reside therein. The oral statement gave rise, the courts concluded, to a collateral contract that could be enforced alongside the lease. (See also *Carrigy v Brook* (1871) I.R. 5 C.L. 501.)

12.4.8 To prove the amount of consideration

Parol evidence may be admitted to prove the amount payable under a contract, if otherwise unstated or unclear. *(Black v Grealy*, unreported, High Court, December 10, 1977.)

12.4.9 The impact of the parol evidence rule

In practice, the parol evidence rule may be of very limited impact. Arguably, the exceptions are so wide and varied that the rule will only apply very rarely. Some commentators suggest, indeed, that the rule is no more than a presumption or a rule of interpretation that may be displaced on the facts. Nonetheless, the parol evidence rule illustrates the dangers that may arise where oral statements are not reduced to writing; in short, for evidential as well as doctrinal reasons, to ensure for certain that a particular understanding will form part of a contract, it is advisable to include it in written form as part of a formal contractual document.

12.5 Conditions precedent/subsequent

In some cases, a contract may be conditional on the occurrence of a particular event. Terms of this nature are generally divided into "conditions precedent" (which must be met *before* the contract comes into operation—see *Pym v Campbell* (1856) 6 E. & B. 370)—and "conditions subsequent" (which must be met subsequent to the formation of the contract, if it is to remain enforceable).

12.6 The relevant importance of contract terms

12.6.1 What is the difference between a "condition" and a "warranty"?

The terms "condition" and "warranty", often used interchangeably in day to day parlance, are assigned specific meanings in contract law. In short, a "condition" is a contractual term the breach of which allows the victim of the breach to regard the contract as having been "repudiated" by the party in breach. In other words, the innocent party is free to walk away from the contract, to regard it as having been terminated (though this right may be waived or lost: see the Sale of Goods Act 1893, s.11). A "warranty", on the other hand, is a term the breach of which does not excuse the victim from fulfilling his or her side of the contract. The sole remedy for the breach of a warranty is the award of damages. The innocent party is, nonetheless, still bound under the contract.

Whether a term is a condition or a warranty generally depends on whether or not the term is deemed to be fundamental to the contract. If the term is central to the operation of the contract, it is more than likely that it will be treated as a condition. Conditions generally go to the core of contractually liability; they are integral or crucial to the agreement entered into. (See, for instance, *Bunge Corporation v Tradax Export* [1981] 2 All E.R. 540.) If, on the other hand, the term is fairly minor or peripheral, it is more likely to be treated as a warranty. Section 62 of the Sale of Goods Act 1893 underlines this point, by defining a warranty as an agreement "collateral [secondary] to the main purpose of [the] contract ...".

It is always possible expressly to indicate, in a contract, that a term is to be treated as either a condition or a warranty. For instance, although it may not be of great consequence to the average consumer, a car buyer who dearly wants to purchase a red car could stipulate that the contractual term as to the car's colour is a condition and not merely a warranty. While such an indication may not be conclusive, the presence of an explicit indication may provide evidence that the term is, in this context, intended as a condition. (See *Schuler v Wickman Machine Tools* [1973] 2 All E.R. 39.) Correspondingly, it is possible (under s.11 of the Sale of Goods Act 1893) for a buyer of goods to waive a condition, or, in the alternative, to treat it as a warranty. The condition, moreover, may, under the aforementioned section, be downgraded to warranty status if the buyer of goods has accepted part or all of those goods (thus, only damages are available).

It is quite common for certain contractual terms implied by legislation to be deemed, by statute, to be either conditions or warranties. For instance, the Sale of Goods Act 1893, discussed below at para.15.2, implies certain terms into all contracts for the sale of goods, expressly stipulating that some (*e.g.* the implied terms as to title, quality and fitness for purpose) are conditions, while others rank as warranties.

12.6.2 Innominate (or indeterminate) terms

There is, however, a third species of term, known as an "innominate" term (literally "a term with no name"). (It is sometimes known as an "intermediate" or "indeterminate" term.) This is a peculiar hybrid, a term the breach of which may result, depending on the circumstances, in either the right to repudiate or alternatively the right only to seek damages. The legal response to the breach of an innominate term depends on how serious the consequences of the breach are—if the effects of the breach are significant, the term is treated as a condition, with the result that the contract will be deemed to have been repudiated by the breach. If the effects, on the other hand, are relatively minor, the term is treated as a warranty and only damages will issue. In other words, the same term can be treated as either a condition (terminating the contract) or a warranty depending on the seriousness of the particular breach.

The *Hong Kong Fir* case (*Hong Kong Fir Shipping Company v Kawasaki* [1962] 1 All E.R. 474) provides the prime example of such an innominate term. The defendants hired (chartered) a ship for two years. A term of the contract required that the ship be "in every way fitted for ordinary cargo service" (*i.e.* seaworthy). Due to various mechanical breakdowns, low staffing levels and inexperienced staff, the ship's first sailing was delayed by nearly five months. The defendants sought to repudiate the contract on this basis, claiming that the condition as to seaworthiness had been breached. The Court of Appeal, however, ruled that in the circumstances, the defendants were only entitled to damages.

The court reasoned that the seaworthiness clause was an innominate term, the status of which could only be determined by reference to the effects of the particular breach after it had occurred. If the breach was sufficiently serious, the term would be treated as a condition, entitling the innocent party to walk away from the contract. If, on the other hand, the breach was not serious, and in particular if it could adequately be compensated in damages, the term would be treated as a warranty. In this case, for instance, the term might be breached in ways which were either quite serious or trifling. If, for instance, the ship had a large hole in its side, and was thus prone to capsize, the breach would entitle the defendants to repudiate the contract. If, on the other hand, the breaches were relatively minor, damages would suffice.

In *The Hansa Nord (Cehave NV v Bremer Handelsgesellschaft)* [1975] 3 W.L.R. 447, a portion of a cargo of 12,000 tons of citrus pellets had been damaged while in transit by ship. The contract under which they were being transported required that they be delivered in "good condition". The Court of Appeal concluded that this was an innominate term. If the entirety of the cargo were destroyed *en route*, undoubtedly the breach would have been treated as a condition. In this case, however, the damage not being particularly extensive, the court concluded that the breach gave rise to damages only, and not a right to treat the contract as having been terminated. By contrast, in *Irish Telephone Rentals v Irish Civil Service Building Society* [1991] I.L.R.M. 880, a telephone system supplied under a service contract broke down. An implied term in the contract to the effect that the goods supplied in the course of the supply of services should be of "merchantable quality" was deemed to be an innominate term. In this case, however, the court concluded that the particular defects were so serious as to give rise to a right to regard the contract as being at an end.

13. The Terms of a Contract: Implied Terms

13.1 Introduction

As a general rule it is assumed that if the parties to a contract want to include a particular term, they will do so expressly. As the Supreme Court pointed out in *Tradax v Irish Grain Board* [1984] I.R. 1, a court's function does not extend to writing the contract for the parties. It is for the parties alone to determine the content of their contract, and the courts will generally be slow to intervene. Nonetheless, in some cases, even though the parties have not expressly included such terms, the courts may imply certain terms into contracts. In other cases, the legislature will require the inclusion of certain terms. There are a number of types of terms that may be implied into a contract:

- terms implied in fact;
- terms implied by reference to custom/trade usage;
- terms implied by common law;
- terms implied by legislation; and
- terms implied by the Constitution.

13.2 Terms implied in fact

In some cases, it is assumed that the parties intended to include certain terms, despite the fact that they were not expressly set out by the parties. In such cases, terms are said to be "implied in fact", the key point being that the parties *intended* their inclusion but omitted these terms either because they were so obvious as not to warrant inclusion, or due to an error or oversight. There are two tests for the implication of terms in fact.

13.2.1 The "officious bystander" test

This test concerns terms that though intended by both parties for inclusion in the contract, are so obvious that they do not need to be expressly stated. For instance, in *Kavanagh v Gilbert* (1875) I.R. 9 C.L. 136, a term was implied into a contract to the effect that an auctioneer would use all due care in completing a sale on behalf of the plaintiff. The test for determining the presence of such terms is called the "officious bystander" test. This test presupposes that, at the time the contract is made, if a hypothetical disinterested bystander were to have asked the parties whether they intended to include a particular term, the parties would both have readily responded in the affirmative.

This was explained by McKinnon L.J. in *Shirlaw v Southern Foundries* [1939] 2 K.B. 206:

> "… that which in any contract is left to be implied and need not be expressed is something so obvious that it goes without saying; so that, if while the parties were making their bargain, an officious bystander were to suggest some express provision for it in the agreement, they would testily suppress him with a common 'Oh, of course!'".

The term must have been obvious to both parties (not just one of them) and must not, moreover, conflict with any express terms of the contract. Nor will a term be implied where it is unclear that it would have been accepted by one of the parties in negotiation. For instance, in *Carna Foods v Eagle Star Insurance* [1997] 2 I.L.R.M.499, the Supreme Court declined to imply into a contract a term requiring the giving of reasons for failure to renew an insurance contract, as it was not likely that the defendant would have accepted it as an express term. (See also *Sweeney v Duggan* [1997] 2 I.L.R.M. 211.) Similarly, in *Spring v NASDS* [1956] 1 W.L.R. 585, a court declined to imply a reference to an agreement between various trade unions into a contract between the defendant trade union and its members, as it was highly unlikely that the members had even heard of the relevant agreement.

13.2.2 The business efficacy test
The business efficacy test permits the courts to imply terms that are required to make a contract effective from a commercial point of view. Again this test requires that the term be obvious to both parties at the time of contracting. *The Moorcock* (1889) 14 P.D. 64 provides a good example of this mechanism in operation. The defendant contracted to permit the use of his wharf by the plaintiff, the owner of a boat called "The Moorcock". In the course of landing, the boat was damaged due to a shallow, uneven ridge of sea bed adjacent to the wharf. Although the contract was silent on this point, the court concluded that, in order to give business efficacy to the contract, a term had to be implied that the jetty was safe for the mooring of boats. Otherwise, it would make no commercial sense for the plaintiff to pay for landing rights: a commercially astute contractor would hardly agree to put his investment at risk in this manner.

In a remarkably similar case, *Butler v McAlpine* [1904] 2 I.R. 445, the Irish Court of Appeal implied into a contract for the hire of a barge a condition that the defendants would use reasonable care in berthing the barge. The barge was damaged when it struck a concrete block lying on the riverbed near the wharf which the defendants had leased. The court concluded that there was an implied duty to ensure that the wharf was safe for this purpose.

Again the court must be able to say with confidence that both parties had intended the term to be included, that it went without saying that it would be included. It is not sufficient, moreover, to show that the contract would work better with the term in question, or that it would have been a good idea to include it. It must be established, rather, that the term is not merely reasonable or sensible but *necessary* in order for the contract to operate, that the contract would not be commercially effective otherwise. For instance, in *O'Toole v Palmer* [1945] Ir. Jur. Rep. 59, Gavan Duffy J. refused to imply a term on the basis that the contract worked perfectly well without it.

13.3 Terms implied by reference to custom or trade usage

In some cases, terms may be implied by reference to a custom in a particular locality or a usage common in a particular trade (see paras 5.2.6 and 12.4.4 for some examples). The onus of proving that a custom exists lies on the person seeking to rely on it; she must establish that the custom is well known and widely accepted. In *Ó Conaill v Gaelic Echo* (1958) 92 I.L.T.R. 156, for instance, a term entitling a journalist to holiday pay, though not expressly included in his contract, was nonetheless implied, as it was a practice common in that profession. Likewise, in *British Crane Hire v Ipswich Plant Hire* [1975] 1 All E.R. 1059, a company that hired a crane was deemed to be bound by terms commonly used in that line of trade, and known to both parties, even though the terms were not expressly included in the contract. This may only happen, however, if it is established that the term is in fact common to the trade, and well known, and that both of the parties were aware of its use. Different considerations clearly would apply, for instance, if one of the parties was not familiar with practices in the trade in question. (See also para.14.5 for examples of terms implied by reference to past dealings between the parties.)

13.4 Terms implied by law

In an increasing number of cases, particularly where consumers are involved, terms are implied by law as a result of legislation, a phenomenon which is addressed in Chapter 15 below. Judges are otherwise very reluctant to imply terms unless clearly intended by the parties, or required by legislation. Nonetheless, in very specific contexts, the courts may at common law imply terms *whether the parties intended them or not*. This will only occur, however, where the term is deemed to be strictly necessary and where it does not conflict with the express intentions of the parties. Such cases, moreover, tend to arise in very specific and specialised contexts, most notably in relation to contracts of employment and leases of social housing.

For instance, in *Liverpool City Council v Irwin* [1977] A.C. 239, a local authority rented out accommodation in a high-rise block. In these circumstances, the Council was held to be subject to an implied term that the tenants would have reasonable access to their properties and that the common areas in the block would be kept in good repair. Although the Council was found not to have breached these terms, the House of Lords concluded that by necessity, such terms were implied by law into the contract with each tenant. A similar conclusion arose in *Siney v Dublin Corporation* [1980] I.R. 400, where the Irish Supreme Court implied into a contract for the lease of council housing a term that the housing was fit for human habitation. At the very least, according to *Burke v Dublin Corporation* [1991] I.R. 341, such housing should not cause a risk to the health of its inhabitants. *Byrne v Marina Investments* [1984] 3 J.I.S.L.L 116 is authority, moreover, for the proposition that a landlord generally has an obligation to keep a property in good repair.

These cases tend to arise most frequently where a local authority is involved (the local authority, after all, having certain statutory obligations to tenants). Indeed, it has proved more difficult to imply similar terms into contracts between private purchasers and builders, though in some cases the courts have indicated that a builder has an implied duty to use all reasonable care in building houses.

Contracts between employers and employees have also been deemed to attract certain terms implied by law, for instance:

- That employers will make best efforts to protect the health and safety of workers (*McCann v Brinks Allied* [1997] 1 I.L.R.M. 461);
- That employers will give reasonable notice of the termination of employment (*Carvill v Irish Industrial Bank* [1968] I.R. 325; *Royal Trust Co. of Canada v Kelly*, unreported, High Court, February 27, 1989);

- That employers and employees owe each other a duty not to breach the trust or confidence placed in each by the other. Thus, employees will not endeavour to undermine their employer's business (by, for instance, simultaneously working for a rival). Likewise, employers will not engage in dishonest activities that may stigmatise their employees or bring them into disrepute (*Malik v BCCI* [1997] 3 W.L.R. 95);
- That employees who resign will receive an accurate reference completed with reasonable care (*Spring v Guardian Assurance plc.* [1994] 3 W.L.R. 354).

Cases in which terms are implied without reference to the parties' supposed intention are in fact quite rare and tend to be confined to specific categories of contract requiring special scrutiny. In fact, in many of these cases, legislation has overtaken the common law, the obligations on landlords and tenants, as well as employers and employees, being quite comprehensively covered by legislation.

13.5 Terms implied by the Constitution

In some cases, terms may be implied into a contract (particularly those involving public bodies) by reference to the Constitution of Ireland 1937. For instance, in *Glover v B.L.N.* [1973] I.R. 388, a contract allowing an employer to dismiss employees for serious misconduct had to be read in the light of an implied term that the employee was entitled to the application of fair procedures. This term was implied by reference to the constitutional principle of natural justice, which dictates that decisions that impact seriously on a person should be made only after that person has had the right to hear and challenge the case against her before an impartial body of persons. (See also *Meskell v CIÉ* [1973] I.R. 121.)

14. Exclusion Clauses

14.1 Introduction

A person who has assumed a contractual obligation may be excused from liability in case of breach by an appropriately worded "exclusion" or "exemption" clause. In the alternative, liability may be limited to a specified sum by means of a "limitation clause". Examples of each are to be found in abundance in daily life. Such clauses may serve, moreover, to exclude or limit liability not only in contract but also in tort, that is, for civil wrongs. Notably, an exclusion clause may be made orally, though it is more common to find it in writing.

Exclusion and limitation clauses effectively serve to assign to one or other party the risk of a particular eventuality occurring. Where two parties with equal bargaining power freely agree the allocation of a risk, such agreements arguably should be enforced. However, exclusion clauses have generally attracted a fair degree of judicial and legislative scrutiny, especially where consumers are involved. Particular concerns arise where exclusion and limitation clauses appear in "standard form contracts" or "contracts of adhesion", commonly found where businesses deal with consumers. A standard form contract is a pre-formulated contract drafted by one of the parties alone (usually a business) and presented to the other party (usually a consumer) on a "take it or leave it" basis. The consumer is afforded no option for the negotiation of specific terms. She must either accept the terms dictated by the business or walk away from the agreement.

There are clearly some benefits in this approach. Contracts of adhesion have the advantage of convenience, greatly increasing the ease with which consumers may purchase products. It would certainly be tedious if every consumer had to negotiate individual terms every time she wanted to buy a product. Nonetheless, as businesses generally exercise a monopoly on the drafting of consumer contracts, the risk arises that the business will use its position unfairly to prejudice consumers.

Thus, while exclusion clauses are quite common, they are nonetheless controversial, as evidenced by the reticence of judges in enforcing such clauses. In particular, the judiciary has adopted a series of principles regarding: (1) the incorporation of such clauses (whether or not they form part of a contract); (2) the interpretation thereof; and (3) the enforceability of such clauses. Each of these matters will be dealt with in turn below.

14.2 Incorporation of exclusion clauses

"Incorporation" is the process by which a statement (in this case an exclusion or limitation clause) becomes part of a contract. In common with all other terms of a contract, incorporation may occur by one or more of the following three methods:

* Incorporation by signature
* Incorporation by reasonable notice
* Incorporation by reference to past dealings

14.3 Incorporation by signature

Where a person signs a contractual document, she is deemed to be bound by everything in that document, including any exclusion clauses therein. The person signing is also bound by any other document to which that contract makes reference. For instance, if a person signs a document stating that she has read and accepted certain terms and conditions external to that document, she is bound by those terms and conditions (whether or not she has read them).

It is important to note that in cases where a signature is appended to a contract containing an exclusion clause, it is no defence to establish that the signer was not aware of the existence of the clause. In fact, a failure to read or to understand the contract does not relieve the person who has signed the document. In particular, a person who is unable to read, or does not speak the language in which the contract is written, will nonetheless be bound by the contract once her signature has been added to the document. The case of *L'Estrange v Graucob* [1934] 2 K.B. 394 illustrates this point. In *L'Estrange*, a woman signed an agreement to purchase slot machines in apparent ignorance of a clause in the agreement excluding liability for express or implied warranties. Although the terms of the contract were written on brown paper and in "regrettably small print", the court concluded that because she had signed the document, the purchaser was bound by everything therein, whether or not she had read it.

This principle only applies, however, if the document can reasonably be expected to contain contractual terms. (See *Grogan v Meredith Plant Hire* (1996) 15 Tr. L.R. 371.) Additionally, the doctrine of *non est factum* may provide some relief in this context. Where a person signs a document under a mistaken belief as to its contents, the person may not be liable under the contract if the signing party exercised due caution in discerning its contents. A very sensible case of some vintage—*Thoroughgood's case* (1584) 2 Co. Rep. 9a—establishes that an illiterate person who signs a document may not be liable if its contents have been misrepresented to her. A similar principle might apply to a person with a visual impairment. A modern manifestation of this principle arose in *Curtis v Chemical Cleaning Co.* [1951] 1 K.B. 805, where the effects of an exclusion clause contained on a dry-cleaning ticket were misrepresented by an employee of the dry-cleaner. Although the clause purported to exclude liability for any damage to clothes, the employee reassured the plaintiff that the clause only applied to certain specific types of damage, thus limiting the legal effect of the clause.

14.4 Incorporation by reasonable notice

Where a contract is not signed, a person may be bound by an exclusion clause where the person is given reasonable prior notice of the clause. Thus, although a party may not be aware of an exclusion clause, and may not have signed a document to the effect that the clause was binding on her, she may nonetheless be bound if reasonable steps were taken to bring the clause to her attention.

The classic test was set out in *Parker v S.E. Railway* (1877) 2 C.P.D. 416. Here, a passenger left his bag for safe-keeping in a railway cloakroom. At the time of deposit, the passenger was issued with a ticket, on the back of which was a clause limiting the railway company's liability in case of damage or loss to £10. (The front of the ticket referred the passenger to the back of the ticket and thus to this clause.) The bag having been lost, the passenger claimed compensation, but was bound by the limitation clause, the Court of Appeal having concluded that reasonable steps were taken to bring the clause to his attention, even if he had not seen it.

In the course of its decision, the court stated first, that if the passenger was aware of contents of the clause, she would be bound by it. Yet, even if she was not aware of the clause, she may still be bound if reasonable steps were taken to bring the clause to her notice.

What constitutes "reasonable steps" depends on the facts of each particular case. While the basic test has not changed over the years, a heightened concern for the welfare of consumers has arguably led to a more rigorous assessment of what is or is not a reasonable step. A number of factors are of relevance in this context.

14.4.1 The timing of notice
Notice of an exemption clause will only be effective where the notice

issues *before* the contract is entered into. Notice will not be effective where it issues after the contract is concluded. In *Olley v Marlborough Court* [1949] 1 K.B. 532, a couple, after booking into a hotel and paying in advance for a week's stay, proceeded to their room. In the room they found a notice exempting the hotel from any liability in respect of lost or stolen goods. The hotel, however, could not rely on this exclusion clause (Mrs Olley's mink coats having been stolen) as it had been brought to the couple's attention after they had concluded their contract to stay at the hotel. Similarly, in *Thornton v Shoe Lane Parking* [1971] 1 All E.R. 686, on entering a car park, an automated machine issued the plaintiff with a ticket which referred to conditions displayed inside the car park. A notice inside the car park purported to exempt the car park owner from liability in respect of damage or personal injury. This was, however, deemed to be ineffective as the clause was only brought to the notice of the car owner *after* the contract to park his car was concluded.

The simple solution is to ensure that the clause is brought to the attention of customers before any contract is concluded. For instance, in *Thornton*, if the exclusion clause had been displayed *outside* the car park, and thus had been available to read *before* customers entered, the clause would have been binding.

14.4.2 The form of the notice

It must also be established that the notice is one that would reasonably be expected to contain conditions such as an exclusion clause. For instance, in *Chapleton v Barry UDC* [1940] 1 All E.R. 356, an exclusion clause was contained on the back of a ticket issued to customers who hired deckchairs for use on a beach. The English Court of Appeal concluded that the exclusion clause was not binding, as it was contained in a document that would not normally be expected to contain such terms. The court reasoned that the ticket was simply a receipt of payment, and that the ordinary reasonable person would not have expected it to contain conditions.

14.4.3 The prominence of the notice

Size and visibility are clearly important factors in this context. The bigger the notice, and the more prominent its location, the more likely it is that reasonable steps will have been taken. For instance, in *Sugar v LMS Railway* [1941] 1 All E.R. 172, the conditions on a railway ticket were deemed not to be binding, as they were obscured by a date stamp.

14.4.4 The onerous nature of the term

Additionally, the more onerous and unusual the term in question, the greater the efforts required to bring it to the customer's attention. For instance, in *Interfoto Picture Library Ltd v Stiletto Visual Programmes Ltd* [1988] 1 All E.R. 348, the defendant had obtained permission to use photographs belonging to a photographic library. On delivery of the photos, the defendant received a delivery note the very bottom of which contained a statement that if the photos were not returned within 14 days, a fine of £5 per photo per day would apply. Having returned the photos a month after receipt, the defendant was presented with a bill for £3,783.50. The term, however, was not binding: the Court of Appeal reasoned that given the very onerous and unusual nature of the term, the plaintiff had not done enough to bring it to the attention of the defendant. The court instead substituted an award of £3.50 per photo per week, holding that this was a more reasonable fine.

The nub of this case is that the more serious the consequences of the clause, the more unusual and onerous its terms, the greater the efforts required to constitute reasonable steps. In this case, the plaintiff was obliged to bring the clause to the explicit attention of the defendant: a written notice in a delivery note was not sufficient for incorporation. This is sometimes termed the "red hand" test, Lord Denning having stated in *Thornton v Shoe Lane Parking* (see above, para.14.4.1) that some exclusion clauses were so unusual that they "... would need to be printed in red ink ... with a red hand pointing to it before they could be considered sufficient".

14.4.5 Reference to conditions that may be obtained elsewhere

Where a notice refers to conditions that may be consulted elsewhere, these conditions may be incorporated if the reader is reasonably able to access those conditions prior to conclusion of the contract. Whether this condition is met, for example, in cases where a bus ticket refers to the "rules and regulations" of the carrier will thus depend on whether the bearer can easily access those rules and regulations. Nonetheless, in *Early v Great Southern Railway* [1940] I.R. 414, a railway passenger was deemed to be bound by conditions referred to (but not listed) on a railway ticket, even though a copy of those conditions was not available at the office where the ticket was purchased.

14.5 Past dealings

An exclusion clause may be incorporated by reference to past dealings.

For instance, in *Spurling v Bradshaw* [1956] 2 All E.R. 121, the defendant had stored eight barrels of orange juice at a warehouse run by the plaintiff. On collection, the defendant discovered that the previously full barrels were now mysteriously empty. A document received by the defendant *after* the contract was made contained a clause excluding the plaintiff from liability in case of "loss or damage occasioned by negligence or wrongful act or default". As this document was received after the contract was entered into, the defendant argued that the clause did not apply. Nonetheless, as the parties had a long history of similar dealings, in which a similar clause had always been included, the plaintiff was not liable for the loss. Similarly, in *Miley v McKechnie* (1949) 84 I.L.T.R. 89, having deposited clothes at a laundry, the plaintiff was given a receipt excluding the laundry from liability for any damage to the clothes. The Circuit Court concluded that although this receipt was issued after the contract was entered into, the plaintiff and defendant had a history of past dealings, on each of which occasions the plaintiff had invariably been presented with a similar ticket. The laundry was thus not liable for damage to the plaintiff's clothes.

In order to give rise to incorporation, past dealings must be: (1) sufficiently frequent, and (2) sufficiently consistent. For instance, in *McCutcheon v MacBrayne* [1964] 1 W.L.R. 125, a Scottish car ferry sank resulting in the loss of the plaintiff's car. The ferry owner had not, on this occasion, required the car owner to sign a risk note (excusing the ferry owner from any liability for loss or damage). On some previous occasions (though not others) the plaintiff had signed such a note. In this case, however, the course of dealing was deemed too inconsistent to incorporate the risk note. Likewise, in *Hollier v Rambler Motors* [1972] 2 Q.B. 71, three or four transactions between the parties over the course of five years were deemed insufficient to create a "course of dealing".

14.6 Interpreting exclusion and limitation clauses

14.6.1 *The* contra proferentum *rule*
The manner in which judges interpret or read exclusion clauses may also serve to limit their application. Exclusion clauses will invariably be read restrictively. In particular, the *contra proferentum* rule requires that any ambiguity in an exclusion clause must be read in the manner least advantageous to the person who is attempting to rely upon the clause (the *proferens*). In other words, in cases of uncertainty, the

benefit of the doubt is given to the person against whom the exclusion clause is being invoked. The European Communities (Unfair Terms in Consumer Contracts) Regulations 1995 contain a similar stipulation requiring that: "... Where there is doubt about the meaning of a term, the interpretation most favourable to the consumer shall prevail".

If correctly and comprehensively drafted, a clause should not be subject to attack, but in order to exclude liability, the exclusion clause must be drafted clearly and expressly to include such a term. The policy here is to dissuade contractors from deliberately designing vague and nebulous exclusion clauses, at the expense, in particular, of unsuspecting consumers.

A few examples of the application of this rule follow:

- In *Andrews v Singer* [1934] 1 K.B. 17, a car with 500 miles on its clock was advertised as "new". A contractual clause excluding "any warranty or condition implied by common law, statute or otherwise" was deemed not to apply in this case, as the statement that the car was new was an *express* contractual term; the exclusion clause only referred to *implied* terms.
- In *White v John Warrick and Co. Ltd* [1953] 2 All E.R. 1021, an exclusion clause to the effect that "nothing in this agreement shall render the owners liable for any personal injury" was deemed not to prevent the plaintiff suing in tort for injury arising from the rental of a defective bicycle (the clause only exempted the owners in respect of liability in contract).
- In *Houghton v Trafalgar Insurance* [1954] 1 Q.B. 247, an exclusion clause exempted an insurance company from liability where an insured car was carrying an excessive "load". The term "load" was interpreted restrictively so that the clause did not apply to an accident involving a car carrying more people than it was designed for. "Excessive load" was deemed to mean an excess of goods, and not an excess of passengers. (See also *Sproule v Triumph Cycle* [1927] N.I. 83.)

In general, however, clauses that *limit* liability to a set amount (as opposed to those that exclude all liability) are not read as restrictively, as evidenced by *Ailsa Craig Fishing Co. v Malvern Fishing and Securicor* [1983] 1 All E.R. 101. In this case, a ship docked at Aberdeen Harbour sank as a result of the negligence of the defendants. A clause limiting the liability of Securicor to £1,000 was deemed enforceable, the House of Lords concluding that the *contra proferentum* rule did not apply with the same rigour to limitation clauses. The courts indeed tend to regard such clauses as reasonable, as they set out the amount of damages that will be awarded in cases of breach, and thus create certain efficiencies, in particular by avoiding litigation on the amount of damages owed in cases of breach. (Though see para.21.2.6 below.)

14.6.2 Extreme eventualities
An exclusion clause may not apply where the circumstances are unusual or extreme. For instance, in *Ronan v Midland Ry. Co.* (1883) 14 I.R. (Ir.) 157, a clause stipulating that cattle travelling on the defendant's ship would travel at "the owner's risk" was deemed not to cover a situation where the cattle had been injured due to the deliberate and malicious actions of the ship's employees.

14.6.3 The main purpose rule
An exclusion clause is generally confined by its "main purpose". In other words, its application may be limited by looking to the purpose for which it was created. For instance in *Glynn v Margotson* [1893] A.C. 351, a contract for the transport of oranges by ship from Malaga to Liverpool allowed the ship to stop en route in various ports. The House of Lords nonetheless concluded that the contract required delivery as soon as possible and that the ship could not be excused unnecessary delays. The main purpose of the clause was to facilitate safe passage, not to allow the captain to circumnavigate the Mediterranean at his leisure.

14.7 Excluding the "core obligation": fundamental breach and other matters

There is some debate regarding the effect of clauses that purport to exclude liability for breach of the "core obligation of the contract". For instance, if Pawel entered into an agreement to sell a motorbike to Odhrán, could Pawel introduce a clause that denied Odhrán the right to sue if the bike was never delivered to him? Such a clause, after all, goes to the very heart of the contract. In fact, the contract may, as a result of such a clause, be said to be totally fictitious, as the fundamental requirement thereunder—delivery of the bike—may be ignored with apparent impunity. Is such a clause enforceable?

The leading Irish case on the point is *Clayton Love v B. & I. Transport* (1970) 104 I.L.T.R. 157. Here, the defendant agreed to transport deep-frozen scampi from Dublin to Liverpool, the parties having resolved that the goods would remain frozen while in transit.

The scampi were, nonetheless, stored at room temperature on board the ship, and thus destroyed. When the plaintiff sued for breach of contract, the defendant sought to rely on an exclusion clause which appeared to be broad enough to exclude liability in this case. The Supreme Court, however, concluded that as *a rule of law*, the clause could not be invoked to excuse a "fundamental breach", that is, a breach of the core obligation of the contract—to transport the scampi in good condition to Liverpool.

Thus, exclusion clauses purporting to exclude liability in respect of a core contractual obligation have been held not to apply to situations where, for instance, a purchased car simply did not run at all (*Karsales (Harrow) v Willis* [1956] 1 W.L.R. 936) or in the case of a tipping truck that did not tip (*Astley Industrial Trust v Grimley* [1963] 2 All E.R. 33). In *Harbutts Plasticine v Wayne Tank Corp* [1970] 1 Q.B. 447, a clause limiting liability to £15,000 was deemed not to apply where plastic pipes, specifically designed to carry molten plasticine, melted, destroying an entire factory and causing £1 million in damage.

While *Clayton Love* suggests that the doctrine of fundamental breach is a rule of law (*i.e.* such clauses can *never* be used to excuse a breach of the core obligation), the UK courts have concluded that the doctrine is merely a rule of interpretation which can be displaced in certain circumstances. In *Photo Production Ltd v Securicor* [1980] 2 W.L.R. 283, the defendant contracted to provide security for the plaintiff's factory. A term in the contract stipulated that "under no circumstances shall [Securicor] be responsible for any injurious act or default by any employee of [Securicor]". As a result of the reckless conduct of one of the defendant's employees, the factory was burnt down. Despite this very obvious breach (the object of the contract being to protect the factory, not to destroy it) the House of Lords ruled that the exclusion clause was enforceable, the plaintiff having freely contracted to accept the risk of such damage, with full knowledge of the risk. In so ruling, the Lords concluded that the doctrine of fundamental breach, while valid, was merely a rule of interpretation. Thus, if an exclusion clause is sufficiently clear and wide enough to cover the loss, and the parties have freely agreed to allocate risk in this manner, the exclusion clause will be enforced.

Therefore, while the doctrine of fundamental breach is considered a rule of law in Ireland, it is deemed merely to be a rule of interpretation in England and Wales. It may be argued that if two businesses of equal bargaining power freely agree (with full knowledge) to allocate risk in such a way as to exempt one party from liability, such an agreement should be enforced. Indeed, although *Clayton Love* remains good law in Ireland, some judges have tentatively suggested a preference for the approach in *Photo Production*. For instance, in *Western Meats v National Ice and Cold Storage* [1982] I.L.R.M. 101, Barrington J. suggested that judges should respect the intentions of parties who freely agree to place the full risk on one of the parties.

14.8 Other limitations on exclusion clauses

In line with the principles of privity of contract, a person generally may not rely on exclusion and limiting clauses in a contract to which she is not a party. (Though see para.8.4.3 above.) By the same token, an exclusion clause may be restricted if its terms have been orally misrepresented as in *Curtis v Chemical Cleaning & Dyeing Co. Ltd* [1951] 1 K.B. 805 (noted above at para.14.3), or if there is an overriding oral promise negating the exclusion clause. For instance, in *Mendelssohn v Normand* [1970] 1 Q.B. 177, a driver was orally reassured that his car would be safe if left unlocked in a car park. The car park owners were thus prevented from relying on a written exclusion clause when items were stolen from the car, the oral statement having superseded the exclusion clause.

15. Statutory Provisions: Contracts with Consumers

15.1 Introduction

In theory, the parties to a contract are free to agree the terms of their bargain. In some cases, however, terms are implied into a contract as a result of Acts of Parliament and other legislative measures. These measures have two alternative purposes:

- Earlier legislation aimed to provide "default" rules in cases where the parties had not provided for particular matters. In such cases, the implied terms will apply unless they are displaced by the express terms of the contract.
- Increasingly, however, legislation has been introduced in order to protect vulnerable parties, in particular consumers when dealing with businesspeople. In such cases, the implied terms tend to be mandatory (i.e. they cannot be displaced by agreement).

Historically, judges and lawmakers proved reluctant to interfere even when a contract seemed lopsided or unfair, preferring the view that the parties to the contract should be held to their bargain. The view was taken that the parties should look out for their own interests—the term *"caveat emptor"* (let the buyer beware) sums up this older perspective. Nonetheless, in more recent decades the view has prevailed that certain terms in contracts should not be permitted, most notably where the contract is entered into between a consumer and a businessperson. The disparity in bargaining power and expertise justified, Parliament considered, laws that offered greater protection to consumers against sharp practices. This view was strengthened by the concern regarding standard form contracts. Consumers generally do not have the time or inclination to negotiate the terms by which they are bound. As such, the task of drafting consumer contracts usually falls to the businesses with whom consumers contract. These businesses often hold the upper hand in that they may present contractual terms on "a take it or leave it" basis.

To this end, a number of pieces of legislation, many being the product of European Union law, serve to imply certain mandatory terms into all contracts between a consumer and a person acting in the line of business. Some of these measures go further still and apply even between businesspeople contracting with each other at arm's length,

119

though the thrust of the legislation is directed at protecting consumers. A summary of the most important examples of such legislation is set out below.

15.2 Sale of Goods Act 1893/Sale of Goods and Supply of Services Act 1980

The Sale of Goods Act 1893 ("the 1893 Act") introduced certain standard terms which would be implied into all contracts for the sale of goods. Initially, these terms were intended only as default measures (*i.e.* to be included in the absence of agreement to the contrary). However, the Sale of Goods and Supply of Services Act 1980 ("the 1980 Act") rendered many of these terms mandatory (*i.e.* they could not be excluded from contracts), in particular where consumers are involved.

While the 1893 Act initially applied only to the sale of goods, the 1980 Act extended its remit to contracts for the supply of services. The Acts involve the *sale* of goods (and not gifts thereof), though in *Flynn v Mackin* [1974] I.R. 101 these measures were applied where a car was traded in as part compensation for the purchase of a new car. The Acts do not apply, however, to the sale of land.

15.2.1 Section 12—good title

In every contract for the sale of goods, s.12 of the 1893 Act (as amended by s.10 of the 1980 Act) implies three terms:

- **Good title:** An implied condition that the seller has the right to sell the goods in question—in other words, that the vendor has "good title".
- **Free from encumbrances:** An implied warranty that the goods are free from any encumbrance or charge (*e.g.* a lien). In other words, the goods are not subject to any overriding claim by a third party.
- **Quiet possession:** An implied warranty that the buyer will have the right to quiet possession of the goods (in other words, no one will have the right to interfere with her use thereof).

The first term is a condition: the remedy for breach is the termination of the contract. The second and third terms, however, are warranties; thus, only damages may be obtained in respect of such a breach.

Section 12(2) of the 1893 Act creates an exception where the parties have agreed that the vendor will transfer only such title as the vendor or a third person possesses. In such cases, there is an implied warranty that the vendor has disclosed all encumbrances and charges (overriding claims) over the goods at the time the contract was made and that the vendor will not, moreover, interfere with the buyer's quiet possession of the goods. Similarly, where the vendor purports to sell that which a third person owns, there is an implied warranty that the third person will not disturb quiet possession.

As a result of s.22 of the 1980 Act, these three terms cannot be excluded (even by agreement) from *any* contract for the sale of goods, whether it is a "consumer contract" or not. Any attempt to exclude the clauses noted above will be void.

15.2.2 Section 13—sale by description

Where goods are sold by description—that is, where they are sold on foot of a written or oral account of their characteristics—section 13 of the 1893 Act (as amended) implies a condition that the items sold will correspond to the description. In particular, s.13 includes descriptions contained on a label or packaging. For instance, if Beata purchases a jar of what is described on the label as "strawberry jam", there is an implied condition that that is what is in fact in the jar. If the jar, instead, contained beetroot, this would be a breach of the condition, and Beata would be entitled to return the goods. This is the case even if the buyer herself picked out the goods or if the goods are shown to the purchaser before purchase (provided the error is not obvious on inspection of the goods). (See *O'Connor v Donnelly* [1944] Ir.Jur.R. 1.)

In this regard, it is important to distinguish between the description of the goods and the quality thereof. The error in description must relate to an essential characteristic of the good; for this purpose, the quality thereof is irrelevant (though quality *is* relevant under s.14). Section 13 would not apply, for instance, if goods described as "the finest quality leather boots" in fact turned out to be of inferior make (provided they were in fact leather boots). If the goods turned out to be plastic, on the other hand, s.13 would apply. For instance, in *Oscar Chess v Williams* [1957] 1 All E.R. 325, a statement as to the age and mileage of a car was deemed not to be a misdescription but to be an error as regards the quality and condition of the car.

15.2.3 Section 14—quality of goods

Section 14 of the 1893 Act (as amended) implies into contracts for the sale of goods a condition that goods are of "merchantable quality". The clause applies, however, only where the vendor sells goods in the

122 *Contract Law*

course of a business. For instance, while a car dealer would be bound by s.14, a private motorist would not be. This clause, moreover, may be excluded if the defect is specifically brought to the attention of the buyer (as where purchasers are invited to buy "shop-soiled" goods). Section 14, likewise, will not apply where a buyer has inspected the goods prior to their purchase, in circumstances where such inspection should have revealed these defects.

"Merchantable quality": Under s.14(3), goods are deemed to be of "merchantable quality": "if they are as fit for the purpose or purposes for which goods of that kind are commonly bought and as durable as it is reasonable to expect having regard to any description applied to them, the price (if relevant) and all the other relevant circumstances ...". Whether goods are merchantable is a question of fact. In particular, age and price may be pertinent in determining what one may "reasonably expect" of a purchase. In *Bernstein v Pamson Motors* [1987] 2 All E.R. 220, for instance, it was suggested that while a second-hand car would be merchantable provided it could be driven in safety, much higher expectations applied to a new car, particularly a prestige model, the purchaser of which could demand: "... the appropriate degree of comfort, ease of handling and reliability, of pride in the vehicle's outward and interior appearance". Thus, in *Rogers v Parish* [1987] 2 All E.R. 232, a brand new Range Rover turned out to have a faulty engine and gearbox, as well as damage to its bodywork, defects that cumulatively rendered the expensive car unmerchantable. (See also *Lutton v Saville Tractors* [1986] N.I. 327 where a three-year-old quality car with low mileage was deemed, due to relatively minor defects, not to be of merchantable quality.) By contrast, where the goods are older and cheaper, the same standard of quality may not be required. In *Bartlett v Sidney Marcus* [1965] 2 All E.R. 753, for instance, Denning M.R. suggested that an older car would be merchantable even if it was not in prime condition, provided that it was safely usable.

"Fit for purpose": Goods sold in the course of a business must be fit for the purpose for which they would normally be bought. The classic Irish example arises in *Wallis v Russell* [1902] 2 I.R. 585. Here the purchaser visited a fishmonger to buy "two nice fresh crabs for tea". The fishmonger had no fresh crabs but instead offered boiled ones, which the purchaser bought. The crabs, however, were defective and caused food poisoning. The fishmonger was deemed to be liable, the goods not being fit for the purpose for which they were purchased.

Here, the fishmonger knew by implication the purpose for which the crabs were bought—to be eaten. Although he had not been negligent, the defect not being evident from reasonable inspection, the fishmonger was nonetheless liable. This conclusion underlines the point that a seller need not be aware of the defect, or negligent in relation to its presence. Once aware of the purpose of use, the fact that the seller did not know, and could not have known, that the goods would not be suitable for that use is irrelevant.

Where a product is sold, then, the expectation arises that it is sufficiently durable and fit for the purpose for which such items would *normally* be purchased. For instance, a kitchen fork would normally be expected not to bend or break when being used to eat food, this being its normal purpose. The buyer could hardly complain, on the other hand, if the kitchen fork failed while being used to dig a tarmacadam road, this not being the usual purpose of such a fork.

The seller, in other words, will not be liable where she could not reasonably have foreseen that the goods would be used for the purpose for which they were bought. That said, s.14(4) of the 1893 Act (as amended) states that where "… the buyer, expressly or by implication, makes known to the seller any particular purpose for which the goods are being bought, there is an implied condition that the goods supplied under the contract are reasonably fit for that purpose, whether or not that is a purpose for which such goods are commonly supplied …". In other words, if the purchaser intends to use the item for an unusual purpose, the seller may be liable if she is aware of that unusual purpose and has accepted liability for such use. In *Stokes and McKiernan v Lixnaw Co-op* (1937) 71 I.L.T.R. 70, alcohol was purchased for use in the testing of milk. While suitable for drinking, the alcohol was unsuitable for the testing of milk. Notwithstanding this quite unorthodox purpose, the supplier was deemed to be liable as it had been expressly told of the use to which the alcohol was being put.

The last clause of s.14(4) opens up the possibility that the seller will not be liable "… where the circumstances show that the buyer does not rely, or that it is unreasonable for him to rely, on the seller's skill or judgement". For instance, in *Draper v Rubenstein* (1925) 59 I.L.T.R. 119, a butcher of 17 years standing purchased cattle which were not, in fact, fit for eating. The butcher failed in an action against the seller, the court concluding that the butcher had relied on his own superior skill and judgment alone, and not that of anyone else. The skill of the buyer, in other words, may displace the liability of the seller.

15.2.4 Section 15—sale by sample

There is an implied condition that where goods are sold by sample, the goods will correspond in terms of quality with the sample. The buyer also has, under this section, an implied right to examine the sample to determine quality. Where both the sample and the bulk are of unmerchantable quality, moreover, the seller will be liable unless it is possible, on inspection of the sample, to determine the presence of such a defect.

15.2.5 Exclusion clauses and the 1980 Act

Under the 1893 Act, the above-mentioned provisions applied only as default rules, and could be displaced by express agreement between the parties. The 1980 Act, however, placed significant restrictions on the parties' ability to exclude such terms. The provisions of s.12 of the 1893 Act, for instance, may never validly be excluded from any contract, and any attempt to do so will be void. In relation to ss.13, 14 and 15 of the 1893 Act, the obligations arising thereunder may never be excluded where the buyer "deals as a consumer", and a clause purporting to exclude liability under those sections will be void. (See s.55 of the 1893 Act.) In a non-consumer contract, by contrast, a clause excluding liability under ss.13, 14 or 15 will be enforceable, but only if the exclusion clause is "fair and reasonable" in all the circumstances. Otherwise, such exclusion clauses will be unenforceable.

15.2.6 "Dealing as a consumer"?

As noted above, the terms of ss.13–15 cannot be excluded where the buyer deals as a "consumer". A person is deemed to be a consumer where she purchases goods or orders services otherwise than in the course of her normal business. A person will only be a consumer for this purpose, however, where the vendor or supplier of the goods is acting in course of her business (and not for instance, when the vendor is dealing as a private person not usually engaged in such business).

The goods or services supplied must be such as would normally be used for private use or consumption. Very often this may be inferred from the circumstances of each case. For instance, a person who buys a bottle of whisky from an off-licence more than likely does so as a consumer. A person who buys 1,000 bottles of whisky from a wholesaler, by contrast, clearly does so with a view to selling on her purchases. Notably, one's status as a "consumer" is determined by reference to the specific transaction. A person may well be cast in the role of a businessperson in her commercial life, but may nonetheless be deemed a consumer in other contexts. A salesman may sell whisky for a living, but if, on his way home from work, he buys a bottle of wine to accompany dinner, he does so as a consumer.

Certain types of contract, however, even where involving consumers, are not considered to be "consumer contracts" within the meaning of the Acts. For instance, under s.3(2) of the 1980 Act, where the sale is by competitive tender, the buyer cannot be treated as a "consumer". By the same token, a contract between two "consumers" is not a "consumer contract" for these purposes. For instance, if Adaobi sells her private car to another consumer, Meredith (neither being in the business of selling cars), the contract is not a consumer contract. Similarly, where a consumer agrees to *sell* an item *to* a businessperson, the resulting contract falls outside the definition of a consumer contract.

15.2.7 What is meant by "fair and reasonable"?

As noted above, the terms of ss.13–15 of the 1893 Act may be excluded in non-consumer contracts, provided that such exclusion is fair and reasonable. The Schedule to the 1980 Act offers some guidance as to what may be deemed fair and reasonable. The term must have been one that, in the context, was "or ought reasonably to have been, known to or in contemplation of the parties when the contract was made". The judge should also have regard to the following factors:

- the relative bargaining power of the parties;
- the availability of alternative methods of acquiring the goods or securing the services;
- whether a party was induced to enter into the contract;
- whether the customer, having regard to a custom of trade or a course of dealing, had knowledge, actual or constructive, of the term or the extent thereof;
- whether compliance with an obligation placed on the customer was practicable; and
- whether the goods in question were made to the customer's order.

In *George Mitchell Ltd v Finney Lock Seeds* [1983] 1 All E.R. 108, the plaintiff had purchased 30 lbs of what it was told was Dutch winter cabbage seed from a seed merchant. In fact, seed of a different and defective variety was supplied and the crop failed. A clause in the contract limiting liability to the price of the seeds alone (£192 as compared to a loss of £60,000 due to the crop failure) was deemed unreasonable. The fact that the loss was so serious, and that the defendant had fully compensated others in similar cases and was better placed to obtain insurance in respect of such losses, were all factors in this conclusion. (See also *Smith v Bush* [1989] 2 All E.R. 514.)

15.2.8 Terms in contract for the supply of services

Though not initially contained in the 1893 Act, the 1980 Act introduced certain implied terms in respect of contracts for the supply of services, save where a service is rendered by an employee to an employer under a contract of employment. Section 39 of the 1980 Act implies a number of terms into contracts where the supplier is acting in the course of her business:

- that the supplier has the requisite skill to supply the service;
- that the supplier will use due skill, diligence and care in the supply of the service;
- that the materials used in the supply of the service are sound and fit for the purpose for which they are being used; and
- that any goods supplied under contract are of merchantable quality.

For instance, if a person holds herself out as being a painter by trade, one may safely assume in law that that person is sufficiently skilled to paint a house, will use skill and care in doing so, and will not use defective products in so doing. These terms only apply, however, where the supplier is acting in the course of her business, that is, where the person is supplying a service as part of her regular professional employment. The terms would not be implied, for instance, where a nurse promises to paint her friend's house as a once-off venture.

It is possible to exclude these terms from a contract by one of three methods:

- by express agreement of the parties;
- if a course of dealing indicates that such terms are normally excluded; or
- if it is common in the relevant trade to exclude such terms and this fact is known or should be known to both parties.

However, in a case where a supplier of a service is dealing with a consumer, the terms implied by the Act may only be excluded if the exclusion can be shown to be "fair and reasonable" and only if it has been expressly brought to the attention of the consumer.

15.3 "Unfair terms"—European Communities (Unfair Terms in Consumer Contracts) Regulations 1995 (S.I. No. 27 of 1995)

Based on EU Directive 93/13/EEC on Unfair Terms in Consumer Contracts, the 1995 Regulations create a framework limiting the use of certain terms in contracts between business people and consumers. A "consumer" for these purposes is defined as a natural person "… acting for purposes which are outside his trade, business or profession". Notably, the Regulations apply only to "consumer contracts", that is, contracts between a consumer and a person acting in the course of her business. The Regulations generally require that such contracts be in plain intelligible language. Any ambiguity will, moreover, be interpreted in favour of the consumer. (Cf. para.14.6.1)

15.3.1 Terms are not "individually negotiated"
Certain conditions arise, the most notable of which is that the Regulations only apply to terms that have not have been "individually negotiated". The Regulations are designed specifically to address the type of situation where "standard form contracts" are presented to consumers on a take it or leave it basis, the consumer being powerless to vary the terms thereof. The onus of proving that a contract has been individually negotiated lies on the seller or supplier. For these purposes, it is irrelevant that some terms of the contract have been individually negotiated if, on the whole, "… an overall assessment of the contract indicates that it is nevertheless … a pre-formulated standard contract".

15.3.2 Term must be unfair
The Regulations apply to any term in a consumer contract which has not been individually negotiated. If the term is unfair, as determined by the Regulations, that specific term will not be enforceable against the consumer.

In order to be deemed unfair, the term must be shown to have resulted in a "significant imbalance in the parties' rights and obligations … to the detriment of the consumer". Where such a significant imbalance arises, the term will be regarded as unfair if the seller is found to have acted "contrary to the requirement of good faith". The good faith concept basically requires that the seller or supplier deal fairly and equitably with the consumer "whose legitimate interests he has taken into account".

A number of criteria must be considered in determining whether a contractual term is unfair:

- the nature of the goods or services;
- the relative bargaining strength of the parties;
- whether there was an inducement to the consumer to enter the contract;

- whether the goods were produced to the consumer's special order; and
- the circumstances attending the conclusion of the contract.

The Third Schedule to the Regulations lists examples of terms that may be deemed "unfair". The list is indicative only, and is not conclusive as to the type of terms that may be ruled unfair, though the broad tenor of the list suggests one key characteristic of an unfair term: that it places an unreasonable and asymmetrical burden on the consumer and, thus, significantly skews the contract in favour of the businessperson.

Blacklisted examples include:

- terms that exclude liability for personal injury or death of a consumer;
- terms that exclude liability in case of the total non-performance of a contract (a "fundamental breach") (cf. para.17.7);
- terms that exact disproportionate penalties for failure on the part of the consumer; and
- terms permitting a businessperson unilaterally to alter the terms of an agreement.

In determining whether a term is unfair, the adequacy of the price paid is not a factor—in other words, the courts will not deem a contract to be unfair solely because it considers the price paid to be excessive. Additionally, the Regulations do not apply to certain types of contract, including employment contracts and family law agreements, nor do they extend to wills.

15.4 "Doorstep sales"—European Communities (Cancellation of Contracts Negotiated Away from Business Premises) Regulations 1989 (S.I. No. 224 of 1989)

These Regulations serve to implement in Ireland the EU Directive on Contracts Negotiated Away from Business Premises (Directive 85/577/EEC). They concern any contract for the sale of goods or supply of services where the contractual negotiation takes place away from the business premises of the trader, in particular, at the home or place of work of the consumer. The classic example might arise where a door-to-door trader is involved—"doorstep sales". The Regulations only apply, however, where the contract is made between a businessperson and a consumer. The policy behind this measure arguably draws from the fact that where a consumer is "doorstepped" he or she may be subjected to particularly sharp sales techniques not normally encountered in a shop or business premises. Whereas the consumer, in the latter case, has voluntarily chosen to attend at the business premises (and may withdraw at any time), in the case of a doorstep sale, the consumer's participation may not be as voluntary and she may not, moreover, so easily remove herself from the sales pitch.

The Regulations do not apply where the consumer has instigated the visit, that is, where it is the result of an express request by the consumer. Nor do they apply to contracts for the sale or rental of land, or the construction of immovable property, to contracts for the supply of food or beverages entered into with a regular roundsman (such as a milk delivery person), insurance and life assurance contracts, and contracts made on foot of a catalogue.

The key element of the Regulations is the presence of a seven-day "cooling off" period for the consumer. Where a contract is entered into otherwise than on business premises, the consumer is free to cancel the contract, without penalty, within seven days of its making. For this purpose, the consumer must be given a dated cancellation notice containing certain information but in particular detailing her right to cancel under the Regulations. In addition, the consumer must be given a cancellation form which, if completed and sent to the trader, serves to cancel the contract. Absent compliance with these Regulations, the contract will be unenforceable against the consumer. If the consumer, moreover, chooses to cancel the contract, the contract will be void, and the trader will be required to repay the consumer in full (though the trader is of course entitled to the return of any goods already delivered).

15.5 "Distance sales"—The European Communities (Protection of Consumers in Respect of Contracts Made by Means of Distance Communication) Regulations 2001 (S.I. No. 207 of 2001)

Based on EU Directive 97/7/EC, the "Distance Sales" Regulations address contracts entered into at a remove from the consumer, where the agreement is facilitated by distance communication (*e.g.* by letter, fax, phone, e-mail or over the internet). In any case where a consumer contracts otherwise than in the physical presence of the seller (or the latter's representative), the Regulations apply, affording consumers some important protections.

Unless there is "simultaneous physical presence of the supplier and consumer", a distance contract arises. Examples are in plentiful supply and include, for instance, purchases made by post, over the telephone, by e-mail and online or made in response to mail order catalogues, newspaper advertisements, order forms (such as those commonly found on the back of cereal packets) and online adverts.

The Distance Sales Regulations, however, apply only where there is contract made between a supplier and a consumer, a supplier being a person entering into contract in the course of her business, a consumer, by contrast, being a person who acts in her personal capacity, *i.e.* otherwise than in the course of her business.

The Directive excludes a number of types of contract from its remit:

- contracts for the construction of buildings or the sale of land and sales made at auctions;
- contracts for the provision of financial services (*e.g.* for banking services or the purchase of insurance);
- purchases from a vending machine;
- contracts agreed over a public payphone.

Where a contract to which the Regulations apply is entered into, Art.4 requires that certain information be given to the consumer. In particular, the consumer has a right to be informed of the following:

- the identity of the supplier and the location of its business;
- the price of the goods, as well as any delivery costs relating to the goods;
- the main characteristics of the goods or services;
- arrangements for payment, delivery or performance;
- the existence of a right of withdrawal from the contract;
- the cost of using the means of distance communication, where it is calculated other than at the basic rate (*e.g.* premium rate phone calls);
- the period for which the offer or the price remains valid; and
- where appropriate, the minimum duration of the contract.

Article 5 of the Regulations requires that these details must be put in writing and sent to the consumer within a reasonable time of entry into the contract. The contract, moreover, is required to be clear and comprehensible having regard to the requirements of good faith.

Under the Regulations, consumers entering into distance sales contracts enjoy certain rights, the most notable of which is the right to withdraw from the contract, without penalty, within seven days of delivery of the goods. The consumer does not have to give a reason for so doing (the goods need not be defective, for instance). She is entitled to cancel the contract and have her money returned. This right cannot be waived. The consumer, furthermore, has a right to be *informed* of this right to withdraw. Although the consumer must bear the cost of returning the unwanted item she otherwise may not be penalised for cancellation of the contract.

Consumers who face lengthy delays in delivery will be pleased to know that, unless otherwise agreed, the Regulations require delivery of the ordered goods within 30 days of the initial agreement, the consumer being entitled to a refund if delivery has not occurred after 30 days.

The right to withdraw is excluded in a number of important cases, usually where cancellation would be impracticable:

- in contracts for services where the performance has already commenced;
- where personalised or custom-made goods are being purchased;
- where the contract involves food, drink or other goods intended to be consumed on the day of delivery (this would apply, for instance, to home pizza delivery); and
- where the contract relates to accommodation, transport, catering, leisure or entertainment where the service is due to be delivered on a specific date (*e.g.* ordering a hotel room by phone, purchasing a plane ticket online, buying a concert ticket online).

15.6 Other relevant measures

The reader's attention is also drawn to a number of measures, inspired by EU Directives protecting consumers in specific circumstances, including the Product Liability Directive 85/374/EEC, the Regulations on Timeshares (S.I. No. 204 of 1997) and the Package Holidays and Travel Trade Act 1995. Additionally, the Consumer Credit Act 1995 strictly regulates credit agreements and in particular the advertisement and supply of credit facilities, such as loans and mortgages.

16. Misrepresentation

16.1 Introduction

A contract will be voidable where a party was induced by a false statement of fact to enter into the contract. This means that the party whose consent was obtained by means of the misrepresentation is entitled (though not obliged) to avoid the contract and escape liability thereunder. Misrepresentation may also give rise to liability in tort, where a party who utters a negligent or fraudulent misstatement may be liable to pay damages for any losses arising.

In para.12.3 above, a misrepresentation was distinguished from a term of the contract. It is important to note that although it may induce a party to enter into a contract, a "misrepresentation" does not form part of the contract. Where a statement incorporated as a term of the contract is not fulfilled or turns out to be false, the appropriate remedy is damages for breach of a contract rather than for misrepresentation.

16.2 When does misrepresentation arise?

In order for a misrepresentation to be "operative" or "actionable" (that is, to give rise to a right to avoid), certain conditions must be met. In particular, the statement must generally be one of fact that, though not incorporated in the contract, nevertheless induced one of the parties to enter into the contract.

16.2.1 Statement of fact vs. statement of opinion

Generally, the statement must be one of fact. By contrast, a statement of opinion will not amount to a misrepresentation unless the party issuing the opinion has knowingly misstated her own opinion. For instance, in *Bissett v Wilkinson* [1927] A.C. 177, a vendor innocently stated that a property could hold 2,000 sheep. Though inaccurate, this statement did not amount to a misrepresentation. The vendor was merely stating an honest opinion. The land, moreover, had never held sheep and the vendor was thus not in a position to give an accurate estimation.

However, a statement of opinion may give rise to a misrepresentation if it did not represent the true state of mind of the person making the statement, or if the person making the statement, given her skills and expertise in the field, ought to have known better. For instance, in *Doheny v Bank of Ireland* (*Irish Times*, December 12, 1997), a bank supplied a reference stating that a customer was "respectable and trustworthy". In fact, as the bank well knew, the customer had a track-record of dishonest dealings. The bank's reference was deemed to amount to a misrepresentation. Likewise, in *Smith v Land and House Prop. Corp.* (1884) 28 Ch. D. 7, the vendor of a hotel represented the then current occupant to be "a most desirable tenant". In truth, the plaintiff had experienced considerable difficulties with the tenant, in particular in extracting rent. The misstatement thus amounted to a misrepresentation.

Similar principles apply where the person expresses what purports to be an "expert opinion" or speaks with the benefit of specialised knowledge. For instance, in *Esso v Mardon* [1976] Q.B. 801, a representative of an oil company, with 40 years of experience in the trade, overestimated the likely sales output of a petrol station. Although stated as an opinion, the estimate was deemed to amount to a misrepresentation, given that the opinion was based on considerable expertise.

16.2.2 Statement of fact vs. "trader's puff"

As discussed above at para.4.3.1, a certain amount of hyperbole (or "trader's puff") is permitted in the course of advertising wares for sale. In *Dimmock v Hallett* (1866) 2 Ch. App. 21, a description of land as "fertile and improvable" was characterised as "sales talk", and thus not actionable as a misrepresentation. Exaggerated claims made on behalf of products will not generally amount to misrepresentation, if, judged from an objective standpoint, they were not intended to be taken seriously. That said, the simple fact that a trader did not intend to be bound in law is not a sufficient defence if, on the facts, a serious promise is made to the consumer—see *Carlill v Carbolic Smokeball Co.* [1893] 1 Q.B. 256.

16.2.3 Statement of fact vs. statement of intention

Generally speaking, a misrepresentation arises only in relation to a statement of past or present fact and not in relation to statements of future intention. A statement of intention is just that—an aspiration or hope that may or may not be realised. Nevertheless, as with statements of opinion, a declaration that knowingly misrepresents a person's current state of mind may constitute a misrepresentation. For instance, in *Edgington v Fitzmaurice* (1855) 29 Ch. D. 459, a company prospectus soliciting potential investors deliberately misrepresented the purpose for which the company intended to use the money. Having lied as to their true state of mind, the promoters were deemed to have been guilty of fraudulent misrepresentation, Bowen L.J. observing that "the state of a man's mind is as much a statement of fact as his digestion".

16.2.4 *Must be a statement of fact, not of law*

This is addressed below in relation to mistake—the applicable principles are the same in each case. (See para.17.2.2 below.)

16.3 The statement must have induced a party to enter into the contract

The misrepresentation must have caused the party complaining of the defect to enter into the contract. The party claiming relief must show that she relied, at least in part, on the misstatement, though it is not necessary to prove that the party who made the statement was aware of such reliance. The misrepresentation need not, however, be the *sole* or even the main impetus to contract, as long as it provides *a* reason why the contract was entered into. For instance, in *Edgington v Fitzmaurice* (*op. cit.*), the prospectors' misrepresentation only partly induced the plaintiff to enter into the contract, the plaintiff's own mistaken belief that he would gain rights over the property of the company also being instrumental. Nonetheless, as the prospectors' statement partly influenced his decision, the misrepresentation was actionable.

It is not possible, however, to avoid a contract where a party was either not aware of the statement, knew it was false, or did not rely on it. (See *Smith v Chadwick* (1884) 9 A.C. 187.) For instance, in *Attwood v Small* (1838) 7 E.R. 684, the vendors of a mine misrepresented its prospects. The buyer, however, had not relied on this misstatement, preferring instead to conduct his own investigation. There having been no reliance on the misrepresentation, the contract remained valid. Likewise, in *Smith v Lynn* (1954) 85 I.L.T.R. 57, a property was advertised as being in "excellent structural condition and decorative repair", in circumstances where it was in fact riddled with woodworm. The plaintiff had only bought the property six weeks earlier, and claimed to be selling for personal reasons. The purchaser in this case was found not to have relied on the advertisement—on the facts, he had wanted to buy the property long before it was offered for sale by the plaintiff. He had, moreover, examined the property himself and was not relying on claims made by defendant. The advert, moreover, was deemed merely to amount to "trader's puff" and thus was not actionable.

Misrepresentation may still arise, however, even where the person to whom the statement was made had an opportunity to discover the falsehood for themselves, provided that they did not in fact discover the untruth. In other words, parties cannot be deemed to have "constructive notice" of the falsity of a statement. In *Redgrave v Hurd* (1881) 20 Ch. D. 1, the vendors of a law practice represented that it was worth £300 per annum, when in fact it was unlikely to yield more than £200 per annum. The buyer was invited to check for himself, but did not do so. If he had done so, he would have discovered that the statement was likely untrue, but the court nonetheless concluded that he was entitled to plead misrepresentation. (See also *Phelps v White* (1881) 5 L.R. Ir. 318; and *Gahan v Boland* (unreported, Supreme Court, January 20, 1984)).

16.4 Can silence amount to misrepresentation?

As a general rule, misrepresentation arises as a result of an express statement, be it oral or in writing. By contrast, *failure to disclose* a material fact does not generally amount to misrepresentation in law. For instance, if Máire advertises old and mouldy potatoes as being "new and in prime condition", this would amount to a misrepresentation. If, however, Máire advertises making no mention of the potatoes' condition, no misrepresentation would arise. In *Fletcher v Krell* (1873) 42 L.J.Q.B. 55, for instance, an applicant for a job as a governess failed to disclose that she had previously been married, a fact that, though irrelevant today, was quite material in Victorian times. As she had remained silent on the point, no misrepresentation arose: had she expressly stated that she had never been married, the situation would have been different.

Yet, despite this general rule, a duty to disclose arises in a number of specific cases.

16.4.1 Conduct of the parties

Silence may constitute a misrepresentation where one of the parties has, by her conduct, indicated that a particular state of affairs exists. In this regard, one must distinguish gestures and other forms of non-verbal communication from silence properly so called. For instance, if the vendor of a cow, when asked if it was in good condition, nodded, grunted affirmatively or otherwise gestured in agreement, this may constitute a misrepresentation if the cow turns out to be in bad condition. In *Spice Girls Ltd v Aprilia World Services* [2002] E.M.L.R. 478, a manufacturer of motor scooters entered into a merchandising contract with the management of the musical group the Spice Girls. Although the band's management knew that one member intended to leave, it nonetheless published promotional photos of the full band, and released a film depicting all five members. This amounted to misrepresentation, the management having indicated by its conduct that the band would continue to comprise five members, when in fact they knew that the number would shortly, and sadly, reduce to four. (See also *Green Park Properties v Dorku* [2001] H.K.L.R.D. 139.)

16.4.2 Half-truths

If a person makes a representation that is partly, but not wholly true, silence as regards the full truth may amount to a misrepresentation. For instance, in *Curtis v Chemical Cleaning and Dyeing Co. Ltd* [1951] 1 K.B. 805, an exclusion clause in a contract made with a laundry was orally represented to exclude liability only for loss of sequins and beads. In fact, the exclusion clause was much more extensive—silence as regards the full extent of the clause was deemed to limit the effect of the clause to loss of sequins and beads only. Similarly, in *Dimmock v Hallett* (1866) 2 Ch. App. 21, a potential buyer of a freehold estate in several farms was informed that the farms were let (which was true), but not that the tenants were scheduled to leave. This amounted to misrepresentation.

16.4.3 Subsequent falsity

Silence regarding a change in represented circumstances may amount to a misrepresentation. In other words, where a statement that is true when made is subsequently rendered false, there is a duty to disclose the fact of the change in circumstances. In *With v O'Flanagan* [1936] 1 All E.R. 727, a doctor had originally stated that his practice was worth £200 a year. While this was true when the statement was made, the practice subsequently declined due to the illness of the doctor, with the result that, by the time the practice was sold, it was worth virtually nothing. Having made the initial representation, the doctor was under a duty to disclose this material change in circumstances.

16.4.4 Property contracts

It is generally considered that there is a positive duty to reveal the existence of covenants in leases, as well as unusual defects in title generally.

16.4.5 Unusual defects

Where a defect is particularly unusual (especially where farm animals are concerned) there may be a duty to reveal its presence. For instance, in *Gill v McDowell* [1903] 2 I.R. 463, a misrepresentation arose where a cattle seller failed to reveal that an animal offered for sale was in fact a hermaphrodite, possessing both male and female organs. The court reasoned that this unusual fact should have been brought to the attention of the buyer. Likewise, in *Kennedy v Hennessy* (1906) 40 I.L.T.R. 84, a failure to reveal that a young heifer (an "unserved" cow) was in fact pregnant was deemed to amount to misrepresentation.

16.4.6 If the contract itself makes disclosure mandatory
Clearly, if the contract itself requires disclosure of certain facts, a failure to disclose will be actionable, but as a breach of contract rather than a tort. See *Munster Base Metals v Bula Ltd* (unreported, High Court, July 27, 1983) and *Geryani v O'Callaghan* (unreported, High Court, January 25, 1995).

16.4.7 Fiduciary relationship
Where a relationship is "fiduciary" in nature, there is a duty to act in utmost good faith, and in particular to disclose all relevant facts to the other party. A fiduciary relationship presupposes that particular trust or confidence is reposed by one person in the integrity and fidelity of another. A key characteristic of such a relationship is that the fiduciary must act for the client's benefit rather than in her own personal interest. Examples of fiduciary relationships include those between a solicitor and her client, a trustee and the beneficiaries of a trust, a parent and her child, and a principal and agent.

16.4.8 Insurance contracts: doctrine of uberrima fides
A duty of full and frank disclosure of all material facts arises where a person seeks to enter into specific types of contract. This is sometimes called the doctrine of *uberrima fides*. Most commonly encountered in respect of insurance contracts, this doctrine requires "utmost good faith" of the parties making the contract. In particular, the party seeking insurance bears a duty of total honesty. Even if not specifically asked to do so, she must spontaneously reveal all material facts that might affect the insurer's decision to insure or the level of the insurance premium. Failure to do so may permit the insurance company to repudiate the contract for lack of candour, even if the non-disclosure is innocent. (Thus, the insurer need not pay out on foot of the contract.)

The insurer, rather unfairly, may refuse to pay out even if the material fact was unconnected to the loss sustained. In *Seaman v Fonereau* (1743) 2 Stra. 1183, a failure to reveal that an insured ship was leaking when last seen rendered a contract of insurance voidable, even where compensation was claimed for capture of the ship by the Spanish, an incident unrelated to the leak.

In *Chariot Inns v Assicurazioni Generali* [1981] I.L.R.M. 173, the Supreme Court noted that, in Irish law, an insured party has a duty to reveal all "material facts", that is, all matters or circumstances:

> "... which would reasonably influence the judgement of a prudent insurer in deciding whether he would take the risk and if so, in determining the premium which he would demand."

In this regard, it is largely irrelevant what the insurer or insured in the specific case considered pertinent. The test is an objective one: what would reasonably influence a prudent insurer's decision.

For instance, in *Keenan v Shield Insurance* [1987] I.R. 113, failure to disclose a previous claim rendered an insurance contract voidable. In *Chariot Inns v Assicurazioni Generali* (*op. cit.*), a similar fate befell a plaintiff who had failed to disclose a previous fire in a building belonging to it. Likewise, silence regarding a prior criminal conviction may vitiate (render voidable) a contract of insurance (*Lambert v Co-op Insurance* [1975] 2 Lloyd's Rep. 485), while a failure to reveal a prior refusal of insurance cover may also be deemed material.

Some exceptions nonetheless apply:

- **Where the right of disclosure is waived.** In *Kelleher v Irish Life Assurance* (unreported, High Court, December 16, 1988), a person seeking life assurance failed to reveal that he had been treated for cancer four years earlier. The contract, however, was the result of a special promotion, under which a regular health questionnaire did not have to be completed. The contract required that the insured confirm only that he had not been treated during the previous six months. The insurance contract was valid, the right to full disclosure having been waived.

- **There is no duty to disclose that of which you are unaware:** In *Keating v New Ireland Assurance* [1990] I.L.R.M. 110, an insured party who was not aware at the time of the contract that he had a heart condition was not liable for failing to reveal this fact. One has a duty only to be honest.

- **"Over-the counter" insurance.** Lower standards apply where the insurance contract is issued quickly and with minimal formality, as for instance where insurance is purchased over the phone. In particular, where there is no detailed form or questionnaire to be completed, the obligation of utmost good faith may not be applied as strictly. In *Aro Road v Insurance Corp. of Ireland Ltd* [1986]

I.R. 403, the Supreme Court ruled that a person issued with insurance subsequent to a quick phonecall, there being no other formalities, was not liable for non-disclosure of material facts. This suggests that more relaxed criteria may apply to "over-the counter" insurance agreements, where full disclosure may not be feasible. This might be the case, for instance, where insurance is included as part of a package holiday deal. Thus in *Aro Road*, an innocent failure to disclose that the insured had, 19 years previously, been convicted for handling stolen goods was deemed irrelevant.

- **There is no duty to disclose matters of common knowledge.** In *Brady v Irish National Insurance* [1986] I.L.R.M. 669, the plaintiff was not liable for failure to reveal that he would be "laying up" his boat for the winter for essential repairs and living in the boat during that time as it was "common knowledge" that boat owners did so in Winter.

16.5 Types of misrepresentation

In considering what remedies will issue for misrepresentation, one must first distinguish between three different types of misrepresentation: Fraudulent, Negligent and Innocent. Different remedies apply depending on the type of misrepresentation arising.

16.5.1 Fraudulent misrepresentation.

A fraudulent statement is, according to the House of Lords in *Derry v Peek* (1889) 14 A.C. 337, a false statement "made (a) knowingly, [with knowledge of its falsity] or (b) without belief in its truth, or (c) recklessly as to whether it be true or false". In other words, if a person makes a statement that they know or believe is untrue, or where they do not care whether it is true or not, the misrepresentation is fraudulent. Likewise, wilful blindness to certain facts, where a deliberate decision is made to ignore certain facts, may amount to fraud. By contrast, if a person honestly believes that her statement is true (whether as a result of negligence or otherwise) the misrepresentation will not be fraudulent.

In practice, it is difficult to prove fraud, though some examples are noted below:

- In *Pearson v Dublin Corporation* [1907] A.C. 351, an agent for the vendor stated that foundations were nine feet deep in circumstances where he didn't in fact know if this was true or not. This was held to be a fraudulent misrepresentation.
- In *Fenton v Schofield* (1966) 100 I.L.T.R. 69, a deliberate

overstatement of the amount of fish caught in a fishery over previous years, made knowing its falsity, was deemed to amount to fraudulent misrepresentation.

- In *Carbin v Somerville* [1933] I.R. 227, the vendor fraudulently misrepresented that a house was dry when he knew it in fact was not.

16.5.2 Negligent misrepresentation

Originally, all non-fraudulent misrepresentation was deemed to be "innocent". Unless one could establish fraud, there was no liability for misrepresentation. In *Derry v Peek*, a company seeking finance claimed in its prospectus that it had permission from the Board of Trade to run steam-powered tramcars. In fact, this was not true, though the directors innocently believed that obtaining such permission was merely a formality. The Board refused to give its consent and the company folded. The plaintiff, who had invested in the company, failed in a claim for damages for fraudulent misrepresentation. Although the representation was incorrect, the directors had honestly believed that it was true.

In *Hedley Byrne v Heller & Partners* [1964] A.C. 465, however, the House of Lords indicated that damages would issue in tort where a negligent misstatement was made, causing economic loss, though only in cases where there was a "special relationship" between the person making the statement and the representee. A special relationship arises if a person with a particular knowledge or skill makes a statement based on this knowledge in circumstances where it is reasonably foreseeable that another party will rely on this statement. In such circumstances, the person making the statement owes a duty of care such that she will be liable for any negligence in making this statement, if the other party in fact relies on the statement to her detriment. In *Hedley Byrne*, for instance, a bank provided an honest but inaccurate credit reference. The reference having been negligently made, the court concluded that, in principle, damages could be sought for negligent misstatement, though as the result of an exclusion clause, the bank was deemed immune from liability. (This principle has been followed in Ireland – *Securities Trust v Hugh Moore and Alexander* [1964] I.R. 417; *Bank of Ireland v Smith* [1966] I.R. 646.)

This doctrine also applies where the representation leads the parties to enter into a contract with each other. (*Esso v Mardon* [1976] Q.B. 801). As *Stafford v Keane Mahony Smith* [1980] I.L.R.M. 53 illustrates, however, where the statement is made to a third party (in this case the plaintiff's brother rather than the plaintiff), no liability arises in respect of a person to whom the statement was not made.

16.5.3 Innocent misrepresentation

Notably, at common law, damages are not available for a misrepresentation which is not the result of either negligence or fraud (though some relief may be available under statute—see para.16.6.4 below). In equity, however, rescission is possible even where the misrepresentation is innocent. (See para.16.6.2.) An innocently made statement inducing the creation of a contract may, moreover, lead to the repudiation of the contract (allowing the wronged party to regard the contract as terminated) but only if there is a complete failure of consideration as a result of the misrepresentation, and not otherwise. In other words, there must be a complete failure to deliver anything under the contract, or the thing delivered must be totally different from that contracted for.

16.6 Remedies

Put simply, an actionable misrepresentation renders a contract voidable. This means that the party to whom a misrepresentation is made has the right to avoid the contract. If avoided, the contract is deemed to be void (invalid), and the duties thereunder are unenforceable. The wronged party, moreover, may be entitled to a remedy, usually either damages or rescission.

16.6.1 Remedies at common law

Traditionally, damages were available for misrepresentation only where it was fraudulently made and not otherwise. Such damages, moreover, lay in tort rather than contract, the court granting relief under the tort of deceit. As a result of the decision in *Hedley Byrne*, however, damages are also available where a negligent misstatement is made, provided that a special relationship existed between the parties, placing a duty of care on the person making the statement.

At common law, innocent misrepresentation does not give rise to damages, though the contract may be repudiated by the wronged party if the misrepresentation led to a complete failure in consideration.

16.6.2 Remedies in equity—rescission

"Rescission" is an equitable remedy that confers a right on the party who has suffered the misrepresentation to "set aside" the contract.

This serves to restore the parties to the position that they would have been in had the contract never been made (a remedy also known as *restitutio in integrum*). Where a misrepresentation occurs (be it fraudulent, negligent or innocent), equity may, at the discretion of the court, grant a remedy of rescission. For instance, in *Gahan v Boland* (unreported, Supreme Court, January 20, 1984), a person buying land was assured that a planned motorway would not affect the land, when in fact it was due to traverse the property. The purchaser was thus entitled to rescind the contract, return the land and recover the money paid.

In theory, rescission is available for all types of actionable misrepresentation, fraudulent, negligent and innocent. Nonetheless, like all equitable remedies, the courts retain discretion to refuse relief. In particular, rescission will not be granted in the following cases:

- If it is not possible to restore the parties to their original position. This may happen, for instance, if the subject matter no longer exists, as in *Vigers v Pike* (1842) 8 E.R. 220, where a mine that was the subject of a voidable contract had been exhausted.
- Where rescission would affect rights acquired by a third party, as for instance where an item has been sold on to a third party.
- Where there has been an undue delay—or "laches"—in seeking relief. In *Leaf v International Galleries* [1950] 2 K.B. 86, rescission was refused where a person discovered five years after purchasing a painting that it had not been painted by Constable, as originally (albeit innocently) claimed. The delay in claiming rescission was a factor in the refusal. Where the misrepresentation is fraudulent, however, even a very lengthy delay may not prevent rescission. (See *O'Kelly v Glenny* (1846) 9 Ir.Eq.R. 25.)
- Where the contract has been "affirmed", that is, where the innocent party became aware of the misrepresentation but nonetheless continued to act under the contract (though this only applies where the party is aware of the misrepresentation and of her right to rescind).
- Where the contract has been executed (performed). Where the duties under the contract have been fully performed, rescission is not possible: *Lecky v Walter* [1914] I.R. 378; *Seddon v North Eastern Salt* [1905] 1 Ch. 326. However, as a result of s.44 of the Sale of Goods and Supply of Services Act 1980, performance is no longer a bar to rescission in contracts for the sale of goods, supply of services or in contracts of hire purchase.

16.6.3 Remedies in equity—specific performance

Specific performance is an equitable remedy requiring that a contractual obligation be performed by one or other party. A remedy of specific performance may be denied, however, where a contract was entered into as a result of a misrepresentation, even if it is innocent. For instance, in *Smelter Corporation v O'Driscoll* [1977] I.R. 305, specific performance of a contract for the sale of land was not granted in circumstances where the agreement was obtained on foot of an incorrect statement that the land would otherwise be compulsorily purchased by a local authority. In *O'Connor v Potts* [1897] 1 I.R. 534, moreover, a statement that a farm was about 15 per cent larger than its true size led a court to grant specific performance only in respect of the true acreage.

16.6.4 Relief under the Sale of Goods and Supply of Services Act 1980

Part V of the 1980 Act grants certain additional and alternative remedies where a misrepresentation has induced a contract for the sale of goods or supply of services, or alternatively a hire-purchase contract. First, s.44 of the Act allows a contract to be rescinded where it has been induced by misrepresentation notwithstanding the fact that either: (a) the misrepresentation has become a term of the contract, or (b) the contract has been performed. Section 45, moreover, creates a statutory right to damages for misrepresentation causing loss, even where the misrepresentation was not fraudulent. Where the misrepresentation has induced entry into a contract, the source of the misrepresentation will be liable to pay damages for loss unless she can prove that she had reasonable ground to believe and did believe up to the time the contract was made that the facts represented were true. This effectively amounts to relief for negligent misrepresentation but with a reversed onus of proof. Whereas *Hedley Byrne* stipulates that negligence be proved by the person alleging it, s.45 requires the alleged wrongdoer to establish her innocence of any negligent act, which may in practice be quite difficult to establish.

Additionally, s.45(2) allows a court to grant damages instead of rescission, if the court considers it equitable to do so. In other words, if rescission would have been available for non-fraudulent misrepresentation, a court may grant damages if it considers this a more appropriate remedy. Unlike s.45(1), it is not necessarily a defence to establish lack of negligence under s.45(2).

If damages are obtained under s.45(2), however, the contract will not come to an end as is the case with rescission, a factor that may render it preferable to rescind the contract. Where damages are sought, the contract remains valid and the parties will still be obliged to perform duties thereunder. Damages will be awarded, moreover, based on principles applicable in tort law, meaning that the wronged party will only be compensated for actual loss sustained, and not for loss of bargain (loss of profit that would have been made had the contract been performed), the usual standard in contract law.

It is important to note, finally, that these statutory provisions only apply to contracts for the sale of goods, for hire-purchase or for the supply of services, and not, for instance, to contracts for the sale of land.

16.7 Exclusion of liability for misrepresentation

A contract may exclude liability for misrepresentation but not where the misrepresentation was fraudulent. For instance, in *Pearson v Dublin Corporation* [1907] A.C. 351, a clause excluding liability for misrepresentation was deemed inapplicable to a fraudulently made statement. By contrast, in *Dublin Port and Docks Board v Britannia Dredging* [1968] I.R. 136, an exclusion clause in a contract was deemed to exclude liability for innocent misrepresentation, made honestly and in good faith. In respect of contracts for the sale of goods, supply of services and for hire-purchase, s.46 of the 1980 Act renders unenforceable clauses purporting to exclude or limit liability for misrepresentation, unless such clauses are shown to be "fair and reasonable".

17. Mistake

17.1 Introduction

Mistake is a complex area of law, the cases on which do not facilitate a particularly coherent summary. In sum, a mistake arises where one or both parties believe that they are consenting to one thing but in fact are consenting to something entirely different. A finding of mistake renders a contract void (as opposed to just voidable, as with misrepresentation and duress). A mistake will, however, invalidate a contract only in very limited circumstances. Here again, one encounters relatively strict rules of common law, mitigated in part by relief in equity.

It is always possible, of course, to include in a contract a term attesting to the accuracy of a statement or understanding. In such a case, where the statement turns out to be false, relief will be available but for breach of contract rather than for mistake. Otherwise, where there is no contractual warranty as to accuracy within the contract, a mistake may invalidate a contract, in which case the mistake is said to be "operative" or "actionable".

There are, basically, three different types of actionable mistake (though some caution is required, as the terminology is not always consistently used):

- **Common** mistake, where both parties are mistaken, each making the same error (the mistake is said to be "shared").
- **Mutual** mistake, where the parties are at cross-purposes, one party believing X, the other Y, there being, objectively speaking, no agreement on the point.
- **Unilateral** mistake, where only one party makes a mistake but the other party either knows or should have known that the mistake has been made.

17.2 Some general points

17.2.1 The mistake must be a cause of the contract
The mistake must have supplied a reason why the party entered into contract, although it need not have been either the sole or the primary reason for having done so. It logically follows that a mistake made after the contract is entered into is not actionable. For instance, in *Amalgamated Investment v Walker & Sons* [1977] 1 W.L.R. 164, a warehouse was sold with a view to being redeveloped, both parties

knowing of the plan to redevelop. A day after the agreement was signed, the building was "listed" as a heritage building. As a result, the planned development was severely restricted, and the value of the property fell dramatically to 11 per cent of its previous value. Yet, because the mistake arose as a result of factors coming into play *after* the contract was made, the contract was valid. At the time the contract was made, there was no error.

17.2.2 Mistakes of law

In line with the general principle that "ignorance of the law is no defence" (*ignorantia juris neminen excusat*), it was once thought that mistakes (or misstatements) as to the existence or meaning of the law were insufficient to invalidate a contract. Thus no relief was available when the mistake related to a matter of law as opposed to a matter of fact. In *O'Loghlen v O'Callaghan* (1874) I.R. 8 C.L. 116, for instance, a contract was enforced notwithstanding the fact that it was entered into under a shared mistake relating to local authority rates set by law.

In practice, however, this distinction between law and fact is very difficult to make, and to a significant extent modern caselaw has mitigated the rule. In particular, equity will permit a contract to be avoided where the mistake relates to the legal consequences of a private transaction or agreement, as opposed to a general principle of law applicable to the public at large. For instance, in *Cooper v Phibbs* (1867) L.R. 2 H.L. 149, a mistake regarding the true ownership of a salmon fishery (a matter of private law between the parties) was deemed to invalidate a contract for the lease of the fishery. Indeed, in many cases an error regarding the effects of a private agreement or will is deemed a mistake of fact rather than law.

In *Kleinwort Benson v Lincoln City Council* [1998] 3 W.L.R. 1095, the House of Lords appeared to mitigate the rule regarding mistake at law further, in holding that restitution is possible in such a case. Restitution is a remedy that permits money to be repaid where it has been unjustly earned. Here, money paid under the mistaken belief that a transaction was legal when it was in fact found to be illegal was deemed to amount to an operative mistake, notwithstanding the fact that the error related to the state of the law.

Indeed, it appears, in Ireland, that mistake of law is no longer a barrier to restitution. In *Lord Mayor of Dublin v Trinity College Dublin* [1986] I.L.R.M. 283, it was held that local authority rates paid in error could be set off against future rates, notwithstanding the fact that the error again was a mistake as to the law. It has, however, been suggested that repayment will only be made where there is some factor additional to the mistake, requiring that the payment be returned. For instance, in *Rogers v Louth County Council* [1981] I.L.R.M. 144, an annuity, overpaid as a result of a mistaken understanding of the law, was returned, partly on the basis that the parties were of unequal bargaining power and partly because the defendant had been responsible for the mistake. The case suggests that if the parties are not *in pari delicto, i.e.* one of them is more to blame for the mistake than the other, a payment made on foot of a mistake as to the law may be recovered. The case also suggests that where pressure is brought to bear on one of the parties, the victim of such pressure may be entitled to repayment of monies paid in error.

17.3 Common mistake

A common mistake arises where both parties share the same mistaken belief regarding a material fact. Such a mistake will only render a contract void if it relates to:

(a) the **existence** of a thing or survival of a person;
(b) title to (**ownership** of) the subject matter; or
(c) in **some limited** cases only, mistakes as to **quality**.

17.3.1 Existence of subject matter (res extincta)
Where, at the time the contract is made, the subject matter of the contract no longer exists (as might happen where it has been destroyed), or simply never existed, the contract will be void. In *Couturier v Hastie* (1856) 5 H.L.C. 673, a buyer contracted for the purchase of corn which both parties believed was on a ship bound for England. The corn in fact had been sold in Tunis *before* the contract was made; the contract was thus void. Indeed, s.6 of the Sale of Goods Act 1893 now stipulates that a contract for the sale of goods will be void if those goods have perished at the time of the contract (provided the seller is not aware that the goods have perished). Similar results arise in cases where life assurance is taken out in respect of persons mistakenly believed to be alive at the time the agreement is made (see *Scott v Coulson* [1903] 2 Ch. 249; *Strickland v Turner* (1852) 7 Exch. 208), the logic being that the person in respect of whom the insurance was taken out no longer exists. In *Galloway v Galloway* (1914) 30 T.L.R 267, likewise, a separation agreement entered into on the incorrect

assumption that the parties were married to each other was deemed void for mistake, as a relationship integral to the contract (the marriage) was absent.

A different conclusion will prevail, however, where, on the facts, one of the parties has knowingly assumed the risk that the item does not exist. In such a case, the contract may not be void, as the parties have agreed that one or other of them will accept that risk. Such a contract is said to be a contract entered into as an "adventure". Thus, where there is "conscious uncertainty" as to the existence of the subject matter, the contract may not be void if the subject matter does not in fact exist. For instance, Sinéad buys a map revealing the location of hidden treasure, on the understanding that the treasure may or may not still be there. More than likely she may not claim that the contract is void if it is not, as she has accepted the risk that the treasure may no longer be present (or may never have existed at all).

As a corollary, if one of the parties has agreed, as a term of the contract, that a thing exists, its non-existence will amount not to a mistake but to a breach of contract. In *McRae v Commonwealth Disposals Commission* (1951) 84 C.L.R. 377, the defendant Commission sold the plaintiff a wrecked tanker reported to be lying on "Jourmand Reef". In fact, the plaintiff discovered, having expended large sums of money searching for its purchase, that there was no such shipwreck. The defendant claimed mistake, but the Australian courts concluded that there was an implied condition that the subject matter existed, which term had been breached. The plaintiff was thus entitled to damages for breach of contract, the court most likely being swayed by the defendant's negligence in relation to the matter.

17.3.2 Mistake as to ownership (res sua)

In *Cooper v Phibbs* (1867) L.R. 2 H.L. 149, an agreement to sell a fishery was deemed void for mistake as, under a private Act of Parliament, the buyer already owned (as tenant for life) what he had been sold. In a contract for the sale of goods, however, an alternative conclusion applies. Nowadays, the Sale of Goods Act 1893 (s.12) implies a condition that the vendor of goods has good title thereto. In case of breach, the contract remains valid but may be repudiated by the innocent party, who make also seeks damages as an alternative.

17.3.3 Mistake as to quality

As a general rule, a mistake as to the quality or attributes of an item will not render a contract void (see *Fitzsimons v O'Hanlon* [1999] 2

I.L.R.M. 551), though there are some very limited exceptions to this principle. In *Bell v Lever Bros.* [1932] A.C. 161, following on a merger, two officers of a company were made redundant, receiving compensation of £50,000 each. In fact, as Lever Bros. subsequently discovered, the two men could have been dismissed without compensation. The company claimed that the contract was void (and the money refundable) on the basis that the money was paid under a mistake as to the validity of the contracts. The House of Lords ruled, however, that the mistake was not sufficiently fundamental to render the contract void.

Does a mistake as to quality ever qualify as an operative mistake? It appears from some statements in *Lever Bros.* that a mistake as to quality may render a contract void for mistake though only in very exceptional cases where the mistake is fundamental to the contract. According to Lord Atkin, a mistake "as to the existence of some quality which makes the thing without the quality essentially different from the thing as it was believed to be" would be enough to render a contract void, though arguably this test sets the bar very high indeed.

In *Nicholson & Venn v Smith-Marriott* [1947] 177 L.T. 189, for instance, table napkins inaccurately described as having belonged to Charles I were sold at auction. This reassurance was deemed a term of the contract and thus damages were awarded for breach. Nonetheless, it was suggested that the contract might also have been treated as void for mistake if the fact that they had belonged to Charles I was "fundamental" to the contract. In the Irish case of *Western Potato Co-operative v Durnan* [1985] I.L.R.M. 5, a serious mistake as to quality of seed potatoes was actionable on the basis that it went "to the root of the contract". Likewise, in *Sherwood v Walker* 66 Mich. 568 (1887), a contract for the sale of a cow believed to be infertile was set aside when it turned out that the cow was pregnant, clearly a very fundamental error as to quality. Nonetheless, it appears that mistakes of quality in common law generally will attract relief only in exceptional cases.

17.3.4 Equity

Where relief is not available in common law, equity traditionally intervenes, either by setting aside the contract (rescission) or in refusing specific performance (enforcement) of a contract made under a mistaken belief. Equitable relief for mistake is much more expansive than that available at common law. In equity, however, the contract would be voidable rather than void, the parties being entitled to set it aside, and seek rescission. In *O'Neill v Ryan* [1991] I.L.R.M. 672, it was suggested that even where relief is not available at common law, equity will set aside a contract entered into under a mistake as to the facts or the rights of the parties, if the mistake is sufficiently fundamental and the party seeking relief is not at fault. This, it appears, may no longer be possible in English law, though it remains good law in Ireland.

In *Solle v Butcher* [1950] 1 K.B. 671, a rent of £250 was charged under the mistaken belief that an apartment was not subject to rent control. In fact, it was subject to such control, the maximum permitted rent being £140. The contract was not void at common law, this being a mistake as to quality and not sufficiently fundamental to render the contract void. The court nonetheless set the contract aside in equity, requiring the plaintiff either to leave the flat or to remain there paying the maximum allowable rent. Lord Denning suggested that if both parties were mistaken either as to facts or to their relative and respective rights, equity would provide relief, if the misapprehension was fundamental and the party seeking to set it aside was not himself at fault. *Solle* was cited with approval in Ireland in *O'Neill v Ryan* and thus still represents good law in Ireland. (See also *Grist v Bailey* [1967] Ch. 532.)

Nonetheless, as a result of the decision in *Great Peace Shipping v Tsavliris* [2002] 4 All E.R. 689, this principle appears to be in doubt. In *Great Peace Shipping* a common mistake as to the proximity of a ship chartered to save a ship in peril was deemed not to be sufficiently fundamental as to amount to a mistake at common law. The court ruled further that once the mistake was not actionable in common law, it would not be possible to grant equitable relief. In other words, it appears that the doctrine of equitable mistake set out in *Solle v Butcher* has been abolished in English law, though it is still current in Irish law.

17.4 Mutual mistake

Fundamentally, a contract is the result of an agreement between two or more parties. If, objectively speaking, there is no agreement, the contract will be void. Mutual mistake basically arises where the parties, unbeknownst to either, are not in fact in agreement on a particular point. However, in this regard, a caveat must be added. In *Smith v Hughes* (1871) L.R. 2 Q.B. 597, Blackburn J. set out the rule that:

"If, whatever a man's real intention may be, he so conducts himself that a reasonable man would believe that he was assenting to the terms proposed by the other party, and that other party upon that belief enters into the contract with him, the man thus conducting himself would be equally bound as if he had intended to agree with the other party's terms".

In other words, if an objective bystander, observing the conduct of the parties, can discern an agreement between the parties by reference to their words and conduct, the agreement will be enforced. If it is not possible objectively to deduce an agreement, the contract will be void. On the other hand, if objectively it can be said that there was an agreement, the parties will be held to that agreement, regardless of the fact that parties may subjectively have expected different conclusions. For instance, in *Wood v Scarth* (1855) 2 K. & J. 33, although the defendant thought he would receive a once-off charge of £500 in addition to rent paid for the lease of a pub, his letter of offer in fact made no reference to this charge. Thus, the contract was (from an objective viewpoint) validly created without the £500 charge. By the same token, a contract will not be void where a party is mistaken as to the effect or impact of a bargain as opposed to the true nature of the agreement. The courts, in other words, will only enforce a party's expectation where it is reasonably well founded, and not otherwise.

Nonetheless, there may be cases where it is not possible to find agreement, where objectively speaking the parties are not *ad idem* ("on the same page"). In *Megaw v Molloy* (1878) 2 L.R. Ir. 530, for instance, the plaintiff offered for sale, by sample, grain being shipped on board one of the plaintiff's ships, the *Emma Peasant*. In fact, the sample of grain produced to the defendant was from a superior batch aboard another ship, the *Jessie Parker*. The parties were thus deemed not to be in agreement—the plaintiff had intended to sell grain from the Emma Peasant, the defendant to buy different grain from the Jessie Parker. The contract thus was void, the parties having been at cross-purposes. (See also *Raffles v Wichelhaus* (1864) 159 E.R. 375.) In *Scriven Bros. v Hindley & Co.* [1913] 3 K.B. 564, the parties had concluded an agreement for the sale of material intended for use in making rope. The plaintiff believed he was selling tow. The defendant, however, believed he was purchasing hemp, hemp being of higher quality than tow. As there was no consensus regarding what was being bought, the contract was void.

17.5 Unilateral mistake

A unilateral mistake arises where only one of the parties is mistaken as to the true situation. The basic rule is that if only one party is mistaken, the contract will be void only if the other party is aware of that mistake, whether or not the mistake was fundamental. If, moreover, the mistaken party can prove that the other party, though not aware of the error, ought to have been aware that the former was mistaken, the contract can be set aside in equity. Otherwise the contract is enforceable. In *Hartog v Colin and Shields* [1939] 3 All E.R. 566, for instance, a vendor mistakenly sold hare skins by the pound. The standard practice was to sell by the piece. The vendor was aware of this mistake, which worked out to his benefit. The contract was thus void. By contrast, in *Centrovincial Estates v Merchant Investors Insurance* [1983] Com. L.R. 158, a landlord mistakenly issued an offer to rent premises at a less than half the price that he had originally intended. As the tenant was unaware of this mistake, the mistake was not actionable, and the resulting contract was valid.

17.5.1 Errors as to identity

The question often arises whether a contract is void for mistake where one of the parties has misrepresented her identity for the purpose of defrauding the other party. There is no argument that, in such circumstances, the contract would be *voidable* for misrepresentation. A finding of operative mistake, however, will render the contract *void*, thus preventing any title from passing to an innocent third party. With misrepresentation, by contrast, title would pass to an innocent third party unless the contract was avoided beforehand. The real question in many of these cases, then, is which of two innocent parties should be granted relief in cases where a rogue has defrauded one innocent party of property and sold it to another innocent party.

First, the mistake must be as to the identity of the individual rather than the attributes or characteristics of a person. For instance, if Mary agrees to sell her farm to John believing John to be a rich company director (when he is in fact unemployed and homeless) her mistake will not be operative. If, on the other hand, she sells the farm to John when in fact she intended to sell only to his twin James, the contract may be void for mistake provided that the identity of the buyer is of fundamental importance to Mary.

This latter point is crucial. A mistake as to identity will not render the contract void unless it can be proved that the identity of the other was of fundamental importance to the seller. In practice, this is difficult to prove, the onus being on the person claiming that identity was fundamental. Indeed, where the parties contract face to face, it is usually assumed that they each intended to deal with the person who was present, their identity not being relevant. In *Phillips v Brooks* [1919] 2 K.B. 243, for instance, a man who claimed to be "Sir George Bullough" purchased a ring from a jeweller, paying by cheque. He subsequently pledged the ring to the defendant, an innocent person. In fact, the man claiming to be Sir George was an impostor, and the cheque subsequently bounced. On the facts, the court concluded that the contract, though voidable for misrepresentation, was not void for mistake as the jeweller had "… in fact contracted to sell and deliver it to the person who came into his shop". The man's identity was not fundamental, though his characteristics (ostensibly being rich and titled) may have been. Thus, as the contract was not void, and the pledge had been made before contract was avoided, the defendant had acquired good title. Likewise, in *Lewis v Avery* [1972] 1 Q.B. 198, the buyer of a car represented himself to be the famous film actor "Richard Greene", showing a movie studio ID card as evidence. Although he was in fact an impostor, the contract was not void for mistake, the court reasoning that the identity of the buyer was not crucial to the plaintiff. The seller had intended to sell to the person before him. The false claim may have persuaded the seller as to the buyer's creditworthiness, but it was not otherwise relevant.

In *Ingram v Little* [1961] 1 Q.B. 31, by contrast, a conman called to the house of two elderly sisters, offering them a £700 cheque for their car. Although they initially refused, the buyer reassured them that he was a "Mr P Hutchinson", giving them his address. Having checked this name and address in the telephone directory, the sisters agreed to accept the cheque, which subsequently bounced. The Court of Appeal concluded that the sisters had intended only to sell to Mr Hutchinson, that his identity was crucial to the sale, a conclusion that rendered the contract void for mistake. Similarly, in *Cundy v Lindsay* (1878) 3 A.C. 459, a Mr Blenkarn sent a letter to the plaintiff asking it to supply him with linen. In the letter, Mr Blenkarn pretended to be representing a reputable company "Blenkiron & Co.", which happened to run a business on the same street where Mr Blenkarn resided. On delivery of the linen, Blenkarn sold it to on the defendants, failing to pay the plaintiff. The court concluded that the plaintiff's contract was void, as the identity of the buyer was of crucial importance.

Cundy v Lindsay is generally taken to be authority for the distinction between contracts made face-to-face (where it is assumed that the wronged party intended to deal with the person before him) and contracts concluded by writing (where the fundamental nature of the writer's identity may be easier to establish). While this distinction was approved by a majority of the House of Lords in *Shogun Finance v Hudson* [2004] 1 All E.R. 215, it does not always hold true. In *King's Norton Metal Co. v Edridge, Merrett & Co.* (1897) 14 T.L.R. 98, the plaintiff received an order for goods from a writer fraudulently claiming to be "Hallam and Co.". This error, nonetheless, did not render the resulting contract void, the court reasoning that the plaintiff had intended to deal with the writer of letter and not with the particular company that the fraudster claimed to be representing. The identity of the writer was not important, the plaintiff being concerned only that the writer was creditworthy.

17.6 Remedies for mistake

Generally, at common law, a contract entered into under an operative mistake is void, and thus of no legal effect. Nonetheless, certain remedies may be available to the parties, both at law and in equity.

17.6.1 Rectification

Certain remedies are available specifically where a document does not accurately reflect the intentions of the parties or where there is a mistake as regards the actual nature of the document. A document that purports to be an account of an oral agreement may be rectified where it is found not to reflect the true agreement. In such cases, the document may be altered to reflect the true intention of the parties. It is important to note, however, that this facility is available only where:

- the parties were in agreement at the time the contract was made;
- the written document was intended only as a record of this agreement (and not as an agreement in its own right); and
- the document failed accurately to reflect that agreement.

Rectification allows the contract to be altered to reflect the true agreement. For instance, in *Craddock Bros. v Hunt* [1923] 2 Ch. 136, two parties had orally agreed to exclude a yard from a house being sold, but the written record of this agreement mistakenly included the yard. The document was rectified so as to exclude the yard.

17.6.2 Non est factum

A person who signs a document is bound by everything in that document, even if they have not read it. However, where a person is tricked into signing a document, the defence of *non est factum* may be available, rendering a contract void. In sum, this defence arises where a person has been misled by trick or fraud into signing a document under a fundamental mistake as to the nature of the document. The signer must, moreover, be blameless as regards the error.

17.6.3 Rescission

A contract entered into under an operative mistake may be rescinded, allowing the parties to be returned to the positions they were in before the contract was made. In particular, rescission may be available where rectification is refused. As with all equitable remedies, rescission is discretionary and may be declined, for instance, if the party operating under a mistake is wholly responsible for her own state of mind, or where there is delay in seeking relief. (See further para.16.6.2 above.)

17.6.4 Damages

Generally, an operative mistake will not attract damages. Damages will only issue if either: (a) the mistake involves a breach of contract, that is, where the contract itself contains a term to the effect that certain facts are true; or (b) the mistake is the result of fraudulent or negligent misrepresentation. In (a) above, the contract itself must contain a term that is breached by the mistake—damages are thus available for breach of contract rather than mistake *per se*.

17.6.5 Specific performance

Specific performance of a contract may be denied if the contract was entered into under a mistaken belief, though again this is a discretionary remedy. It appears that if a party seeking performance is responsible for the mistake, specific performance will not be granted, but otherwise the matter is for the discretion of the court.

18. Duress, Undue Influence and Unconscionability

Contracts generally arise from an agreement between the parties, the supposition being that the agreement is the product of the parties' free choice. As a general principle, a contract may be voidable where one of the parties acts under illegitimate pressure or undue influence, though certain restrictions apply. Where unlawful force is used to create a contract, it goes without saying that the contract will not be enforced. However, when pressure and influence of a more subtle nature are brought to bear, the question arises whether the resulting contract may be enforced.

18.1 Duress at common law

Duress is a defence rendering a contract voidable. Duress may basically be defined as illegitimate pressure brought to bear on one of the parties with the result that the latter has no reasonable alternative but to enter into the contract.

In some cases, it has been suggested that relief will only issue where the will of one of the parties has been "overborne" by the conduct of the other party. This suggests, misleadingly, that the wronged party does not make any intentional decision. It is suggested that the better view is that the pressure must be such as to foreclose access to any reasonable alternative; in other words, the affected party has no practical alternative but to do what the other party has demanded. For instance, Maria, a cheesemonger, threatens to shoot Pól, a would-be customer, unless he agrees to buy a consignment of camembert. Pól's will is not in fact "overborne" in these circumstances. He is faced with a choice— he can buy the camembert or risk death—but in reality, he has only one reasonable option—to buy the camembert. Thus, it might be said that duress arises where, due to the illegitimate conduct of one party, the other party has no reasonable alternative open to him but to do the former's bidding.

18.1.1 The traditional limits of duress

All sorts of pressure, influence, cajoling and convincing may be brought to bear to induce people to do business. Notably, only certain types of pressure are treated as amounting to "duress". Indeed historically, duress only arose where there was a threat to "life, limb or liberty", that is, a threat to kill, maim or unlawfully incarcerate a person. For instance, in

Barton v Armstrong [1975] 2 All E.R. 465, a contract entered into as a result of threats to injure or kill a man and his family members was deemed voidable for duress. In *Blackwood v Gregg* (1831) Hayes 277, the relatives of an elderly man abducted him with a view to getting him to execute a deed in favour of one of their number, the resulting contract being deemed voidable as a result of the unlawful incarceration.

Generally, the pressure must be of a type which is deemed illegitimate in law. In *Griffith v Griffith* [1944] I.R. 35 (a case involving the validity of a marriage), for instance, a marriage was deemed invalid where the groom, falsely accused of paternity in respect of an underage girl, was threatened with prosecution if he did not marry her. The groom had not, in fact, done anything illegal, though, being innocent in matters sexual, he wrongly believed he was the father nonetheless. The High Court made it clear that if he had, in fact, broken the law, and impregnated the girl, the marriage would have been valid, as the threat to incarcerate would have been justified. (Notably, the rules relating to marriages have changed considerably since *Griffith*, though the basic point, that the threat must be illegitimate, remains valid in contract law.)

18.1.2 Economic duress and threats to breach a contract
In more recent years, the initial restrictions on the scope of duress have been relaxed. In particular, it has been acknowledged that certain forms of economic pressure may constitute duress, even where there is no threat to life, limb or liberty. Although "normal commercial pressure" will not suffice, an illegitimate threat to break a contract, or to commit a tort, may amount to duress if it leaves the party no economic alternative but to submit. For instance, in *North Ocean Shipping v Hyundai ('The Atlantic Baron')* [1979] Q.B. 705, the parties had entered into an agreement for the purchase of a ship. While the ship was being built, the sellers demanded a 10 per cent increase in the price payable under the contract, to compensate for a devaluation in the dollar (the currency in which the price was to be paid). This constituted duress, the court reasoning that economic pressure could give rise to a voidable contract just as easily as physical force. The contract, nonetheless, stood, as the buyers had delayed in avoiding the contract.

In '*The Universe Sentinel*': *Universe Tankships of Monrovia v International Transport Workers Federation*, [1983] A.C. 366, the defendant trade union blockaded or "blacked" a ship, refusing to let it leave port until such time as its owners agreed to certain demands made on behalf of the ship's workers. Having agreed under pressure, the ship's owners sought to avoid the contract on the basis of economic duress. The House of Lords concluded that the contract was voidable as it had been entered into as a result of illegitimate pressure. Lord Diplock elaborated on the basis for relief, noting that although a choice was available to the shipowners—agree to the terms, or face a lengthy blockade—practically speaking, the only feasible economic option was to agree to the terms. The House concluded that the pressure was unlawful and not, moreover, excused or justified by UK trade union law. The contract was thus voidable for duress.

In the course of his decision, Lord Scarman (although dissenting on the conclusion) laid out a useful series of tests for duress:

- Did the person alleging duress protest?
- Was there a feasible alternative to succumbing to the pressure?
- Was the person alleging duress independently advised?
- Did she seek to avoid the contract at the first available opportunity? (This last point, for instance, was not satisfied in *'The Atlantic Baron'* as the buyer had delayed seeking relief once the pressure was lifted.)

Atlas Express v Kafco [1989] 1 All E.R. 641 illustrates the requirement that there should be no feasible alternative but to submit to the pressure. Here, a company won a contract to supply products to Woolworths, a large retailer. It contracted with a carrier for the delivery of its products. The carrier initially quoted a price per product based on its own inaccurate calculation of the number of products it could carry in each van. On discovering that the quoted price was less profitable than originally envisaged, the carrier threatened not to deliver the products unless an increased price was secured. The producer reluctantly agreed, but later sought to avoid the contract for duress. Given the proximity to Christmas, they had no choice but to accept, as they were otherwise unlikely to achieve delivery and thus risked losing their contract with Woolworths. Given the illegitimate nature of the threat (a threat to breach the contract between the parties), the contract was voidable for duress. Similarly, in *B. & S. Contracts v Green* [1984] 1 I.C.R. 419, a threat not to erect stands at an exhibition, as agreed, unless extra pay was secured, was also deemed to constitute duress. The threat having been made days before the exhibition was due to commence, there was no reasonable alternative but to submit.

Where money is obtained under duress, restitution may be available (requiring the return of monies unjustly earned) as illustrated by *Great Southern and Western Railway v Robertson* (1878) 2 L.R. (Ir.) 548. Under legislation, railway companies were obliged to transport soldiers at a fixed rate. A railway company that refused to transport soldiers unless a higher rate was paid was required to refund the excess, as it had been extracted under duress. The important point here is that the attempt to charge a higher rate was illegitimate, as it was in breach of legislation.

18.2 Duress in equity

Equity may refuse to grant specific performance of a contract entered into under duress. For instance, in *Smelter Corporation v O'Driscoll* [1977] I.R. 305, the plaintiff had effectively forced Mr O'Driscoll to enter into a contract allowing the plaintiff to buy O'Driscoll's property. The plaintiff did so on the basis of a false claim that if Mr O'Driscoll did not do so, the land would be subject to a compulsory purchase order. The Supreme Court refused to grant specific performance on the grounds that the circumstances in which the contract was concluded were substantially unfair. The misrepresentation effectively left Mr O'Driscoll in a position where he felt he had no choice but to sign. Equity has also allowed contracts to be set aside where they are entered into under a fear of prosecution. (See *Rourke v Mealy* (1879) 13 I.L.T.R. 52).

18.3 Undue influence

Equity provides some relief in cases where one party to a contract has inappropriately exercised influence over the other party. In Irish law, a distinction is still made between two different categories of undue influence:

- Actual undue influence where, on the facts, undue influence has been proved; and
- Presumed undue influence, where undue influence is presumed to arise from a relationship in which one party places significant trust and confidence in the other. Where such a presumption arises, the onus is on the person presumed to have exercised undue influence to prove that the contract was the result of an exercise of free will by both parties. This category is further subdivided into two sub-categories:

- Where the relationship is one that, by its very nature, is automatically deemed to attract the presumption;
- Where the relationship is one that normally does not attract the presumption but where, on the facts, the relationship is one in which one party places significant trust and confidence in the other.

In the overwhelming majority of cases, undue influence arises on foot of the presumption noted above.

The use of such a categorisation has been questioned by the House of Lords in *Royal Bank of Scotland v Etridge (No. 2)* [2001] 3 W.L.R. 1021, though for the time being it remains good law in Ireland. The House of Lords suggested that whether undue influence arose in any particular case was a matter of evidence only. Although it might be easier to prove undue influence where a particular type of relationship exists, some of the judges appear to suggest that a distinct category of presumed undue influence is not required. Some of their Lordships also suggest that the distinction between relationships where the presumption arises automatically from a relationship and those where the relationship must be proved on the facts is unhelpful and should be abolished. While these are valid points, Irish law remains unchanged as a result of this decision.

18.3.1 Actual undue influence
The first category of undue influence is in fact the least commonly invoked. With actual undue influence, the claimant must prove affirmatively that the wrongdoer exerted undue influence on the complainant to enter into a particular transaction.

In *Bridgman v Green* (1755) 2 Ves. Sen. 627, a butler was found to have so "completely dominated" his master that a conveyance made by the latter to the former was set aside as having been made *de facto* (in fact) as a result of undue influence. The master was in such "a state of vassalage" to his servant that he even submitted to the latter's inducement to separate from his wife. In a more modern Irish case, *O'Flanagan v Ray-Ger Ltd* (1963–1993) Irish Co. Law Reports 289 (1983), two businessmen, Messrs Pope and O'Flanagan, were joint shareholders of a company. Knowing that his business partner was close to death, Pope prevailed upon the more impressionable O'Flanagan to agree that, on either's death, the survivor would take full control of the company, free from the claims of the deceased's family. The agreement was made in a pub, at a time when the deceased was seriously ill with terminal cancer. Upon O'Flanagan's death, Costello P. concluded, on the facts, that undue influence had in fact been exercised by Pope, who "... had a strong and forceful personality and had obviously exercised considerable influence amounting to domination of the deceased on previous occasions."

18.3.2 Relationships automatically attracting the presumption

Certain relationships are deemed automatically to attract the presumption of undue influence. These include relationships between:

- Parents and their children. In *McMackin v Hibernian Bank* [1905] 1 I.R. 296, a young woman living with her mother signed two promissory notes securing debts owed by the mother. A presumption arose that the mother had unduly influenced her daughter to sign the notes. As the daughter had not received independent professional advice, the settlement was set aside.
- Guardians and their wards. In *Mulhallen v Marum* (1843) 3 Dr. & War. 317, a transfer of land from a ward to his guardian was set aside for presumed undue influence.
- Solicitors and their clients (the presumption is particularly strong in this context).
- Religious advisers and their followers. In *Allcard v Skinner* (1887) 36 Ch.D. 145, a gratuitous transfer of property from a young nun to her religious order, on the prompting of the mother superior, was deemed subject to the presumption. As the gift had been made without the benefit of external advice, the court was satisfied that the presumption had not been displaced (though, due to delay in seeking relief, the court refused to set the agreement aside). (See also *White v Meade* (1840) 2 Ir. Eq. R. 420). In *O'Neill v Murphy* [1936] N.I. 16, the presumption arose where a priest asked an architect to forego his normal fees for building work done for a parish and a local convent.
- Trustees and beneficiaries.
- Doctors and their patients.

In the case of these relationships, the presumption is deemed automatically to arise, such that the party in whom trust is reposed is assumed to have exercised undue influence unless she proves otherwise.

18.3.3 Relationships that attract the presumption on the facts

Although the presence of a particular type of relationship may not automatically give rise to the presumption in every case, if, on the facts, the relationship is such that one party reposes trust and confidence in the other, the presumption will apply to the relationship. For instance, although the relationship between a husband and wife does not automatically attract the presumption, a particular spousal relationship may be deemed subject to the presumption if, on the facts, one spouse places a strong degree of trust and confidence in the other. Similar principles apply to other intimate relationships, whether based on marriage or not:

- In *Carroll v Carroll* [2000] 1 I.L.R.M. 210, the presumption arose in a case where an elderly father transferred a pub to his son. Although this was not a situation typically attracting the presumption, on the facts, the son had a relationship with the father from which the presumption arose that he had exercised undue influence, the onus being cast on him to prove that the transfer was the result of the father's independent judgment.
- In *Inche Noriah v Shaik Allie Bin Omar* [1929] A.C. 127, an aged and illiterate woman gifted land to her nephew, who took considerable responsibility for his aunt's financial affairs. In such circumstances, the presumption was deemed to arise and in order to rebut it, evidence had to be adduced that the donor acted freely and not under the influence of her nephew. The nephew was unable to rebut the presumption and the transaction was set aside.
- In *Gregg v Kidd* [1956] I.R. 183, the presumption arose in respect of an elderly farmer and his sister, to whose sons he had transferred his farm. Mentally infirm and physically ill, the farmer depended heavily on his sister for care, factors which gave rise to a presumption that she had exercised undue influence in her sons' favour.
- In *McGonigle v Black* (unreported, High Court, November 14, 1988), the presumption arose from a relationship between an elderly farmer (who was lonely, ill and unable generally to cope) and his neighbour, a relationship that on the facts was one in which the farmer placed considerable trust and confidence in his neighbour.

18.3.4 Manifest disadvantage
It has been suggested that for the presumption to arise, the party alleging undue influence must have been placed at a manifest disadvantage by the contract. In other words, one must establish a significant contractual imbalance to the detriment of the party alleging undue influence. This requirement was first proposed in *National Westminster Bank v Morgan* [1985] A.C. 686. The House of Lords, however, has since doubted

this proposition on several subsequent occasions. Most recently, in *Royal Bank of Scotland v Etridge (No. 2)* [2001] 3 W.L.R. 1021, the House strongly intimated that manifest disadvantage is at best to be treated as an evidential aid in determining whether there has been undue influence. Although not yet followed in Ireland, *Etridge* suggests that the absence of manifest disadvantage may not be fatal to the raising of the presumption.

That said, as a matter of common sense, it is arguable that evidence of disadvantage will make it easier to shift the onus of proof to the dominant party. In *Goldsworthy v Brickell* [1987] Ch. 378, for instance, Nourse L.J. commented that certain gifts may be so large, or certain transactions so improvident, that standard motives of "... friendship, relationship, charity or other ordinary motives ..." are displaced. "Although influence might have been presumed beforehand ..." he continues, "... it is only then that it is presumed to have been undue". (See also *Allcard v Skinner, op. cit.*). Indeed, in *Provincial Bank v McKeever* [1941] 1 I.R. 471, Black J. suggests that "the less improvident the bargain, the less strong the presumption."

It is clear, of course, that the mere fact of undervalue, without more, will not be sufficient to give rise to an inference of undue influence. In *McCrystal v O'Kane* [1986] N.I. 123, for instance, a sale of land was upheld despite the existence of a substantial undervalue, there being no other factors permitting the court to upset the transaction. The fact of transactional imbalance in itself is not sufficient to trigger the presumption.

18.3.5 How to displace the presumption

Where the presumption applies, the onus is on the party alleged to have exercised undue influence to prove that no influence was brought to bear. Unless the presumption is displaced, the contract may be set aside for undue influence. The presumption may be displaced ("rebutted") where the evidence establishes that the alleged victim in fact entered into the contract as a spontaneous act of her free will and not under any pressure. The alleged wrongdoer is required to show that the transaction was the product of a mind unencumbered by influence, that there was a free and informed exercise of independent judgment on the part of the donor.

One of the most obvious ways (though not the only way) to rebut the presumption is to establish that the gift was made after the nature and effect of the transaction has been fully explained to the donor by some independent and qualified person. By definition, such advice must emanate from an independent source. Where, as often happens, the adviser is an agent of the opposite party, such advice as is given may not suffice. A solicitor may not, for instance, be regarded as independent if she acts for both parties in the matter, but primarily represents the interests of the dominant party. In *Carroll v Carroll* [2000] 1 I.L.R.M. 210, a solicitor who had acted for both the donor and recipient (but primarily for the recipient) was held not to have been sufficiently independent for these purposes. It may not, however, be necessary to show that the solicitor in question has *never* previously acted on behalf of any of the other parties in other cases. (See *Bank of Nova Scotia v Hogan* [1996] 3 I.R. 239).

It is not necessary that the advice be taken or otherwise heeded. The advice, however, must be such that the donor is fully and competently informed; any material deficiency in the information conveyed or the competence of the adviser will render the advice insufficient. In particular, the advice must be such that an ordinary, reasonable lawyer of adequate skill would have given in the same circumstances. As noted in *Inche Noriah*, the advice "must be given with a knowledge of all the relevant circumstances and must be such as a competent and honest advisor would give if acting solely in the interests of the donor". Thus, in *Inche Noriah* itself, the court set aside the impugned transaction on the ground that, while independent legal advice was given to the aunt, it was so given in ignorance of the fact that the transaction conveyed almost all of her property to the nephew. Similarly, in *Gregg v Kidd* [1956] I.R. 183, advice given in ignorance of the mental deficiencies of the donor did not displace the presumption.

Although the absence of independent advice may be fatal to the validity of a contract (see *McMackin v Hibernian Bank* [1905] 1 I.R. 296), it is not always conclusive. If on the facts the transaction is the result of the spontaneous act of the donor, it may be upheld even in the absence of independent advice: see *Provincial Bank v McKeever* [1941] 1 I.R. 471 and *Kirwan v Cullen* (1856) 4 Ir. Ch. Rep. 322.

18.4 Undue influence and third parties

Many cases concern the effects of undue influence on persons who benefit from a transaction entered into by a person under third party undue influence. This most often occurs where a spouse (usually, though not exclusively, a wife) enters into a surety or guarantee agreement with a bank, guaranteeing a debt assumed by her husband.

If the husband has exerted undue influence on the wife, what is the effect on the validity of the transaction with the bank?

This matter was considered by the House of Lords in *Barclay's Bank v O'Brien* [1993] 3 All E.R. 417, the main principles of which were broadly accepted by the Irish Supreme Court in *Bank of Nova Scotia v Hogan* [1996] 3 I.R. 239. In *O'Brien*, the House of Lords suggested that:

- Where the creditor had actual knowledge of the existence of an intimate relationship involving cohabitation between the guarantor and the person receiving the benefit of the guarantee, the creditor will be "put on inquiry". This will arise not only between a husband and wife but in respect of any intimate relationship, including those between opposite sex and same sex cohabitants, respectively.
- The bank will not, however, be put on inquiry unless the transaction was *not "on its face"* to the financial advantage of the guarantor. In particular, if a loan ostensibly appears to be for the benefit of both husband and wife, the bank is not put on inquiry.
- Once the creditor is put on inquiry, it will be fixed with notice of any wrongdoing (such that it will be unable to enforce the guarantee) unless it has taken *reasonable steps* to minimise the risk of undue influence or misrepresentation. A creditor will be regarded as having taken reasonable steps if the guarantor is properly appraised by a representative of the creditor as to:
  - the extent of the liability;
  - the consequences for the guarantor should the debtor default on the loan; and
  - the importance of acquiring competent independent legal advice before entering into the agreement.

In England and Wales, these rules have been modified by the decision of the House of Lords in *Royal Bank of Scotland v Etridge (No. 2)* [2001] 3 W.L.R. 1021. Though it is unclear whether these new procedures will be followed in Ireland, it is worth considering them in summary: *Etridge* suggests that a bank will be put on inquiry in all cases where a person guarantees a loan on behalf of an intimate partner. The only exception arises where the loan is made jointly to the partners.

Where the creditor is put on inquiry, it must take reasonable steps to satisfy itself that there was no improper influence or misrepresentation brought to bear on the guarantor. The House of Lords clarified in further depth what would constitute reasonable steps for this purpose:

- Prior to entering into the contract, the creditor should inform the guarantor directly of the need for confirmation from a solicitor acting for her that she has been given advice on the transaction. The guarantor should be informed that the purpose of this advice is to prevent her from subsequently disputing the validity of the guarantee.

- The guarantor should be asked to nominate a solicitor. Although this may be the same solicitor as that of her partner or spouse, in giving advice to the guarantor, the solicitor must act solely with the guarantor's interests at heart. If, however, the creditor suspects wrongdoing by a spouse seeking the guarantee, it should insist on the appointment of a totally independent legal advisor who has not acted for the party seeking the guarantee.

- Once the guarantor has nominated a solicitor, she should inform the bank, in writing, as to the solicitor's name and address.

- The bank should then send certain information to the solicitor, including information on the purpose for which the loan is sought, the amount of the loan and any terms and conditions attached and the current level of debt of the party for whom the guarantee is sought.

- The solicitor should meet face-to-face with the guarantor in the absence of her partner. The solicitor should, in particular, explain the nature and practical consequences of the loan as well as the risks involved, clearly indicate that the guarantor has a free choice whether to sign or not and, finally, inquire as to whether the guarantor nonetheless wishes to proceed.

- Finally, the creditor should get written confirmation from the guarantor's solicitor that she has received appropriate advice.

Provided that the lender follows these steps, it will be entitled to rely on a guarantee even if it subsequently transpires that there was undue influence or other wrongdoing.

18.5 Unconscionability

A third form of relief arises in the form of unconscionability. This remedy addresses situations where a party under some disadvantage has entered into a contract that, on the whole, is improvident or not to their benefit. Indeed, this type of relief is often described as the doctrine of "improvident bargains". The predominant features of such bargains are that:

- one party is at a disadvantage relative to the other; and
- the resulting bargain is unfairly imbalanced to the detriment of the weaker party.

Equity requires that the stronger party was aware, or ought to have been aware, of the weaker party's disadvantaged state. (*Hart v O'Connor* [1985] 2 All E.R. 880).

Although it is not necessary to show fault or improper behaviour on the part of the stronger party, equity will intervene where it considers it unconscionable or unfair to allow the latter to retain a substantial advantage arising from a bargain that significantly disadvantages a weaker party. In such cases, equity will set aside the contract, or refuse to enforce it, unless it can be shown that the contract is fair and reasonable overall, and, in particular, that it is the product of the weaker party's free and informed choice.

The party claiming relief must have been in a position of disadvantage at the time of the agreement, of which, moreover, the stronger party was aware or ought to have been aware. Put a different way, there must be an inequality of bargaining power between the parties such that there is a risk that one party will exploit the weakness of the other. Many earlier cases involved young, impressionable heirs persuaded to sell reversionary interests in land for a pittance, but it is clear that the doctrine goes further. It includes, according to Fullager J. in *Blomley v Ryan* (1956) 99 C.L.R. 362, a situation of "... poverty or need of any kind, sickness, age, sex, infirmity of mind or body, drunkenness, illiteracy, lack of education, lack of assistance or explanation".

Such disadvantage is not, however, sufficient in itself. The agreement must involve a significant imbalance in favour of the stronger party. For instance, in *Haverty v Brooks* [1970] I.R. 214, a transaction involving a man with a history of mental illness, the same solicitor having acted for both parties, was upheld, there being nothing to indicate that the contract was substantively unfair. By contrast, in *Fry v Lane* (1888) 40 Ch. D. 312, a transaction under which £170 was paid for consols worth £475 was struck down as unconscionable. Likewise, in *Filmer v Gott* (1774) 4 Bro. P.C. 230, a transaction under which an elderly woman conveyed her entire estate to her nephew for less than 5 per cent of its market value was struck down as unconscionable. (See also *Rooney v Conway* (unreported, NI Chancery Div., March 8, 1992), where a sale of a farm for a quarter of the market price was set aside as unconscionable.)

Some further examples follow:

* In *Grealish v Murphy* [1946] I.R. 35, an elderly, illiterate farmer of some wealth but limited mental proficiency agreed to transfer his farm to a younger man, Mr Murphy, who had agreed to work the land in return. Although he retained a life interest in the farm, Grealish assigned the remainder to Murphy in fee simple. The court set this bargain aside, concluding that it was improvident. The farmer lacked competence to look after his own affairs, and he had entered into an agreement under which his interests were not sufficiently protected. He was thus left "for the remainder of his life very much at the mercy of a rather impecunious young man, who had no ties of blood and was still unproved as a friend".
* In *Slator v Nolan* (1876) I.R. 11 Eq. 367, a young, reckless, bankrupt man with next to no wealth sold his inheritance for a fraction of its value to his brother-in-law, an experienced businessman with some legal training. The contract was set aside as unconscionable.
* In *Rae v Joyce* (1892) 2 L.R.(Ir.) 500, a pregnant woman on a low income took out a mortgage on property, paying 60 per cent interest. The bargain was set aside with a more reasonable rate of 5 per cent being imposed instead.

If, on the other hand, the stronger party can show that the bargain was fair and reasonable, the bargain may stand. This may be proved, for instance, by showing that the weaker party acted of her own free will and with independent expert advice (though the absence of adequate independent advice will not render the contract unconscionable if it is otherwise shown to be a fair transaction). In *McCormack v Bennett* (1973) 107 I.L.T.R. 127, a contract made by an elderly father, though improvident in certain respects, was upheld as it was entered into of the donor's free and informed will. Likewise, in *Kelly v Morrisroe* (1919) 53 I.L.T.R. 145, an elderly eccentric woman of limited means sold premises for full value, having received independent advice from her former employer, an experienced businessman. The transaction was upheld. Independent advice will not, however, be considered sufficient where it is given, as in *Grealish v Murphy* [1946] I.R. 35, in ignorance of certain important facts, or where it is otherwise inadequate.

19. Illegal and Void Contracts

19.1 Introduction

The concept of "freedom of contract" presupposes that the content of an agreement is the business solely of the parties to the contract. Clearly, however, there are limits to this proposition. In particular, the courts obviously will not enforce contracts that would involve the doing of something that is illegal or contrary to public policy. Contracts of this type fall into two categories—those that are illegal and those that are void. This distinction may appear somewhat academic, though an important difference arises:

- Illegal contracts are unenforceable in their entirety—no part may ever be enforced.
- By contrast, a void contract may be severed such that the offending parts may be removed and the remainder enforced.

19.2 Illegal contracts under legislation

Contracts may be rendered illegal by legislation or by virtue of the common law. Statutes (Acts of Parliament) very often declare certain activities to be illegal. As a logical consequence, a contract requiring the performance of an act deemed illegal under statute will generally be unenforceable, unless the statute clearly exempts such a consequence. For instance, in *Gray v Cathcart* (1899) 33 I.L.T.R. 35, an agreement to lease unsanitary premises was deemed unenforceable on the ground that it was an offence under statute to occupy unsanitary lodgings. Thus, it was "a contract to do an illegal thing". In *Cope v Rowlands*, (1836) 2 M. & W. 149, an unlicensed stockbroker failed in an action to recover payment for stockbroking services. As the plaintiff did not have a licence to work as a stockbroker, the contract could not be enforced as it involved breaking the law requiring stockbrokers to be licensed.

Yet a contract involving the breach of a statute may nonetheless be enforced in certain circumstances. If the legislation does not expressly ban contracts to do that which is deemed illegal, the court will look to the purpose for which the legislation was created. For instance, in *Hortensius Ltd v Bishops* [1989] I.L.R.M. 294, the trustees of a bank invested funds in a manner that contravened a statute. The High Court determined, nonetheless, that the contracts were not illegal as the purpose of the legislation was to render the trustees liable for any breach, and not to make the contracts illegal. It has been further suggested that where legislation imposes a fine for breach, a contract in breach of the legislation may be enforced, as the penalty intended is the fine. Likewise, laws banning unlicensed taxis are designed partly to protect the public. As such, it could hardly be maintained that an unlicensed taxi driver could, in breach of contract, abandon a fare without liability. The purpose being to protect the public, the passenger could likely sue for breach even of the illegal contract.

In considering such purposes, a distinction is sometimes made between measures that are intended to protect the public interest (in which case a contract will be unenforceable) and those that merely serve to collect revenue for the State. A contract designed to circumvent a revenue-collecting measure may thus be upheld. In *Smith v Mawhood* (1845) 14 M. & W. 452, for instance, the sale of tobacco without a licence was prohibited by statute. Nonetheless, an unlicensed tobacco seller successfully recovered payment from a purchaser, the purpose of the legislation not being to ban the sale of tobacco, but to raise revenue therefrom.

A further distinction may be made between a contract that on its face requires a breach of legislation (illegal in formation), and those where the breach arises in the course of performance. The latter may still be illegal if the statute expressly or impliedly bans illegally performed contracts, though otherwise the illegal performance may not prevent enforcement. The leading case in this arena is *St. John Shipping v Rank* [1957] 1 Q.B. 267. The plaintiffs agreed to transport cargo belonging to the defendants. Contrary to legislative requirements, the plaintiff's ship was deliberately overloaded, the plaintiff reasoning that the excess profit would outweigh any possible fine it might incur. The court concluded, on a reading of the particular statute, that the contract was enforceable. The contract itself was not contrary to law, though there was illegality in the manner in which it was performed. Such illegality was not fatal to the enforcement of the contract. Yet it is clear again that such a conclusion depends on the purpose of the relevant legislation, the question being whether the legislation intended expressly or impliedly to ban illegally performed contracts.

19.3 Illegal contracts at common law

Certain types of contract are deemed to be illegal at common law. The category of contracts illegal at common law is not closed, but included among the most prominent examples are the following:

19.3.1 A contract to commit a crime or a tort

In this context, the principle of *ex turpi causa non oritur actio* arises, suggesting that from the circumstances of a crime there can arise no action in law. In *Everet v Williams* (1725) (see (1893) 9 L.Q.R. 197), for instance, a contract between two highway robbers to divide the proceeds of their heists was deemed unenforceable. Similarly, in *Beresford v Royal Insurance* [1937] 2 K.B. 197, the heirs of a man who had committed suicide were denied the benefit of a contract of insurance on his life, on the basis that suicide was then an illegal act.

19.3.2 A contract involving immorality

A contract that tends to encourage or reward conduct regarded as "immoral" may also be illegal. In *Devine v Scott* (1931) 66 I.L.T.R. 107, rent on a premises knowingly let for the purposes of illegal gambling was deemed irrecoverable, as the contract was illegal. Likewise, in *Pearce v Brooks* (1866) 1 Ex. 213, a contract for the hire of a carriage for use by a prostitute was deemed unenforceable. As the owner had been aware of the purpose for which it was hired, he was thus prevented from suing in respect of damage to the carriage. In former times, any contract involving extra-marital sexual relations was liable to be struck down on this ground. Nonetheless, moral standards may evolve and what may have been considered immoral in Victorian times may not be so treated today. For instance, in *Armhouse Lee v Chappell, The Times,* August 7, 1996, a contract under which telephone sex lines were advertised was upheld, the court reasoning that there was no reason of public policy requiring the avoidance of this agreement. Likewise, a contract facilitating a meeting of atheists, deemed illegal in 1867 (*Cowan v Milbourn* (1867) L.R. 2 Exch. 230) was in a subsequent case deemed legal (*Bowman v Secular Society* [1917] A.C. 406), the change undoubtedly reflecting intervening changes in social attitudes.

19.3.3 A contract prejudicial to the administration of justice

While the law generally permits the compromise of private and civil claims, public law (and in particular, criminal law) litigation is treated differently. In particular, a contract seeking an end to proceedings may be illegal if those proceedings involve criminal matters or matters that have a bearing on the public at large. Thus, in *Keir v Leeman* (1846) 9 Q.B. 371, an agreement not to bring criminal prosecutions in respect of a riot was deemed illegal and thus void. Similarly, in *Nolan v Shiels* (1926) 60 I.L.T.R. 143, an Irish court refused to enforce a contract under which the plaintiff had accepted £50 in exchange for agreeing to drop a prosecution for sexual assault. (See also *Brady v Flood*, (1841) 6 Circ. Cases 309). The situation may be different, however, if the contract is made in circumstances where no prosecution has commenced. Thus, in *Rourke v Mealy* (1879) 13 I.L.T.R. 52, an agreement by the defendant to honour a cheque forged by the defendant's relative was held to be valid as no proceedings had been instigated in the matter.

19.3.4 Maintenance

Maintenance involves "improperly stirring up litigation and strife by giving aid to one party to bring or defend a claim without just cause or excuse". Basically, this is illegal—common law frowns on agreements under which one party attempts to encourage speculative litigation by another party. For instance, in *Uppington v Bullen* (1842) 2 Dr. & War. 184, a solicitor sold land to a Mr Fleming for £400 but agreed to accept £100. The remainder of the proceeds was to be used by the solicitor to take a case on Fleming's behalf. The agreement was deemed illegal, as it involved supporting or "maintaining" a third party in pursuing litigation.

19.3.5 Champerty

Champerty, like maintenance, concerns agreements to fund speculative litigation, but with an added twist. A contract is champertous if it involves providing financial support for litigation in exchange for a right to share in the winnings. For instance, in *McElroy v Flynn* [1991] I.L.R.M. 294, a contract to share an inheritance in exchange for helping to make a legal claim upon it was deemed illegal. Likewise, in *Fraser v Buckle* [1996] 2 I.L.R.M. 34, the plaintiffs had approached the defendants suggesting that the latter may have been heirs to the estate of a deceased American. The plaintiffs offered to assist in pursuing a claim against the estate, on the condition that the plaintiffs would receive one-third of any share the defendants might gain. This being champertous, the contract was deemed illegal and thus unenforceable.

19.3.6 A contract encouraging corruption

In *Lord Mayor, Aldermen and Burgesses of Dublin v Hayes* (1876) 10 I.R.C.L. 226, Hayes had been appointed City Marshal and Registrar of Pawnbrokers. As Registrar he was entitled to certain fees which he had agreed, as a condition of his appointment, to pay to the Treasurer of the City of Dublin. This being an agreement to pay money in exchange for appointment to public office, it was illegal as it had the potential to encourage corruption. Likewise, in *Parkinson v College of Ambulance* [1925] 2 K.B. 1, a contract under which £3,000 was paid in an attempt to secure a Knighthood was deemed to be illegal and thus unenforceable. Clearly a contract to pay a member of parliament or a county councillor to vote a particular way would be similarly illegal. See *Osborne v Amalgamated Society of Railway Servants* [1910] A.C. 87.

19.3.7 A contract to defraud the Revenue

A contract that is created with a view to evading taxes owed to the Revenue is illegal in Irish law. This arises most commonly where employment contracts purport to represent salary as "expenses". In *Lewis v Squash Ireland Ltd* [1983] I.L.R.M. 363, for instance, an employment contract under which a salary top-up was misrepresented as "expenses" was deemed unenforceable as it was designed deliberately to evade tax.

19.3.8 A contract liable to endanger diplomatic relations with a friendly country or to attack a friendly state

For instance, a contract involving a breach of foreign law will not be enforced. Thus, in *Foster v Driscoll* [1929] 1 K.B. 470, a contract to smuggle whisky into the United States during Prohibition was deemed illegal.

19.4 Consequences of illegality

The consequences of illegality depend on whether the contract is:

- illegal in itself or "on its face"; or
- illegal as performed.

19.4.1 Illegal in itself

A contract illegal in itself is null and void and unenforceable. This is the case even if the illegality is confined to part of the contract only; nonetheless, the contract as a whole is deemed unenforceable. For instance, in *Murphy & Co. v Crean* [1915] 1 I.R. 111, the defendant leased a pub from the plaintiff, agreeing as part of the contract to source all its stout from the plaintiff. A covenant in the lease permitted the plaintiffs to nominate a person to whom the pub licence should be transferred. Such transfer, however, was illegal under licensing law. Notwithstanding the fact that the bulk of the contract was otherwise in compliance with the law, the contract was unenforceable in its entirety. Likewise, in *Re Mahmoud and Ispahani* [1921] 2 K.B. 716, a buyer falsely stated that he was licensed to buy linseed oil (as required by law), but subsequently refused to accept such oil under a contract for its purchase. As the contract contemplated a sale in breach of the law, it could not be enforced.

As a general rule, any property that passes under an illegal contract cannot be recovered. The general rule in this regard is summarised in the Latin phrase *in pari delicto, potior est conditio possidentis.* Roughly translated, this means that where the parties are equally at fault in respect of the illegality, the loss will lie where it falls. The courts, thus, will generally not come to the aid of a party to an illegal contract, where both parties are equally guilty of wrongdoing. There are, however, certain exceptions to this rule:

- Where the parties are, however, not *in pari delicto, i.e* not equally at fault, the court may intervene on behalf of the party bearing less of the blame, in particular by restoring to the less guilty party property transferred under the agreement.
- A party may be able to recover if she "repents" before the illegal purpose has been carried out.
- Property may be recovered if there is another cause of action available that does not concern the illegal contract. For instance, in *Tinsley v Milligan* [1993] 3 All E.R. 65, two women, both of whom had provided money for the purchase of a house, agreed to put the house in the name of Tinsley only, so that Milligan could continue (unlawfully) to claim social welfare. Nonetheless, an understanding existed that ownership of the house would be shared. Although the agreement was illegal, the House of Lords concluded that, independently of the contract, a trust arose in favour of Milligan on foot of her payments towards the purchase (in Ireland, this would arise on foot of a "resulting trust").

19.4.2 Illegal in performance

A contract that is legal on its face but illegal as performed may be unenforceable if both parties intended the illegal performance. However, where one of the parties is innocent of any wrongful intent, the contract may be enforced by that party, provided she took steps to repudiate the contract on discovering the illegal performance. For instance, in *Marles v Trant* [1954] 1 Q.B. 29, the defendant sold what though described as spring wheat, was in fact winter wheat. The defendant having failed to supply an invoice with the delivery, the contract was deemed illegal. Nonetheless, the plaintiff, being innocent of any wrongdoing in the matter, was permitted to sue for breach of contract. Likewise, in *Whitecross Potatoes v Coyle* [1978] I.L.R.M. 31, a Meath farmer agreed to sell potatoes to the owner of a chain of English fish and chip shops. Anticipating certain restrictions on cross-border trade in potatoes, the parties agreed a higher than normal price. On the evidence, the plaintiff believed that the restrictions would be avoided legally by sourcing the potatoes in Northern Ireland. The defendant, however, had intended illegally to smuggle the potatoes across the border. As the defendant alone intended to act illegally, the plaintiffs were allowed to sue on foot of the contract, the potatoes not having been delivered.

19.5 Void contracts

Terms in contracts may be void under statute or void at common law. Many examples of such terms arise under consumer legislation (as, for instance, where an exclusion clause unlawfully purports to exclude certain statutory terms from consumer contracts). Another good example arises in connection with legislation requiring financial support ("maintenance") of family members. Section 27 of the Family Law (Maintenance of Spouses and Children) Act 1976, for instance, renders void any term in a contract purporting to oust the right to claim, through the courts, maintenance from a spouse or parent. Though the remainder of any such agreement will be valid, the specific clause attempting to oust this right will not be enforceable.

Contracts void at common law broadly fall into three categories.

19.5.1 Contracts that oust the jurisdiction of the courts

A contract that seeks to deny the courts their ordinary jurisdiction in resolving legal disputes will be void at common law. For instance, in *Baker v Jones* [1954] 1 W.L.R. 1005, a contract that sought to give an association exclusive power to interpret the law was deemed void, as it excluded the possibility of judicial review or other recourse to the courts. In this regard, a distinction must be made between rules that seek to prevent access to the courts in matters of law (which are void) and those that nominate an independent arbitrator to officiate on factual matters in cases of dispute (which are valid). In *Scott v Avery* (1856) 5 H.L.C. 811, for instance, a clause that referred contractual disputes to an arbitrator was deemed acceptable as the contract still allowed for ultimate access to the courts. In short, the parties should always have access to the courts in order to clarify matters of law. It is worth bearing in mind that the right of access to the courts is a constitutionally protected right.

19.5.2 Contracts that "subvert" marriage

A contract may be deemed void if it is considered that it may "undermine" the institution of marriage. It is well established in Irish law, for instance, that an agreement made in contemplation of the potential future separation of spouses (for example, in a pre-nuptial contract) will not be enforced. (*Marquess of Westmeath v Marquess of Salisbury* (1830) 5 Bli. (n.s.) 339; *Cohane v Cohane* [1968] I.R. 176). The (rather unconvincing) reasoning is that such agreements tend to destabilize marriages, and moreover, may incentivise the parties to split. By contrast, an agreement that is made where the parties intend to separate with immediate effect will be enforced.

It appears also that a contract of cohabitation between unmarried persons will not be enforced in Ireland. In *Ennis v Butterly* [1997] 1 I.L.R.M. 28, Kelly J. concluded that an agreement between an unmarried couple contemplating the payment of financial support in a case of relationship breakdown was prejudicial to the institution of marriage, and thus unenforceable. This view was strengthened, in the judge's view, by the provisions of Article 41.3 of the Constitution requiring the State to safeguard the institution of marriage.

Contracts that involve marriage brokerage (under which a broker arranges to secure a spouse for another party, for a fee) or which otherwise restrict a person's right to marry will also be void. It is worth noting that an agreement to marry is no longer enforceable in Irish law, as a result of the Family Law Act 1981.

19.5.3 Contracts in restraint of trade

A contract may be deemed void where it unreasonably restricts the right of a person to trade, or to carry out a business or profession. Similar principles apply where a contract purports unreasonably to limit an employee's right to work after an employment contract is terminated. The basic principle is that such restraints will be void as a matter of public policy unless they can be justified as being: (a) reasonable having regard to the interests of the parties; and (b) reasonable having considered the interests of the public. (See *Nordenfelt v Maxim Nordenfelt & Co.* [1894] A.C. 535.) In this regard, the courts essentially seek to strike a balance between a number of competing rights:

- On the one hand is the right of the business/employer to protect its legitimate interests. An allied concern is the issue of freedom of contract; if a party has freely agreed to a particular restraint, arguably that party should be held to the bargain.
- On the other hand, one must consider the right to earn a livelihood (which is, after all, a constitutional right) as well as the interest of society as a whole in the promotion of free trade and competition and the benefits derived thereby.

It is worth bearing in mind, of course, that these rules are now supplemented by competition legislation and other measures governing restrictive practices, in particular the Competition Acts 1991–2002 as well as the competition provisions of Articles 81–82 of the EC Treaty.

The basic common law rule applicable in this context was elaborated upon in *Esso Petroleum v Harper's Garage* [1968] A.C. 269, holding that restraints on trade would be upheld only if the impugned measure:

- Is reasonably required to protect the legitimate interests of the beneficiary (the business/employer);
- Goes no further than is necessary to protect those interests (*i.e.* is proportionate);
- Is reasonable having regard to the rights of the restricted party; **and**
- Is not inconsistent with the public interest (a point emphasised in *Macken v O'Reilly* [1979] I.L.R.M. 791).

The onus of proof differs depending on whether the interests of the parties or those of the public are being considered: the onus of proving that the restraint is reasonable having regard to the parties is on the person wishing to rely on the restraint. On the other hand, the onus of proving detriment to the public interest lies on the person seeking to avoid the restraint. In considering such matters the courts will have regard to:

- **The scope of the restriction:** the wider the restraint, the more extensive the range of tasks to which it refers, the less likely it is that it will be upheld.
- **The duration of its application:** the longer the restraint is scheduled to last, the less likely it is that it will be upheld. For instance, in *Esso Petroleum v Harper's Garage*, the defendant owned two petrol

stations. Both were subject to an "exclusivity agreement" requiring that the defendant only purchase petrol from Esso. In the case of the first garage, the agreement was to last 4.5 years, 21 years in respect of the second garage. While the exclusivity agreement was deemed reasonable in respect of the first garage, it was void in respect of the second, as it went much further than was required to protect Esso's legitimate interests.

• **The geographical scope of the term:** a clause preventing a former employee from setting up a business in the same street as the former employer might be reasonable. A clause that extended to the entire of Ireland arguably might not be.

Established commercial practice is relevant in this context. The courts have upheld long-standing practices within particular trades, for instance, exclusivity contracts involving pubs and brewers (*Murphy & Co. v O'Donovan* [1939] I.R. 457, where a contract to source stout exclusively from the plaintiff was upheld) and contracts involving oil companies and petrol stations (solus agreements). For example, in *Continental Oil v Moynihan* (1977) 111 I.L.T.R. 5, a garage owner's five-year agreement to source oil only from the plaintiff was upheld as reasonable. It is clear, however, that such agreements may not go further than is required to protect the interests of the parties, as in *McEllistrem v Ballymacelligott Co-op* [1919] A.C. 548, where the House of Lords struck down an agreement restricting members of the co-op from selling their milk to any other creamery or from unilaterally leaving the co-op.

19.6 Severability

Where a contract is void at common law, it is nonetheless possible to sever the offending portion from the remainder of the contract, thus upholding the rest of the contract. For instance, in *Skerry's College v Moles* (1907) 42 I.L.T.R. 46, a contract restricting a teacher from teaching within seven miles of Dublin, Cork and Belfast for three years was upheld insofar as it related to Belfast but struck down in relation to Dublin and Cork. Severance thus allows the offending portion of the contract to be "extracted". Provided that the remainder of the contract is not unreasonable, it can still be enforced absent the offending provision.

20. Discharge of a Contract

20.1 Introduction

This chapter concerns how a contract is terminated, in other words how it is "discharged." Where a contract is discharged, the parties are deemed free of any further obligations towards each other. There are four different ways in which a contract can be discharged—agreement, performance, frustration and certain types of breach. Each of these options will be considered in turn.

20.2 Agreement

A contract may be terminated where the parties agree that it should come to an end. A distinction must be made, however, between an agreement to terminate under which both parties benefit ("bilateral discharge") and an agreement under which only one benefits ("unilateral discharge"). While a bilateral discharge will generally be valid (as consideration has been provided, both giving a benefit under the contract), a unilateral discharge will only be upheld if it is either contained in a deed or separately supported by consideration. Thus, it is said that there must be "accord and satisfaction", the "accord" referring to the agreement to terminate and the "satisfaction" alluding to the consideration required.

Where certain formal requirements applied to the original contract (such as a requirement of written evidence in respect of a contract for the sale of land), an agreement to discharge will not necessarily need to follow the same formalities. Where the discharge is intended to be complete (that is to terminate all obligations thereunder), an oral agreement will suffice. On the other hand, if the parties wish to *alter* the agreement (rather than completely terminate it), any relevant formal requirements will need to be met. Similar requirements apply if the parties wish to replace their old agreement with a new one; the new contract will only replace the old one if the formal requirements are complied with.

20.3 Performance

Where all obligations under a contract have been performed, the contract is deemed to come to an end. Traditionally, at common law, it was said that a contract was not performed until every element thereof was completed exactly as anticipated by the contract. Thus, in strict theory, even very minor deficiencies in performance may prevent the contract from being deemed "performed." *Cutter v Powell* (1795) Term Rep. 320 provides a rather stark example of this rule. A sailor died while working on a ship *en route* from Jamaica to Liverpool. He had been promised 30 guineas if he completed the voyage. His widow claimed payment for the time that he had served before his death. On a construction of this particular agreement, the court concluded that it was an "entire contract", that is, that payment was not to be made unless it was performed in its entirety. The sailor was deemed to have accepted the risk that he might not perform the contract in full, in exchange for which he was offered a wage at some four times the average rate. Likewise, in *Coughlan v Murray* (1905) 39 I.L.T.R. 153, a builder who had agreed to build a house was deemed to be entitled to nothing when he failed to complete work on the partly built house some nine months after the agreed deadline. In *Re Moore & Co. v Landauer* [1921] 2 K.B. 519, the parties had agreed that tins of fruit to be supplied to the buyer would be packed in boxes of 30. Some of the tins were boxed in cases with 24 tins each. The buyer was thus entitled to repudiate the contract as, although the buyer had received the correct number of tins, the contract had not been performed as agreed.

There are, however, some exceptions to this rather harsh rule.

20.3.1 Substantial performance

Equity may require payment where the contract is substantially performed, subject to a clawback in respect of the unperformed portion of the work. This exception, arising from *Boone v Eyre* (1779) 1 Hy. Bl. 273n, stipulates that where a contract is performed with minor deviations, payment will be due less the amount needed to address the deficiency. In *Hoenig v Isaacs* [1952] 2 All E.R. 176, a builder completed all but a small portion of redecoration work on the defendant's home. The parties had agreed a fee of £750, but the defendant refused to pay as a book shelf remained incomplete. The court nonetheless ordered payment of the full fee less £55, the amount of money required to finish the book shelf. The court reasoned that, unless the breach went to the root of the contract, it could order payment, subject to a deduction in respect of the incomplete portion of the work. Lord Denning added that even where a lump sum was agreed as payment, the courts would lean against requiring complete performance.

However, this exception applies only where what has been received is in fact of substantially the same value as what was promised. For instance, in *Bolton v Mahadeva* [1972] 2 All E.R. 1322, a central heating system which cost £560 coughed out fumes and ran inefficiently. It was estimated that it would cost £124 to fix the system, in which circumstances the court concluded that there had not been sufficient performance to justify even part-payment of the agreed fee. Another way of putting this is that the substantial performance exception only applies where the breach is relatively minor in the context of the whole contract.

Likewise, where the contract has been abandoned prior to completion, it may not be possible to exact payment. In *Kincora Builders v Cronin* (unreported, High Court, March 5, 1973), a builder refused to complete insulation work, as agreed, on the attic of a house he was building for the defendant. Although this represented a relatively minor deviation from the agreement, the court refused to find that substantial performance had occurred, on the ground that the plaintiff builder had abandoned the work, refusing to complete it.

20.3.2 *Severable/divisible contracts*

To a large extent, the harsh results in cases like *Cutter v Powell* turn on the interpretation of the relevant contracts. If the contract requires that payment only be made on entire performance, partial performance will not suffice. If, on the other hand, the parties can be said explicitly or implicitly to have agreed that partial performance would attract partial pay, the courts may grant some relief.

A contract may thus be interpreted as divisible such that payment will be required for the performance of discrete obligations thereunder. If the contract can be regarded as involving a series of discrete obligations, it may be possible to order payment in respect of the performance of obligations that have been performed, even if other obligations remain outstanding. For instance, if Ruaidhrí agrees to supply carrots on a weekly basis for a year, he would arguably be entitled to payment for each week's supply that he has delivered, even if he were to withdraw from the contract after a month.

This is the case, for instance, with most employment contracts and tenancy agreements. Indeed, as a result of the Apportionment Act 1870, rents, annuities, dividends, salaries and pensions are deemed to accrue on a daily basis. Thus, if a contract of employment is terminated before it is due to end, the employee is still entitled to a proportionate payment of salary. See *Treacy v Corcoran* (1874) I.R. 8 C.L. 40. Likewise, if a tenancy ends prematurely, the landlord is entitled to recover for the period during which the tenancy lasted.

It is often a matter of interpretation whether the contract is an "entire agreement" requiring performance of every element, or whether it is divisible. If, on the facts, the parties are deemed to have agreed to make payment for performance of specific elements, the rule in *Cutter v Powell* will not apply. In *Brown v Wood* (1864) 6 Ir. Jur. 221, the plaintiff agreed to weave cloth from the defendant's yarn. Some but not all of the cloth was delivered, the remainder of the yarn being discarded. The court concluded that the plaintiff was nonetheless entitled to be paid for the cloth that was delivered, subject to the defendant's right to recover for the yarn not processed.

20.3.3 Prevention of performance

Where one of the parties is required to complete performance, which the other party is deliberately preventing, the former may be entitled to part-payment in respect of what has been completed to date. In *Arterial Drainage v Rathangan River Drainage Board* (1880) 6 L.R. (Ir.) 513, the defendants asked the plaintiffs to drain land, the contract requiring that this be performed with "due diligence". The work did not progress as quickly as planned, and the defendants attempted to terminate the contract. However, as the actions of the defendant had considerably stalled the plaintiff (the defendant having failed to grant prompt access to the land and plans), the court concluded that the plaintiff was entitled to part-payment for work already done. The contract was thus deemed to have been rescinded, the plaintiff receiving part-payment for its endeavours. In *Planché v Colburn* (1831) 8 Bing. 14, the plaintiff agreed to write one of a series of books, but before he had finished, the publisher decided to stop publishing the series. The plaintiff's entire performance having been precluded by the publisher's decision, the plaintiff was entitled to £50 for work done, half the agreed price for the completed book.

20.3.4 Tender of performance

Where a person's attempts to perform under a contract are rebuffed by the other party, this may relieve the former of any further obligation. A tender of performance, even if rejected, may result in discharge. In *Startup v MacDonald* (1843) 6 Man. & G. 593, the defendants ordered oil from the plaintiff, with a stipulation that it be delivered by March 31. The plaintiff attempted to deliver March 31 at 8.30 p.m., but the defendants did not accept, alleging that the delivery was too late. The court held that as performance had been tendered, the plaintiff had done everything it could to fulfil its obligation. It was entitled to be paid notwithstanding the failure to accept. Where a tender is made, however, it must comply with the terms of the contract. For instance, if a contract requires payment in cash, an offer to pay by cheque or credit card will not amount to an adequate tender of performance.

20.3.5 Time

Generally speaking, a contract may be successfully completed even where performance occurs after a stipulated deadline has passed. In short, unless time is deemed to be of the essence, a failure to perform on time will not discharge the contract. In *United Scientific Holdings v Burnley Borough Council* [1978] A.C. 904, the plaintiff claimed that the defendant, as landlord to the plaintiff, had lost the right to pursue a 10 yearly rent review, as the Council had sought such a review two months after the deadline stipulated in the lease. The court nonetheless allowed the review to proceed, on the basis that, unless otherwise agreed, time generally is presumed not to be of the essence.

There are, however, three ways in which time may be deemed to be of the essence, such that a failure to perform on time will discharge the contract, entitling the wronged party to sue for damages:

- If the parties have expressly agreed that the time of performance is crucial, the failure to meet a deadline will result in discharge of the contract.
- Although there may not be express agreement on the point, the nature of the contract's subject matter may necessarily imply that time is of the essence, where, for instance, the subject matter is perishable (such as organic mushrooms) or subject to sharp price fluctuations (*e.g.* oil).
- Even where the parties did not initially agree that time is of the essence, a contracting party may, after the deadline has passed, notify the other party of a further deadline, compliance with which is deemed to be essential. In such a case, provided the time for completion is reasonable, a failure to complete by the stipulated date will result in discharge. In *Nolan v Driscoll* (unreported, High Court, April 25, 1978) for example, the plaintiff had agreed to buy the defendant's house but some 15 months later the sale remained outstanding. Although time was originally not deemed to be of the essence, the defendant served notice requiring completion of the sale within a month of the notice. The court ruled that failure to complete within the month served to terminate the contract.

20.4 Frustration

As a general rule, contractual liability is absolute: a person who agrees to do something is bound by their agreement, even if they are and never were able to perform. This latter rule is exemplified in the rather extreme case of *Parradine v Jane* (1647) Aleyn 26, where rent paid under a lease was deemed payable notwithstanding the fact that the tenant had been ejected from the land as a result of the English Civil War.

This stance is tempered, however, by the doctrine of frustration. A contract may be deemed to have been discharged where it has been frustrated, that is, where the core obligation under the contract can no longer be performed because of some intervening event for which neither party is responsible. The parties are thus relieved of their obligations under the contract. This occurs where one of the following conditions is met.

20.4.1 Impossibility of performance

If due to an intervening event, the performance of a contract is rendered impossible, the contract will be deemed frustrated. A classic example arose in *Taylor v Caldwell* (1863) 3 B. & S. 826. A music hall, hired for use as a concert venue, was destroyed in a fire six days before the first concert was due to take place. The destruction of the hall rendered the parties unable to perform, thus frustrating the contract. Similar principles apply where a person is unable to perform due to death or illness in circumstances where the contract requires personal performance—the death or illness will, if it entirely prevents performance, render the contract frustrated. Likewise, if the method of performance stipulated in the contract subsequently becomes impossible, the contract may be frustrated, though not if the agreement can be interpreted as permitting an alternative mode of performance.

It is important in this regard to distinguish between events that make performance impossible and those that render it more onerous or difficult to perform. Put simply, mere hardship or inconvenience is not enough to frustrate a contract. For instance, in *Tsakiroglou v Noblee Thorl* [1962] A.C. 93, a contract was made to ship ground nuts from the coast of Sudan to Hamburg. It was originally envisaged that the goods would travel via the Suez Canal (the shortest route), but due to an outbreak of war, the canal was closed, necessitating a much lengthier journey around the southernmost tip of Africa. Despite the added time and cost involved (the cost in fact doubled), frustration had not occurred. The House of Lords ruled that the fact that performance was rendered more difficult did not mean that frustration had occurred. Similarly, in *Davis Contractors v Fareham UDC* [1956] A.C. 696, the plaintiff had agreed to construct 78 houses for £94,000. Severe problems involving the supply of materials and labour disputes resulted in a 14-month delay in completion and a final bill which exceeded the contract price by £21,000. These factors nonetheless were deemed not to have frustrated the contract, the key point being that although the performance was rendered more difficult, it was not made impossible—the houses were still built.

20.4.2 Frustration of purpose

A contract entered into for a specific reason may also be discharged if, due to intervening events, the reason or purpose no longer applies. For instance, if Mel pre-books a taxi to take him to the airport for a flight, the contract would be frustrated if his flight was cancelled prior to the taxi ride. Mel may still enjoy a jaunt to the airport, but given the cancellation, such a trip would be pointless and without purpose.

In *Krell v Henry* [1903] 2 K.B. 470, a hotel room was hired specifically because it overlooked the route of King Edward VII's planned coronation procession. The procession having been cancelled due to the King's illness, the contract was deemed to have been frustrated. Although the defendant still had the use of the room, the specific purpose of the contract was to watch the procession, and this was now postponed. Watching the procession, the court concluded, went to the "root of the contract" and the cessation of the procession thus led to its discharge. Contrast this with *Herne Bay Steam Boat v Hutton* [1903] 2 K.B. 683. Hutton hired a steam boat in order to watch a naval review celebrating the coronation of Edward VII. When Edward fell ill, the review was cancelled. Nonetheless, the court concluded that the contract remained valid and enforceable, as it was still possible to take trips on the steam boat. The reasoning appears to have been that watching the review was not fundamental to the contract to hire the boat. One might say that in *Krell*, the thing contracted for was a view of the coronation procession, whereas in *Herne Bay* the thing contracted for was the hire of the steamship, though the distinction seems remarkably difficult to justify.

20.4.3 Intervening illegality

A contract that is legal when entered into may be frustrated due to the fact that the performance contracted for is subsequently deemed illegal.

For instance, in *Fibrosa Spalka Akeyjna v Fairbairn Lawson Combe Barbour* [1943] A.C. 32, a contract between an English firm and a Polish company was deemed frustrated when Poland was invaded by the Germans. At common law, it is illegal to contract with citizens of an enemy state; as the contract was now illegal, it was deemed to have been frustrated. (See *Ross v Shaw* [1917] 2 I.R. 367 for a similar Irish example.) By the same token, where an Act of Parliament invalidates a contract, this may be deemed a frustrating event. For instance, in *Ó Cruadhlaoich v Minister for Finance* (1934) 68 I.L.T.R. 174, a judicial position created by the first Dáil in 1919 was subsequently revoked by a statute of the Irish Free State. The contract was deemed to have been discharged by the intervening statute.

20.4.4 *Where frustration will not occur*
Frustration will not occur in certain circumstances:

* Where changed circumstances render performance more difficult or onerous but not impossible.
* Where circumstances have changed due to the conduct of one of the parties. In *Herman v The Owners of S.S. Vicia* [1942] I.R. 304, a ship was unable to dock in Britain, as planned, due to its owners' negligence in not obtaining the requisite documentation for this purpose. As the failure of the contract was self-induced, no frustration arose. Similarly, in *Maritime Fish Ltd v Ocean Trawlers* [1935] A.C. 524, the defendant owned five trawlers and had rented one to the plaintiff for the purpose of fishing. A licence was required for this purpose, but the defendant only had three licences, which it had applied to three of its other ships. The failure to obtain a licence was not a frustrating event, as the absence of a licence was the result of a choice made by the defendant to apply the licences received to its other ships.
* If a contract makes specific provision for a particular event, for instance by assigning the risk of its occurrence to one or other party, the occurrence of such an event will not constitute frustration. In *Mulligan v Browne* (unreported, Supreme Court, November 23, 1977), a doctor's contract of employment at a Donegal hospital was made expressly conditional on the availability of funds for the running of the hospital. As this eventuality was foreseen by the parties, and provided for in the contract, the hospital's subsequent funding crisis was not deemed to be a frustrating event.

- If the event was actually foreseen, its occurrence will not amount to frustration. In *McGuill v Aer Lingus and United Airlines* (unreported, High Court, October 3, 1983), the first defendant had booked passengers on board a partner airline despite being aware of an imminent strike at the latter airline. As predicted, the strike went ahead, but because it had been foreseen, the contract was not frustrated.

20.4.5 *Effects of frustration*

The effects of frustration are relatively stark and sometimes quite unfair. Put simply, the contract is deemed discharged, with both parties being relieved of all future obligations. In *Appleby v Myers* (1867) L.R. 2 C.P. 651, a contract to install a machine was frustrated by a fire destroying the building in which the machine was being installed (the installation not having been completed in full). The manufacturers of the machine were deemed unable to recover for work already done on the machine, as the obligation to pay fell due after the frustrating event.

However, an obligation that falls due *before* the frustrating event occurs will stand: in other words, if a payment is due, or an obligation arises prior to the event in question, such payment or obligation may still be enforced. For instance, in *Krell v Henry* (*op. cit.*) the hotel could not pursue the balance owed in respect of the hire of the hotel room as the obligation to pay this arose after the frustrating event. On the other hand, in the same case a deposit paid *before* the frustrating event could not be recovered, as the obligation to pay it arose prior to the event.

Similarly, where a payment is made under the contract prior to the frustrating event occurring, such payment is not recoverable—the loss essentially "lies where it falls". Nonetheless, where no consideration at all is received under the contract, it may be possible to get relief. In *Fibrosa* (*op. cit.*), for instance, under a contract to provide machinery to a Polish factory, £1,000 was paid in advance to an English firm. However, because of the outbreak of World War II, the machine could not legally be delivered. Because the Polish company received no benefit at all, the £1,000 had to be returned.

20.5. Discharge by breach

Although a breach of contract normally entitles a party to damages, there are certain types of breach that may additionally permit the innocent party to treat the contract as being discharged. It is important to note that the party in breach may not rely on her own breach as discharging the contract. If the breach is sufficiently serious, however, the innocent party may opt either to have the contract discharged or to let it stand.

20.5.1 Breach of a condition

A breach will only permit discharge of a contract where it is sufficiently serious. In this regard, the distinction between conditions and warranties noted at para.12.6.1 above should be revisited. A breach of a warranty does not permit discharge—the contract stands, though the wronged party is entitled to damages for breach. Breach of a condition, on the other hand, or of an innominate term in circumstances where the effects of the breach are serious, will entitle the wronged party to regard the contract as having been terminated. However, even in such a case, the innocent party may elect to allow the contract to stand, and seek damages for breach.

20.5.2 Repudiatory breach

Where a party repudiates a contract or threatens to do so, the innocent party may choose to discharge the contract. A contract is "repudiated" where one party clearly intimates, by words or conduct, that they intend not to be bound by its terms. This is sometimes called "repudiatory breach". For instance, in *Athlone RDC v Campbell and Son (No. 2)* (1912) 47 I.L.T.R. 142, half way through the performance of a contract for excavation services, the local authority wrote to the defendant indicating that its services were no longer required. This was deemed to be a repudiation of the contract between the parties, allowing the defendant to treat the contract as having been discharged.

A repudiatory breach may be committed even before performance falls due, as where a person indicates in advance that they do not intend to perform an obligation under the contract. This is called an "anticipatory breach"'. It may entitle the innocent party to seek discharge, as illustrated by *Hochster v De La Tour* (1853) 2 E. & B. 678. A courier was due to start work under a contract securing his services. Before the date nominated for the commencement of work, the defendant indicated that he would not be employing the courier after all. This was deemed to amount to repudiation. Although the date on which the obligation commenced had not yet passed, the courier was deemed entitled to discharge the contract for breach.

20.5.3 *"Fundamental breach"*

A "fundamental breach" (which, confusingly, is totally different from the type of fundamental breach described above in para.14.7) is a breach of an essential term of the contract. In other words, the breach of such a term will have serious consequences that go to the root of the contract. Such a breach will entitle the innocent party to choose to regard the contract as being discharged. For instance, in *Dundalk Shopping Centre v Roof Spray Ltd* (unreported, High Court, March 21, 1979), a contract requiring that a roof be made watertight was deemed to have been fundamentally breached in circumstances where the defendant failed, within a reasonable time, to eliminate leaks.

20.5.4 *The effects of a breach*

As noted above, only certain types of breach lead to the discharge of a contract, and even then only at the instance of the innocent party. The latter may, moreover, choose to waive this right and allow the contract to stand (in which case the contract is "affirmed"). Similarly, the right may be lost through delay as in *Bord Iascaigh Mhara v Scallan* (unreported, High Court, May 8, 1973). That said, the innocent party, even where the right to discharge is lost or waived, does not lose the right to sue for damages. It is also important to note that a discharge in case of breach releases the parties from the obligations under the contract only with *prospective* effect. In other words, the innocent party may still sue for damages in respect of a breach prior to discharge. Additionally, the parties may still rely on certain terms in the contract insofar as they relate to events that occurred before discharge.

21. Remedies

Where a breach of contract occurs, certain remedies are available to the innocent party. Although one might think that the most obvious remedy would be enforcement of the contract (a remedy termed "specific performance"), in practice the most common remedy available is damages. It is, in fact, relatively rare for a court to require performance from a reluctant or recalcitrant defendant; instead damages tend to be the preferred remedy.

21.1 Damages

The most common remedy for breach of contract is an award of a sum of money called "damages". In this regard it is important to distinguish between the purpose of damages in the context of tort (for civil wrongs) and the purposes of damages in contract law.

- In tort law, an award of damages generally addresses only the actual loss sustained as a result of the tort. In this context, damages seek to restore the injured party to the position she would have been in had the tort not been perpetrated.
- In contract law, by contrast, judges generally seek to address the expectation loss or loss of bargain sustained. The purpose of damages in this context is to place the wronged party in the position she would have been had the contract been performed as agreed. This may include compensation in respect of the profit that the person would have made had the contract been performed.

However, in order for damages to issue, a number of matters must be considered.

21.1.1 Causation
The party in breach must have caused the loss in question. It is not necessary that the breach be the only cause provided that it contributed in some manner to the loss. As a result of the Civil Liability Act 1961, s.2, however, the amount of damages may be reduced in cases where the person claiming damages shares some responsibility for the loss, the reduction being in proportion to her level of responsibility for the loss.

21.1.2 Remoteness of damages
A breach may have caused a loss, in the sense that the loss would not have been sustained but for the breach. Nonetheless, contract law will

not compensate for *all* losses that flow from such a breach. In particular, contract law will not provide compensation for losses that are too "remote" from the breach. For instance, if a passenger is "bumped" from a flight due to overbooking, she would arguably not be entitled to compensation if she lost a major business contract as a result, as this is neither a typical result of such an event nor will it have been within the contemplation of the airline.

In the main case on this point, *Hadley v Baxendale* (1854) 9 Exch. 341, the Court of Exchequer explained that a loss would only result in damages if it was either:

- A loss that a reasonable person would consider to be the natural consequence of such a breach, *i.e.* that the loss "arose in the usual course of things"; or
- A loss that was within the reasonable contemplation of both parties, at the time the contract was made, as a loss that would result from a breach of the contract.

For instance, in *Wilson v Dunville* (1879) 6 L.R. (Ir.) 210, a court concluded that injury to animals was a natural consequence of supplying adulterated feed, containing lead pellets, to cattle. In *Stock v Urey* [1955] N.I. 71, damages were awarded where a smuggled car, sold under a contract, was seized by the customs authorities (this being a natural consequence of smuggling). In *Lee and Donoghue v Rowan* (unreported, High Court, November 17, 1981), a failure to complete a shed to be used for drying potatoes prompted a court to order payment of damages for the cost of finishing the shed and what it would have cost to transport the crops to storage in another shed (both eventualities being foreseeable). However, in this case, the farmer was unable to source alternative storage facilities, with the result that the crop was completely destroyed. Nonetheless, the farmer was unable to get damages for the crop as a whole as such an eventuality was neither foreseeable nor within the contemplation of the parties.

In *Hadley,* the owners of a mill sued in respect of the late delivery of an iron shaft which had been dispatched for repair and was being transported by the defendant. The mill having stopped all operations pending delivery, the owners sued for the loss of profit they would have made had the machine been delivered on time. This loss, however, was neither the natural consequence of the breach nor was it within the contemplation of the parties. The defendant could not have expected that the mill would cease operations; it would not have been unreasonable to assume, for instance, that the mill owners had a spare shaft for use in such eventualities. Nor could the loss be said to have been within the defendant's contemplation, the mill owner having failed to clarify that the mill would lie idle pending delivery. Similarly, in *Victoria Laundry v Newman Industries* [1949] 2 K.B. 528, a laundry lost a lucrative State contract as a result of a five-month delay in the delivery of a boiler. Although the laundry secured damages for loss of normal profits, the loss in respect of the government contract was deemed too remote, as this was neither a natural consequence of such a breach nor was the defendant aware that such a contract was at stake. Likewise, in *Kemp v Intasun Holidays* [1987] 2 F.T.L.R. 234, due to an overbooking of holiday accommodation, a woman was placed in dusty accommodation that brought on an asthma attack. As this was a reaction particular to sufferers of asthma (and not the public at large) and as the condition had not been brought to the defendant's attention beforehand, the damage was deemed too remote.

21.1.3 *Mitigation*

Where a party stands to lose as a result of a breach of contract, that party is not permitted to stand idly by. The innocent party is required to do everything reasonably within their power to mitigate or reduce the loss, though only where the loss has actually been sustained and not where the breach is "anticipatory". For instance, if a butcher refused to accept meat supplied by a farmer under a contract for supply, the farmer would be obliged to find another buyer to mitigate his losses. The farmer would not be compensated if he let the meat rot simply because the butcher would not accept it, as required.

Thus, in *Brace v Calder* [1895] 2 Q.B. 253, a manager who was wrongfully dismissed on the dissolution of a partnership declined an offer by two of the partners to re-employ him. As the manager had failed to mitigate his losses, he was deemed unable to recover damages for dismissal. In *Malone v Malone* (unreported, High Court, June 9, 1982), the plaintiff had taken out a loan to buy property—he was not entitled, however, to recover interest paid in a case of breach of contract as the court held that he should have repaid the money to mitigate his losses once the breach transpired. Similarly, in *Bord Iascaigh Mhara v Scallan* (unreported, High Court, May 8, 1973), the plaintiff was deemed unable to recover for damage to a ship abandoned by its hirers, as it had failed to take steps to recover the ship speedily on abandonment.

21.2 Types of damages

21.2.1 *Expectation loss and speculative damages*

The general measure of damages is the amount that the wronged party stood to make if the contract was carried out as planned. Notably, this includes the projected profit that would have been made had the contract been fulfilled. In many cases, however, it may not be possible to tell whether a profit or loss would have been made. *Afton v Film Studios of Ireland* (unreported, High Court, July 12, 1971) appears to be authority for the proposition that damages for loss of expectation will not issue where it is unclear whether a particular contract would result in a profit or loss. (In such a case, though, the appropriate remedy may be based on reliance loss. See para.21.2.2 below.)

The courts will nonetheless generally strain in favour of estimating the probable loss, provided that it is established that the contract was likely to result in a profit. For instance, in *Hawkins v Rogers* (1951) 85 I.L.T.R. 129, in breach of contract, a racehorse was prevented from taking part in a series of races. Despite the fact that it might never have won a race, the court granted damages based on an assessment of the horse's general performance in other competitions. Similarly, in *Manubens v Leon* [1919] 1 K.B. 208, a plaintiff succeeded in claiming in respect of a lost opportunity to make tips (a wholly discretionary matter). In *Blackpool and Flyde Aero Club v Blackpool Borough Council* [1990] 3 All E.R. 25, the plaintiff won damages in respect of the Council's omission to consider the club's tender, even though there was no guarantee that the club would have won the tender, if considered.

21.2.2 *Reliance loss*

Damages are generally awarded on the basis of the loss of bargain, the wronged party being entitled to recoup the profit she would have made had the contract been fulfilled. Where it is not possible, however, to calculate losses on this basis, an alternative method of assessing damages lies in the concept of "reliance loss". This allows the innocent party to sue for damages in respect of losses incurred due to her reliance on the contract, that is, to recover damages in respect of expenses incurred on foot of the wronged party's performance of obligations that would not have arisen had the contract not been made. For instance, where a top actor is contracted to appear in a film, but, in breach of contract, withdraws therefrom, it may not be possible to determine the extent of expectation loss (the film might have been a box office success or a

flop). In *Anglia Television v Reed* [1972] 1 Q.B. 60, a famous actor
(Oliver Reed) who had agreed to star in a film withdrew from production
at a late stage, with the result that the film was not completed. As it
would have been difficult to establish the likely profit lost (if any), the
television company sued based on reliance loss. The court thus allowed
it to recoup any losses sustained making the film on the basis that it
had relied on its contract with the actor. It was also deemed, however,
to be entitled to claim for pre-production costs including those sustained
in advance of the contract with Reed. The court reasoned that the
latter costs would have been within Reed's contemplation when he
entered into the contract.

Where it is obvious, however, that a venture would not have made
a profit at all it may be possible to avoid damages on this ground. For
instance, in *Bowley Logging v Domtar* (1982) 135 DLR (3d.) 179, a
haulier hired to transport logs succeeded in establishing that its breach
of agreement actually *lowered* the losses that the logging company
would have made had the contract been fulfilled. The logging company
had contracted to sell the logs at a significant undervalue, and actually
stood to make a greater loss if the haulier had fulfilled its side of the
bargain. As there had been no expectation loss, the logging company
could not claim reliance loss.

21.2.3 Restitution loss and consequential loss

Damages may be awarded in the form of restitution loss, in order to
prevent a party from deriving an unjust enrichment from the contract.
This would occur, for instance, if a party pre-paid for goods or services
that were not delivered: the court would order restitution (repayment)
of monies paid.

It appears also that, provided the damage is not too remote,
damages may issue for consequential loss. For instance, in *Stoney v
Foley* (1897) 3 I.L.T. 165, in consequence of the purchase of diseased
sheep, the land on which they were grazed was deemed unfit for use
for four months (including the Spring and early Summer). The buyer
was permitted to recover for his inability to use the land as well as for
the loss of the sheep.

21.2.4 Compensation for non-financial loss

Generally, contract law is concerned only with financial loss.
Traditionally, damages for hurt feelings, disappointment and mental
distress flowing from a breach of contract were not the subject of
compensation in contract law. Certainly in a commercial context, it is

extremely rare to encounter awards in respect of non-financial loss—even where a breach of contract causes upset, stress or disappointment, a remedy in contract is generally not forthcoming. In *Kelly v Crowley* (unreported, High Court, March 5, 1985) for instance, owing to the negligence of his solicitor, a man purchased what he thought was a pub licence. In fact it was a drinks licence for a hotel. While this error caused him some considerable upset, he was unable to recover for mental distress, only for financial loss. The injured sensibilities of a business person, it seems, cannot be the subject of compensation in contract law at least (though a remedy may be available in tort).

Nonetheless, in more recent cases, the courts have granted relief in respect of non-financial losses, such as mental distress or loss of amenity, in cases where the provision of recreation or peace of mind is at the root of the contract. The rule appears to be that where the parties reasonably expect some enjoyment or relaxation to arise from the contract, a loss of enjoyment may be the subject of damages. If, for instance, the owner of a health spa insisted on constant powerdrilling in one of its treatment rooms while clients were present, one might feasibly claim that compensation should be available for the resultant stress, the purpose of attending a health spa being to relax and unwind.

Jarvis v Swan Tours [1973] 2 Q.B. 233 is one of a number of cases in which the courts have provided compensation for mental distress in cases where travel agents fail to deliver on promises relating to holiday packages. Although the plaintiff was transported to and accommodated in a Swiss holiday resort, specific entertainment events promised as part of the package fell far short of what was promised and in some cases did not materialise at all. Damages were awarded for the plaintiff's disappointment. Similarly, in *Dinnegan and Dinnegan v Ryan* [2002] 3 I.R. 178, the distress and humiliation arising when a bride and groom and their guests were turned away from a planned reception, on their wedding day, resulted in an award of damages.

It appears, however, that this principle is not confined to contracts involving travel or entertainment. In *Johnson v Longleat Properties* (unreported, High Court, May 19, 1976) for instance, damages were awarded for the inconvenience and loss of enjoyment arising from the defective performance of a contract to build a house. To put the defects right, the homeowner would have to put up with considerable disruption, including the presence of builders in his home for a considerable period, as well as the lifting of carpets and tiles and the excavation of the concrete sub-floor. The homeowner was awarded damages in respect

of the inconvenience arising. Similarly, in *Farley v Skinner* [2001] 3
W.L.R. 899, a pensioner bought a house for his retirement. A surveyor
secured by the pensioner failed to advise of the high levels of noise
emanating from a nearby airport. The pensioner succeeded in claiming
damages for distress and loss of amenity arising from this error. The
House of Lords reasoned that a major objective of the contract was to
confer pleasure and relaxation through the provision of comfortable
accommodation for the pensioner's retirement.

21.2.5 Punitive damages
Although there is a public interest in holding people to their bargains, it
is not the function of contract law to punish people for breaking
contracts. In fact, it would be extremely unusual for an Irish court to
award punitive damages (damages that seek to punish a party for a
particularly flagrant and "high-handed" breach of contract). *Garvey v
Ireland* (1979) 113 I.L.T.R. 61 provides a rare Irish example, where
punitive damages were awarded in respect of the wrongful dismissal
of a Garda in breach of constitutional principles of natural justice.
Nevertheless, the courts tend to regard punitive damages as
inappropriate in contract cases (a point underlined by the courts' dislike
for penalty clauses noted below).

21.2.6 Liquidated damages and penalty clauses
In some cases, the contract itself may attempt to stipulate the amount
of damages that will be payable in cases of breach (termed "liquidated
damages"). On the one hand, this can be useful in providing clarity
and reducing litigation on the amount of damages, as well as limiting
liability in cases of breach. In particular, in cases where damages may
be difficult to estimate, the courts will appreciate the efforts of the
parties in agreeing a fixed sum in advance.

On the other hand, the courts will not enforce even an agreed
sum where the purpose or effect of the imposition of damages is to
penalise a party for breach of contract. Such "penalty clauses" are
frowned upon by the courts, contract law not having as its purpose
the penalisation of parties in breach of contract. In *Dunlop Pneumatic
Tyre v New Garage and Motor Co.* [1915] A.C. 79, Lord Dunedin
noted that a clause will be deemed to be a penalty clause if:

- It lists a sum that is "extravagant and unconscionable" when
  compared to the greatest actual loss that could conceivably occur
  in respect of the breach.

- The breach consists only of a failure to pay a sum of money, and the stipulated damages exceed the former sum. In *O'Donnell v Truck and Machinery Sales* [1998] 4 I.R. 191, for instance, the Supreme Court ruled that a failure to pay a fixed sum cannot result in damages exceeding that sum with interest. This situation must be distinguished from situations where, on failure to pay an instalment, an entire debt falls due under what is called an "acceleration clause". Such acceleration clauses are valid provided that the sum claimed does not exceed the entire sum due with interest.
- The amount of damages stipulated for is the same regardless of the nature and extent of the damage caused by the breach. In *Schiesser International v Gallagher* (1971) 106 I.L.T.R. 22, the plaintiff had paid to train the defendant as a textile cutter. In return, the defendant committed to working for the plaintiff for three years; if he left their employment within three years, he would have to reimburse the cost of the training. As this clause applied equally regardless of the departure date (*i.e.* whether he left within a day or a month or two years, the consequences were the same), the clause was deemed to amount to a penalty clause and was thus unenforceable.

21.2.7 *Other matters relating to damages*

As a general rule, the date by reference to which damages are assessed is the date on which the contract is breached, though there are exceptions to this rule. Interest may be awarded by the court in respect of the period between the date of breach and the date of the judgment.

21.3 Remedies other than damages

Although damages would be the most common type of remedy available where a breach of contract occurs, other remedies are available and are summarised below:

- **Specific Performance.** In exceptional cases, the court may, exercising its equitable jurisdiction, order the party in breach to perform the contemplated obligation. In practice, the courts are quite reluctant to order specific performance. In particular, the courts will not generally order performance in respect of contracts involving personal performance, for instance, employment contracts. Specific performance will only be granted where damages are not adequate to provide relief and where the person seeking relief will suffer hardship unless specific performance is ordered.

- **Injunctions.** An injunction may be issued in order to prevent a party from doing something that they have contracted not to do (a prohibitory injunction) or to force a party to reverse the effects of a breach of contract (a mandatory injunction). However, an injunction generally will not be granted where it has the effect of compelling performance. For instance, in *Page One Records v Britton* [1968] 1 W.L.R. 157, an injunction was refused in circumstances where the manager of a rock band sought to prevent his replacement in breach of contract. The court reasoned that to grant the injunction would effectively force the band to keep their manager, and would thus require specific performance of a contract involving personal performance.
- **Restitution.** Where money is paid under a contract, and nothing is received in return, an action for restitution may be available. This permits the donor to recover monies paid, on the basis that a failure to recover would result in the recipient being unjustly enriched. Restitution will generally only be granted, however, where there has been a total failure of consideration (*i.e.* nothing of value has been received in exchange for the payment).
- ***Quantum Meruit.*** The remedy of *quantum meruit* (literally meaning "as much as is deserved") permits a person, who has performed duties under a contract, to be paid a reasonable price for performance in circumstances where the parties have not agreed a fee, or where the fee is unclear. Provided that the parties intended that the performance would be remunerated, the court may order such payment as it considers reasonable in the circumstances.
- **Rescission.** Rescission is an equitable remedy requiring that a contract be terminated and that the parties be restored to the position they were in before the contract was made. This remedy is usually available in cases of contracts entered into under actionable misrepresentation, mistake, duress or undue influence as well as in certain cases of breach, though usually only where the breach is serious. Rescission is an equitable remedy and will thus only be awarded at the discretion of the court (see para.16.6.2 for further details).

Appendix

Answering Exam Questions

I. GENERAL POINTS

Before the examination:

- **Try to anticipate likely questions.** In some (though by no means all) subjects, certain exam questions tend to repeat themselves. This may either be because the issue is central to a study of the relevant area of law, or because the particular examiner has a strongly manifested interest in that topic. While one should *never* assume, unless told otherwise, that a question will definitely come up, it is always worth consulting past exam papers to spot popular questions or motifs. Where one is studying contract law as part of a programme with set tutorials, the tutorial questions may also offer a guide to the type of question that may come up in the exam.
- **Don't bank on certain questions definitely coming up.** No matter how sure you are that a particular question is a "banker", always be prepared for an unconventional examination. Make sure you have revised enough course material in case the questions you anticipated do not appear. For these purposes, it is generally useful to prepare for likely questions, with safety questions in reserve should your preferred options not materialise.

During the examination:

- **Answer the required number of questions.** You are more likely to pass with the required number of mediocre answers than with a lesser number of excellent answers. It is worth noting (as a rule of thumb) that students *tend* to drop one potential grade for every unanswered question. More candidates fail exams for this reason than for any other. Correspondingly, it is usually ill-advised to attempt more than the required number of questions. If you find yourself with time left, work on improving and re-checking the questions that you have already answered.
- **Timing is of the essence.** If you have three hours to answer five questions, don't spend the first hour and a half answering one question. Plan your time in advance. Once the allotted time for a particular question has passed, move on to a new question, even if the previous answer is not yet complete.

- **"Cut your cloth to fit the measure".** Sometimes questions consist of more than one part. Do not spend more time on a part of a question than it is worth. If, for instance, the first part of a question is worth 16 per cent and the second part 4 per cent, it makes sense to spend most of your allocated time answering the first part of the question.

Style points:

- **Clarity is the key.** Exams tend to be rushed affairs. Examiners, thus, can hardly demand especially polished answers. Your aim, however, should always be to make yourself understood. The key to a good mark is, almost invariably, clarity in the presentation and explanation of the key concepts and rules. Try to structure your answer so that you are making one point at a time. Avoid complex sentence structures.
- **Avoid "wordy" answers.** Contrary to popular perception, legal exams do not demand the use of elaborate words and phrases. Simplicity in the use of language lends itself to clarity and, thus, to good marks.
- **Precision.** Precision in the use of language is very obviously a key feature in the study of law. The use of slack or slang language is thus to be avoided. It is not necessary, however, to be able to remember the precise subsection of an obscure legislative provision. As a general rule the examiner is more concerned that you understand the principles at stake than that you can memorise a series of numbers.
- **For (nearly!) every rule there is an exception.** One should be careful not to engage in sweeping generalisations. For virtually every legal rule, there is at least one exception, and this is particularly true of contract law. Use phrases like "generally", "ordinarily" or "in most cases" when outlining general principles of law to which there are exceptions.
- **Offer constructive opinion.** Where relevant you should try to give your own opinion on the area of law that is being discussed. Be careful, however, not to allow your opinions to replace a full discussion of the relevant legal principles. Opinion should always be supported by argument. Do not be afraid to argue with received wisdom or with what you know to be the opinion of the examiner … but if you do so, you must be especially well-prepared to back up your arguments.

- **Irrelevance.** Irrelevant content may not necessarily lose you marks, but it is unlikely to gain you any credit. If someone, for instance, asks you how much the bus to Navan costs, it will not be of much use to give them the cost of the train to Cork. Likewise, if you are asked a question about consideration, a lengthy dissection of the rules of offer and acceptance will merit few if any marks.

II. ESSAY QUESTIONS

The basic purpose of an essay question is to give you an opportunity to display your understanding of the law on a particular topic. Hence, a typical question will ask you to "discuss", "outline and comment upon", "evaluate" or "critique" the law. In each case, the first thing to do is to outline, as clearly and concisely as possible, the law in that area. Try to cite at least one case as authority for every important legal point that you make. If there is a particularly significant case in that area, it must at the very least be mentioned and should preferably be cited and discussed at some length. By "citation" one means that one should:

(a) Give the **name** of the case (the year and place where the case is reported generally do not have to be given), *i.e. Dickinson v Dodds*;
(b) Outline the **basic facts** of the case;
(c) State the **decision** in the case; and
(d) Explain the **reasons** given by the judges for their decision(s).

A good answer will continue, having explained the law, to critique it. Do you think that the law in this area is fair and just? Is it workable? Could it be usefully reformed and if so how? It is worth noting, however, that such a critique should never precede or replace a clear and cogent explanation of the law.

Long unwieldy sentences and complex formulations of language should be avoided; contrary to popular perceptions, the very best legal writing is simple and clear. Sentences should not be overlong—if you find yourself taking a deep breath in the middle of a sentence it is probably too long. Imagine always that you are explaining the law to an educated person without legal experience.

III. PROBLEM QUESTIONS

Problem questions are a common and useful tool of assessment. The purpose of this type of question is to assess your ability in applying legal principles to new (usually unseen) fact scenarios. These questions usually pose a hypothetical legal problem that the candidate is expected to solve. Very often, such problem questions quite closely replicate or mirror the facts of an important case ("a precedent") that you have studied. In such a case, the purpose of the exercise would be to discuss the precedent, apply the precedent to the new fact scenario and to suggest a likely outcome to the problem posed.

There are three steps to the resolution of such problem questions:

1. **Identifying the legal issues.** The key to answering this type of question lies in identifying the problem thrown up by the fact scenario. Very often such problems will resemble a case or (an amalgam of cases) that you have studied in class.

2. **State and explain the law.** The next approach is to outline the applicable law clearly and concisely. If there are any applicable cases (especially if they involve a very similar fact scenario), the facts should be briefly outlined, followed by a summary of the decision in the case. In particular, remember to explain the reasoning of the court in such cases.

3. **Apply the law to the problem.** Many students make the mistake of treating a problem question as if it were an essay on the law, thus forgetting to apply the law, as stated, to the problem. You should imagine that you are a lawyer advising a client: you will thus be expected to spell out the implications of the legal situation for the hypothetical party with the legal problem. There may not be one definitive legal solution to a problem. The law may be uncertain, or there may be no direct precedent on the point. The job of a lawyer in such cases is simply to give an educated assessment of what a court is most likely to do, based on more indirect precedents, on the merits of the case and on one's general knowledge of the legal principles.

A good acronym for this approach is "ISLA"—**I**dentify, **S**tate **L**aw, **A**pply. It is always useful, in conclusion, to give your own opinion on the state of the law—is the solution to the problem a fair one? Opinions, however, should always be delivered with caution. They should, in particular, be supported by relevant argument. Do not, moreover, allow excess personal sentiment to override your answer. As a student of law you are being asked to explain and apply the law, and not solely to espouse your personal opinions.

IV. STUDYING CASES

Cases vary in importance and significance and the study of cases should be approached accordingly. A footballing analogy may help to explain this. Some cases are clearly "premier division" cases. Their significance to contract law is vital. Often, such cases represent an important new innovation in the law or the establishment of a fundamental principle of contract law. Such cases frequently touch on more than one aspect of contract law and knowledge of these cases is, thus, essential to an understanding of the subject.

Other cases are "first division" cases, useful to elaborate upon a point but not crucial to your answer. While such cases may add to the law as it stands at any one time, the innovation is less significant than that of a "premier division" case. Then there are the "non-league" cases, cases that simply follow precedent and add nothing to the law as it stands. While it is also useful to be able to cite such cases, the priority in any exam answer is to identify the "premier" cases first and to spend most time dealing with these before citing less significant cases.

Discussing cases in an exam

Examiners are often asked by exam candidates, "how much do I need to write on a particular case?" While there is no one definitive answer to this question, the basic response is that the candidate should convey a broad understanding of the facts of the case, the decision taken and (most crucially) the reasons for that decision. In most situations, where a case is being used simply to explain a principle of law, one or two sentences on the facts, a sentence on the decision and a sentence or two explaining the reasoning of the case will usually suffice. Where the case is central to the exam question being answered, however, a more detailed exposition of the case will be expected, perhaps a half to three-quarters of a written page.

Index